...CK'S

IMPROVED

FRONT,

d Flat or Built.

TOP

THE ENCYCLOPEDIA OF TOYS

THE
ENCYCLOPEDIA
OF
TOYS

Constance Eileen King

NEW
BURLINGTON
BOOKS

A QUARTO BOOK

© Copyright 1978 Quarto Limited
First published in Great Britain 1978
ISBN 0 90628 667 0

Reprinted 1985

Published by New Burlington Books,
The Old Brewery,
6 Blundell Street,
London N7 9BH

This book was designed and produced by
Quarto Publishing Limited
Picture Research: Anne-Marie Ehrlich

Phototypeset in England by
Filmtype Services Limited, Scarborough
Printed in Hong Kong by
Leefung-Asco Printers Limited

Frontispiece: **'Bonzo', a soft toy made
in printed plush, probably by Dean's
Rag Book Company of Rye,
England. Height 10 inches.
Betty Harvey-Jones Collection**

Contents

Introduction

Adults have found it convenient to amuse their children with toys from the earliest times, and examples of bronze miniature furniture, earthenware dolls and animals with simple articulation have survived from the ancient civilizations. Curiously, some of these very early pieces are quite lightly considered by collectors and a good example of a Greek doll, for instance, can command a fraction of the sum raised by a late 19th century mass-produced figure that is more decorative in appearance.

Medieval children were supplied with the playthings that are still the basic toys of today such as kites, balls, toy soldiers, hobby horses and pull- and push-along animals. The ordinary child owned only the simplest versions that were roughly carved from wood or bone, but the wealthy were presented with exquisite bronze or even silver armies and small painted earthenware and glass figures. Much of our knowledge of this period is derived from prints and paintings, as there are few actual examples in comparison with those which have survived from the ancient civilizations. One of the most interesting toys is illustrated in the *Weiskunig* of Hans Burgkmair, dating from 1516, which shows the young Maximilian I

playing with articulated jousting figures; these were propelled by hand and serve to indicate the very high standard of workmanship that was available. Maximilian is also connected with one of the first recorded toymakers, as in 1516 he ordered from Kolman, a helmet maker and master smith of Augsburg, two knights armed with lances and mounted on wooden horses, which he gave to the ten-year-old Ludwig II of Hungary.

Germany was established as a producer of good quality toys on a commercial basis from the 16th century, the Council of Nuremberg authorising pewterers and jewellers to make tin figures as playthings for children in 1578. A few years earlier August, the Elector of Saxony, had commissioned a hunt from a Nuremberg carver that was to consist of wild boar, dogs and horsemen – an indication of how the wooden toy industry was flourishing even at this period. Nuremberg became a great toymaking centre whose ascendancy was to last into the 20th century, because of its proximity to lead mines and its position near the medieval trade routes across Europe. Woodcarving was a traditional folk craft in the surrounding mountain areas and the Nuremberg merchants were able to assemble their work and send it across Europe, so

This group of beautifully carved musicians illustrates the skill of German woodcarvers. Made in the 19th century, it was probably intended for use as an ornament as well as a toy. Bethnal Green Museum of Childhood, London.

Facing page: 'Punch on a bicycle', an exquisite Victorian toy made by William Britain around 1890. Punch rides realistically round a central weight which contains a clockwork motor. Height 8¼ inches. David Pressland Collection.

Christmas Presents, **a painting by Hugo Oehmichen, dating from 1882 and showing a typical selection of toys from the Victorian era. Victoria and Albert Museum, London.**

Facing page: **A concertina-folded peepshow dating from the early 19th and representing the Coronation of Napoleon. Ipswich Museums.**

that by the 18th century German-made toys were common in the nurseries of England, America, Italy and Russia.

The demand for attractive toys increased substantially in the 18th century because of the gradual improvements in the living conditions of artisans, who were able to buy modest commercially produced playthings for their children. The great divergence of standard between toys for rich and poor also begins to narrow from this time, though there were obviously still a few extravagant princely commissions, in particular for well equipped dolls or complete armies of model soldiers. It is from this period that the collectors of today are able to acquire their earliest examples, as toys made before this time rightly belong in museums where, hopefully, they can be correctly preserved. Rocking horses on splendid curved rockers, packs of cards, dissected puzzles, baby houses that are complete representations of domestic life, paper dolls and toy soldiers all occasionally appear on the market and are bought to form the cornerstones in representative specialised collections. These 18th century pieces are acceptable even if somewhat damaged, whereas later examples usually need to be in almost perfect state before they are wanted by the more advanced

collectors. Many toys produced in the 19th century were modelled retrospectively, so great care has to be taken in establishing the true date of an item before a high price is paid. Many general antique dealers are misguided by the battered and worn appearance of toys and optimistically attribute an early manufacture. Despite the rising price of antique toys, it is still very possible to specialise in the products of the 18th century, as their cost is often lower than that of items from the Victorian period. A good display of 18th century dissected puzzles, cards, wooden games and books could represent less expenditure than a single late 19th century train or doll's house.

In the second half of the 19th century, wooden toys were steadily ousted from popularity by those of metal, though the main area of production remained in Germany, particularly in Württemberg and Nuremberg. Large toys that were expensive to ship, such as horses, doll's houses, wheelbarrows and prams, tended to be made in the country of sale and were termed 'strong toys' by their 19th century makers. The Americans in particular found it economical to produce their own doll's houses, and the firm of Bliss made the brightly coloured lithographed versions that are among the most desirable toys produced in that

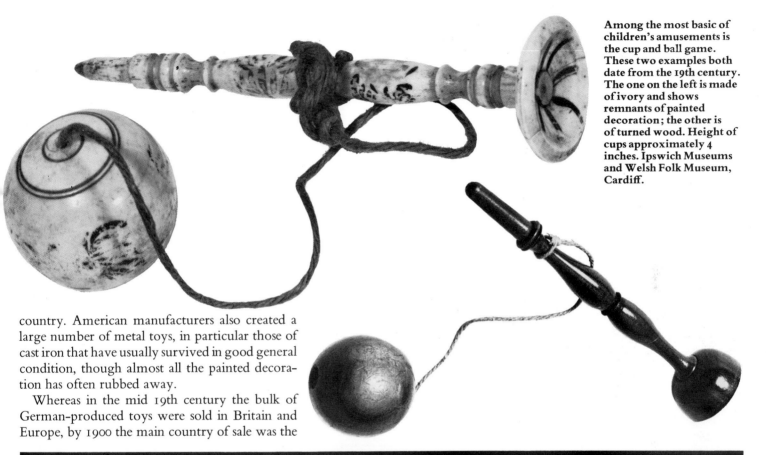

Among the most basic of children's amusements is the cup and ball game. These two examples both date from the 19th century. The one on the left is made of ivory and shows remnants of painted decoration; the other is of turned wood. Height of cups approximately 4 inches. Ipswich Museums and Welsh Folk Museum, Cardiff.

country. American manufacturers also created a large number of metal toys, in particular those of cast iron that have usually survived in good general condition, though almost all the painted decoration has often rubbed away.

Whereas in the mid 19th century the bulk of German-produced toys were sold in Britain and Europe, by 1900 the main country of sale was the

COSTUME GAME, CIRCA 1860.
Presented by Mrs Madden.

R.1950-44.27

USA and this accounts for the fact that some of the finest toys of this period are now found in that country and that the prices asked by American dealers are frequently lower than in Europe. American toy makers placed great emphasis on the durable qualities of their work and the pieces made before 1915 have a tremendous air of permanence. Examples include the cast-iron kitchen ranges with names such as the Gem or Pet and money boxes that have remained in excellent working order despite their age.

In comparison, the French contribution to the development of toys has a distinctively ephemeral quality. That country is characterised by, for instance, the detailed Epinal prints from which, with a little patience, the child could construct an elegant picture gallery or a farmyard scene. A number of good quality tin toys were also made, particularly those working figures of characters seen in the streets of Paris which were created by Fernand Martin at the end of the 19th century. In the early 20th century realistic cars were made by Jouets de Paris and the firm of Citroën, who used these children's toys to promote the full-sized adult versions. Above all, the French are famed for their automata, many of which had fine heads made by the leading dollmakers. These figures

A colourful Pope Jone board on the usual swivel base with a central covered compartment. English, late 18th century. Author's Collection.

were finely costumed and when activated formed charming parlour amusements, while the cheaper versions were sold as toys. A wide variety of wind-up toys with simple movements were produced and these are often characterised by coloured metallic wheels of a rather flimsy construction. This lack of solidity is also sometimes seen in the doll's houses made in France, but this is compensated for by their lavish and colourful decoration, and their small doll inhabitants are among the best produced.

Britain concentrated mainly on the so-called strong toys until the First World War made the manufacturers aware of the necessity of producing some novelty pieces. After this time several firms, including Chad Valley and Wells, made acceptable tin model transport and there was a more significant native production of board games and constructional kits of various kinds. The doll's houses and rocking horses that furnished the large nurseries in the 19th century are among the most important toys, but probably the most significant contribution was in the field of printed games. Many publishers from the 18th century made really high quality dissections, picture blocks, card games and a whole range of well presented and often moralistic board games. The engagingly

primitive model theatres, with the actors in stylised Regency stage postures, are also peculiarly British; good early examples are now difficult to find, though not necessarily very expensive.

When purchasing a toy of any type, the general condition is very important and it is usually far better to buy a later example that is within your price range than an early piece that it may not be possible to restore satisfactorily. Many of the specialist collectors undertake their own restoration, as they find that only in this way can their own requirements be adequately served. It is also extremely difficult to locate high quality restorers, as once they are discovered by collectors they have so much work that they have to turn down many new customers and hardly ever find it necessary to advertise. Tin toys in particular have to be dealt with sensitively, otherwise the hard effect of a reproduction piece may easily result. Generally the beginner is advised to leave the object in its original state, even if it is very battered, as resale to an enthusiast is more difficult if he first has to remove amateurish paintwork. In some cases, such as with doll's houses, repainting and decorating is acceptable if it is carried out tastefully, as this was after all one of the functions of the toy. Many children were provided with sheets of

Facing page, top: **Printed games popular in the 19th century included items such as this group of dressing dolls dating from around 1860. Ipswich Museums.** *Bottom:* **This sand toy is a rare example of a labelled toy made by William Tower, one of the prime instigators of the Tower Guild of South Hingham, Mass. (see page 57). When sand is fed through the hopper with the shovel, the wheel turns, activating the figure.** *Circa* **1840-1850. Margaret Woodbury Strong Museum, Rochester, New York.**

A rare American doll's
house made completely of
sheet metal in about 1880.
The outside is painted
white with green
trimmings and the roof is
corrugated. The tin
chimneys are painted to
represent bricks. The
staircase is of metal also,
but most of the furnishings
are wooden and of the
German type, probably
added over a long period
up to the Second World
War. Width 50⅜ inches.
Margaret Woodbury
Strong Museum,
Rochester, New York.

wallpaper with the house when new so that its appearance might have changed several times even in the childhood of the original owner. Obviously houses in completely original condition are preferred, but repainting in this area is not as significant as for instance in the field of tin.

Fashions among collectors often cause quite rapid fluctuations in price and two eager people competing for an object that has suddenly appealed to them in the salerooms can cause quite radical shifts of emphasis. The number of leading collectors who set values in Europe and America is fairly limited, and if one of these loses interest in a particular item, its price can rapidly fall, pinpointing the necessity for the average collector to buy what he really appreciates rather than what is currently fashionable. Until very recently, toy collectors have been in the enjoyable position of finding that all their possessions are escalating in value every year but at the time of writing the mad scramble to buy almost anything old has died down and more logical prices are being realised. In a few instances values have actually dropped, though interest has not waned, and the impression is given that collectors are now considering purchases much more carefully.

It was once predicted that as the quality early toys disappeared from the market or became very expensive, collectors would turn to those made more recently, but this has not happened in Europe, where the toys of the 1940s and 1950s are viewed with some distaste. Enthusiasts obviously prefer to aquire fewer pieces rather than accept items made when standards of toymaking were becoming completely geared to mass-produced cheap products. Collecting in America is somewhat different in this respect, as more people collect toys rather than antique toys. But even in that country later examples have not risen in value as fast as was originally predicted and the beginner is strongly advised to buy pieces from as early a period as he can possibly afford.

Primitive toys, perhaps carved by a father out of a piece of scrap wood for the amusement of his own children, are very lightly considered in Europe and pass through the hands of dealers and auctioneers at remarkably low prices. In the USA, by contrast, such pieces are very highly regarded and will often command substantial prices. This is because the motivation behind the making of such toys is more appreciated whereas in Europe the interest is in the professional finish of an example. Roughly carved animals made by the early settlers, home-made checkers and cribbage boards and sets of gaudily decorated skittles, all made with the minimum number of tools, appeal greatly if

they can be positively attributed to an American source.

The collecting of marbles is also idiosyncratic to the USA, where there is even a specialist society of enthusiasts. American glass of all types is avidly collected, particularly the products of the numerous factories set up in the 19th century. Several of these produced marbles, some to a very high standard, and it is inevitable that interest should have developed in any examples which can be attributed by documentation or appearance to a particular glass house. Marbles attributed to the Bennington pottery in Vermont usually have a characteristic mottled brown glaze, though a few are known in shades of blue. *The Boys' Own Book*, published in 1829 by Munroe & Francis of Boston, describes the sports and games enjoyed by boys at the time, and deals with marbles, which were then mostly imported, in some detail. The best available were taws made of pink marble with dark-red veins, known originally as blood alleys and later as alleys. The cheapest, and the most inferior, were apparently those of Dutch origin, which were made of variegated clay. Another type was made of yellow stone with brown or black spots and circles. There is no mention of glass marbles at this time, and as late as the 1880s and 1890s

S. C. Dyke and M. B. Mischler of Ohio were selling clay marbles in some numbers.

It seemed appropriate when writing this book to deal with the subject in relation to the main collecting fields rather than listing individual makers. In certain areas, such as doll's houses and wooden toys, there are only a handful of marked examples, and these sections have been set out in a way I thought would be most helpful. Patent office records and old magazines often contain lists of firms, but where their actual products are not known or when no accurate descriptions or illustrations were included, I have ignored their presence as they served only to cloud the general picture. Whereas dolls would tend to be classed with toys by the general public, collectors consider the two fields quite separately, though in some cases the distinction between doll and toy becomes blurred, as in the case of automata or clockwork figures. This encyclopedia follows the collectors' and dealers' distinction and excludes dolls, which are in any case very adequately covered by several specialist books. Toy collecting appeals to people of all income levels so the cheapest acquisitions such as battered soft toys are included as well as expensive items such as automata. Each section contains individual comments on care and advice on purchase.

An ivory chess set dating from the 17th century and once the property of the Venerable Benjamin Millingchamp (1756–1829), Archdeacon of Carmarthen. Welsh Folk Museum, Cardiff.

I

MINIATURE LIVING

Continental doll's houses

The Gontard cabinet house in the Historisches Museum, Frankfurt am Main. Originally made in Holland around 1750, it was evidently very much a plaything, containing a wide selection of furnishings added by successive generations of German girl owners. Characteristic items include the earthenware stove in the bedroom at top left, and the kitchen, unusually placed on the first floor, with its fine display of miniature metal jugs and dishes.

The earliest surviving doll's houses are of German origin, and the first written references also relate to houses made in that country, such as the prestige cabinet which Duke Albrecht V of Bavaria purchased for his daughter in 1558. Continental houses made before the 19th century have survived in a fairly limited number, and the more ordinary versions that were the everyday playthings of children do not appear to have been preserved. Wealthy merchants and princes equipped cabinet-type houses as expensive curiosities with fine silver and porcelain from the East, and it is mainly the results of their interest that can now be seen in the breathtaking selection at the Germanisches Nationalmuseum in Nuremberg and in the Rijksmuseum, Amsterdam.

A number of the German cabinet houses were,

in fact, constructed quite roughly but have a great impact on the viewer because of the degree of surface decoration, which must have been quite brilliant in colour when new. Though the majority were set out by collectors as lavish display pieces, there are a few houses that were constructed purely with the aim of teaching children their household duties, such as that assembled by Anna Köferlin, a Nuremberg burgher's wife, in 1631. The earliest cabinet in the Nuremberg Museum dates from 1600 and represents a three-storey town house. It is unique because of the figures of guards which are painted on the walls on either side of some inner doors. A wall around a courtyard is painted with several scenes showing a brief amorous encounter between a monk and a nun which results in them both doing penance –

a clear indication that the cabinet was intended for adults. These early German houses are characterised by their large kitchen fireplaces with an arched storage space for fuel and a wealth of miniature brass, copper and pewter dishes arranged on shelves on the canopy. Though originally intended to carry away the smoke from the pans, this was almost invariably utilised as a decorative display feature. The reception rooms and bedrooms often contain the very heavily glazed green earthenware stoves that were originally sold as ornamental pieces but were of a size that made them ideally suited for a doll's house. Nearly all the houses also contain good quality miniature silver and porcelain, and though the problem of scale was of less concern to the German than the Dutch creators of such pieces, the combined effect of the

A large scale two-roomed Nuremberg cabinet house with its original inhabitants. The structure dates from the second half of the 17th century and presents an exact picture of an interior of the period. Note the canopy over the kitchen range with its display of dishes, and the green earthenware stove in the bedroom (*detail below*). Germanisches Nationalmuseum, Nuremberg.

The splendid interior of the Stromer cabinet house with its date, '1639' painted on the upper window. The balustrading along the fronts of the rooms is cleverly painted to simulate depth. Germanisches National-museum, Nuremberg.

rich furnishings and the gleaming metals is splendid.

The most famous of the German cabinets is the Stromer house, which carries the date 1639, and is remarkable because the scale of the house changes entirely in the lower third, where eight small rooms are closely packed. This part of the house contained the nursery and servants' rooms and one section forms a stable with two finely carved horses and a cow. Although the furniture is not constructed in very precise detail, it is more lively in effect than the perfectly made pieces in the Dutch houses simply because the German collectors crammed their rooms with so much interesting detail. An example is a gentleman's room where a barber's bowl hangs on the wall and a freshly laundered nightcap and nightshirt lie on the bed. A wash bowl is placed below a finely made water container that pivots downwards, and a rather dainty sponge hangs from a ribbon alongside.

Another well-known German cabinet, the Kress house, dates from the second half of the 17th century, and this is particularly memorable because of the correctly carved balustrading across the front of the various rooms. Although the maker has kept fairly closely to scale, the lower part of the house contains the same small out-of-proportion rooms as the Stromer house, though in this case they are more integrated as they are at the end of several flights of stairs which appear to lead right through the house from the attic area. This cabinet has one great advantage as it still contains the dolls, including an unusual bent-limb baby with painted black hair and an elegant lady doll in undress with items of her costume, including a green corset, lying around her room. The well made furniture includes two tables in the dining room that are inlaid with bone or ivory. There is a painted sundial on a wall dated 1785 – an indication of how, as in so many houses, extra pieces were added over a period of years.

The Dutch houses are more in the nature of items of furniture than the German and the most important are contained in exquisitely made cabinets so that the valuable contents can be protected from light by closing the doors. Another house was originally curtained when not on display, again indicating the seriousness with which these adult toys were regarded. The oldest Dutch cabinet at the Rijksmuseum is that once owned by Margaretha de Ruyter and constructed in the mid 17th century. As in most early Dutch houses, there is a well equipped laundry room in the attic area with an abundance of finely stitched and correctly

made garments drying on the clothes lines or waiting for ironing. The nursery is situated next door and the furnishings include a fine bed surmounted by rather over-large pineapples – a symbol of hospitality. Most of the walls in this well set out cabinet are hung with silk, which gives the structure a particularly rich effect and accentuates the contrast between the exquisitely furnished reception rooms and the practical kitchen and work rooms. The house exactly mirrors a Dutch burgher's home of the period and is complete even to a mouse lying captive in a trap.

The other house in the Rijksmuseum is much more sophisticated in concept, as the structure itself is carefully designed to simulate depth. The effect is given of a basement leading off the down-

The interior of the cabinet house once owned by Margaretha de Ruyter and dating from the last quarter of the 17th century. The cabinet itself is of heavy walnut and the inhabitants are finely made with wax heads. The laundry room on the top floor is typically Dutch. Rijksmuseum, Amsterdam.

stairs hall and passages running behind the rooms in the foreground. The cabinet itself is a splendid piece decorated with marquetry of pewter on tortoiseshell and it is necessary to climb a set of library steps to look at the top floor rooms. It is thought that the house was made for Petronella Oortman, who married Johannes Brandt in 1686, and the whole structure is of great interest as it is accompanied by a portrait of itself, painted by Jacob Appel (1680 to 1751). This painting shows that it was originally provided with a family of the realistic dolls that are also a feature of Margaretha de Ruyter's house. No expense was spared in the creation of this exquisite structure and the woodwork, panelling, chimneypieces and murals are all of the very highest standard. The 'best kitchen' in which the mistress of a Dutch house sat during the day is one of the most memorable rooms, as the cupboards are filled with the fine silver and porcelain that would have formed part of a bride's dowry. Most of the rooms are supplied with small rectangular foot warmers that are again a feature of the Dutch cabinets and give a touch of realism to the exquisite structure.

There is another great cabinet house at the Hague dating from the mid 18th century which is of interest as it was so fully documented by its original owner, Sara Rothe. It was described after her death as 'A cabinet of Art Curios with all those household articles appertaining to the same'. This cabinet was constructed from the parts and the contents of three older houses which Sara bought at auction and amalgamated in a walnut cabinet for which she paid 230 florins. Carpenters and painters were engaged to carry out the work, while some of the furnishings such as a rug were sewn by the lady herself. One of the most impressive features of the house, apart from its massive size, is the porcelain room, where a wealth of china and glass miniatures are displayed on specially shaped shelves.

There are few early recorded houses from other European countries, though there are written references, one to a Strasbourg house dating from 1680 and another to a fine example owned by Marie Antoinette. A rare survivor is an entrancing miniature palace dating from the 17th century that can be seen in the Museum of Industrial Art at Bologna. This is an arresting piece because so much accurate detail has been packed into a very small construction. The reception rooms are entirely those of a noble family and furnished with a classical elegance that contrasts effectively with the extremely primitive kitchen.

Advances in colour lithography in the 19th century opened up new possibilities in the decoration of doll's houses. The complex and decorative house shown *left* was probably made in Germany. The surface is a combination of lithographed paper and painted wood. Few commercially made houses are finished with such care – each window, for example, was provided with curtains that matched the decoration. *Circa* 1880; height 3 feet 6 inches. *Below:* The interior of the same house showing part of the interesting arrangement of the attic area and the original wallpapers. The furnishings are mainly late 19th century German with several pieces of imitation rosewood. Betty Harvey-Jones Collection.

Facing page: **An effective brightly lithographed miniature doll's house with a simple two-roomed interior and a painted roof. German, late 19th century; height 10½ inches. Author's Collection.**

Individual rooms for the display of miniatures and furniture were particularly favoured by French and German children, and these survive in far greater numbers in Europe than in Britain. The development of these settings, from accurate craftsman-made versions possibly for adults, to cheaply made, commercially furnished examples made purely as toys in the late 19th century, can be traced in the large number of examples at the Spielzeugmuseum in Nuremberg. These cannot be illustrated as the museum is reluctant to allow its exhibits to be reproduced. The number of exhibits however makes a visit to this town a necessity for the miniature enthusiast.

There are far more examples of Continental houses made after 1850 and the trade exhibitions and fairs that became so much a part of commercial life after the Great Exhibition of 1851 meant that the names of manufacturers and the nature of their wares were recorded. An example is a certain

Dutch cabinet houses were generally more formal and exquisite than their German counterparts. The lavishly equipped interior of the Utrecht cabinet house shown here includes an art chamber on the first floor and a formal garden on the ground floor. The latter is a feature seen in early houses of both German and Dutch origin. *Circa* **1680. Centraal Museum, Utrecht.** *Right:* **This massive Dutch cabinet house dates from the mid 18th century and is of particular interest as its contents were fully documented by the original owner Sara Rothe, who died in 1760. Escher Foundation, Haags Gemeentemuseum, The Hague.**

Facing page: **The particularly ornate Dutch cabinet house made for Petronella Oortman in the late 17th century. The exterior is decorated with marquetry of pewter on tortoiseshell. The detail shown at the top features some exquisite miniature porcelain and an interesting mural in the first floor drawing room. Rijksmuseum, Amsterdam.**

M. Kopp of the Rue du Temple, Paris, who was mentioned in the *citations favorables* for his fine model of a dining room at the Paris Exposition of 1844.

Late 19th century French doll's houses have a very charming lightness of design and the manufacturers made great use of delicate balconies, sometimes simply made of painted cardboard and applied transfer-type motifs. Mansard-type roofs with printed paper tiles and impressive double doors are also features of the French designs, which were furnished with bright silk upholstered furniture and dainty wall mirrors. Few of the houses were marked in any way, and where a house is without documentation the country of origin is assessed by the general characteristics of the structure. Furniture is of little help in establishing provenance, as it was obtained from a variety of sources and many French houses were mainly equipped with German-made pieces.

The most elegant of the Continental furniture is that painted to resemble gilded rosewood and produced in the Waltershausen area, where the finest doll's house furniture was still made well into the 20th century. These rosewood furnishings were made from the first quarter of the 19th century until around 1900. They are extremely popular because of their precise detail and the fact that three distinct sizes were made, so that the collector can usually find a piece exactly in scale for the house that is being furnished. Sewing tables, chiffonniers, pianos and even small key cupboards were made by this firm, whose work was well within the price range of middle class children. One of the greatest producers of metal pieces was the firm of Märklin (see German Tin Toys) who included an almost unbelievable assortment of quite unusual kitchen equipment in their catalogues. In the early years of the 20th century, Gebrüder Schneegass of Waltershausen in Germany made a range of very stylised Art Nouveau furniture including fashionable art pot stands and longcase clocks in high Art Nouveau. Their wash stands, for instance, were provided with marble tops and all cupboards and drawers opened realistically, thus providing the child with a completely satisfying model. The majority of doll's-house furniture is completely unmarked, though it can sometimes be identified by comparison with the drawings in old catalogues. These are now being reproduced in greater numbers because of the interest shown by collectors in correctly identifying their possessions, and are a useful source of information.

British doll's houses

The interior of the late 17th century cabinet house given to Ann Sharp by her godmother, the future Queen Anne. This photograph is of particular interest as it shows the house reassembled for the first time in many years. Courtesy of William Bulwer Long.

The concept of a cabinet house did not appeal to the English as much as to the German and Dutch merchants and the only surviving early house in cabinet form is that which once belonged to Ann Sharp, goddaughter of Queen Anne. This is contained in a very poorly made pine cupboard that is very much a country cousin to the elegant Continental structures. The great difference, however, is one of intention, as the Sharp house was played with by a child and was intended as a toy, not merely a repository for fine miniatures. Ann Sharp was born in 1691 and most of the contents of the house date from the years of her childhood, though she continued to add individual pieces until the mid 18th century. At the top of the house is a shelf that appears to have been constructed purely for the display of curiosities,

such as cut-out paper figures, a small theatre, a tiny card doll's house, adult size gloves and even shoes and a muff. The house, despite its very basic structure, contains a most impressive assortment of contemporary wooden dolls all labelled by Ann herself according to their station in life. Scale was obviously of little concern and this contributes to the appeal of the house, in which huge Leeds creamware plates contrast with small Bristol blue glasses and decanters. There are several commercially made pieces of furniture that still carry their original prices and are mainly finished in imitation lacquer, though there is also a table painted with a delicate scene and an assortment of very crudely made chairs as well as an intricately carved chandelier protected by a glass shade. The alabaster table, with its matching tea pot and tea

The massively proportioned 'baby' house at Uppark in Dorset, which belonged to Sarah Lethieullier and carries her family coat of arms on the pediment. *Circa* 1730.

Some details of the interior of the Ann Sharp house. The lacquered furniture was commercially made and sold from toy shops of the period, and various items were added by the owner throughout her life.

Probably the most beautiful English baby house is this example from Nostell Priory in Yorkshire dating from around 1735. Of particular interest are the fine chimney pieces and the wax and wooden dolls.

bowls, is decorated with a simple leaf design and similar sets are also seen in early Continental cabinets. As the original wallpapers and hangings are untouched, the house has a most evocative atmosphere and reflects its period with complete truthfulness.

In 18th century England, dolls were described as 'babies' and doll's houses were therefore termed 'baby houses', a title that is still used by native collectors as a means of differentiating these early houses from later examples. The highly elegant baby house at Uppark, in Dorset, is a complete contrast to the Sharp house, and was made originally for Sarah Lethieullier, who became the wife of Sir Matthew Fetherstonehaugh, whose home was at Uppark. This splendid baby house has one of the most impressive façades and the furniture is exquisitely made, in many cases especially for the rooms. The actual paintings of animals and game were also especially fitted into the panelling, as in a full-sized house of the period, and contribute

greatly to the realistic effect. The construction of the house is believed to date from 1730 and is very ingenious, in that the front opens in nine separate sections, so that each room can be viewed independently. Inside, all the connecting doors are correctly panelled and are provided with well made brass model locks. The dining room is arresting, as it is furnished with miniature chairs of extremely high quality and wooden serving men, while on the table is an assortment of fine silver. Although wood was quite acceptable for the servant dolls, it was thought necessary to make the family of wax that gave a much more realistic and delicate effect.

The baby house at Nostell Priory in Yorkshire is thought to have been originally constructed around 1735 for the children of the 4th baronet, who rebuilt Nostell Priory itself, though it is probable that the doll's house was not in fact finished until 1743. The furnishing of the house, which is very loosely based on Nostell itself, was

supervised by Lady Winn and her sister Miss Henshaw, the ladies adding a label to this effect in one of the first floor rooms. The whole of this house is still in original condition and the two parts of the front slide to the sides to give a view of the contents. Various stories associate this house and its furnishings with the names of Chippendale and Adam, but their actual involvement is very unlikely though the high standard both of design and workmanship makes it easy to see why the tradition arose. It was in all probability made to the design of James Paine, with an interior divided into nine rooms and a staircase in the lower hall. The kitchen still retains its original spits and there is a fabric dog and a wooden cook carved by a British craftsman. The marble chimney pieces in the reception rooms are perfectly made, especially one in the Chinoiserie drawing room carved in grey marble and surmounted by a bust. This room is quite beautiful in effect, its gold walls being painted with the most perfectly proportioned scenes and

the correctly panelled door enriched with gilt along the mouldings and panels. All the doors have correctly made working locks, a detail very rarely seen even in the finest baby houses.

The two ladies who furnished this house obviously enjoyed sewing the bed linen and curtains, the quilts in particular being stitched in very correct detail. Though the effect of this house is lavish, the furnishings are in fact fairly sparse, as they were in the actual interiors of the period, where chairs and tables were set out around the sides of a room and brought forward when required. It is now virtually impossible to find 18th century furniture for houses purchased without their contents, so that most collectors have to resort to adding much later pieces.

Although the 18th century is mainly associated with such fine houses as those already discussed, it should be remembered that much simpler structures were also available for more ordinary children, though these have only occasionally

Some of the furniture produced for doll's houses was exquisitely detailed despite its small scale. Shown here is a group of delicately carved doll's house furniture which includes a needlework box fitted with mother of pearl tools. The dressing table has opening doors. Luton Museum and Art Gallery, Bedfordshire.

Many English doll's houses in the 19th century were equipped with Continental furniture. Shown here is a late 19th century doll's house kitchen with mainly German furnishings. Ipswich Museums.
Below: This late Victorian Gothic villa is an example of the simple but none the less decorative designs which were the result of commercial production in the 19th century. It has additional round windows at the sides and contains five rooms and a staircase. Height 21 inches. Author's Collection.

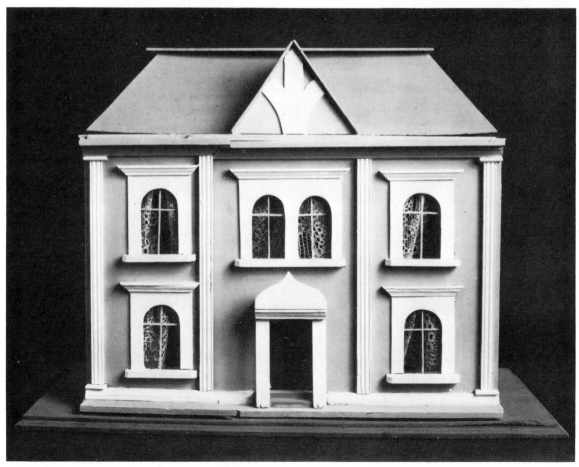

survived. A few, illustrated in prints, are of a most basic type and would be very lightly regarded by the majority of collectors, who expect a doll's house to be decorative. The Georgian house with painted brickwork and pedimented windows at the Norwich Museum and the small example with mock attic windows at the Bethnal Green Museum in London are probably more in line with the houses played with by children than the splendid houses at Uppark and Nostell. Even in these cheaper examples, however, there is often a wealth of correct but unobtrusive detail not seen in late 19th century houses, such as correctly panelled doors and chimney breasts that really do connect to the chimneys. Quite a number were provided with locks so that the child could not play with the contents when unsupervised, and later to stop her rough younger brothers and sisters damaging the china. When the construction of the house was weighty, carrying handles were sometimes fixed to the sides and the style of these fixtures, if contemporary, is often an aid in dating.

The houses of the Regency period became much simpler in form and only occasionally, such as in the house at Audley End, Saffron Walden, do we see a really large structure with many rooms. These houses are sometimes provided with keys but a more usual closing device was a centre panel which pegged into place and prevented the side

doors from opening. The danger of damage from younger brothers was still very obvious and an example in my own collection has a notice painted on the back: 'Warning. Boys throwing stones against the back of this house will be prosecuted with the utmost severity'. Changes in architecture seem to have affected doll's house designers only slightly, and the basically Georgian shape continued in use well into the 19th century, so that many houses are optimistically dated to an earlier

Top: **A set of home-made doll's house furniture created out of feathers for a child in Norfolk.** *Circa* **1850. Ipswich Museums.**
Above: **This music room from a South Kensington style doll's house contains a set of gold and black lithographed paper-on-wood furniture, probably of German origin. Author's Collection.**

A typical 19th century doll's house interior, 'Miss Bradshaw's doll's house', with contents obtained from several countries in the second half of the 19th century. Note the tin bath at the top of the stairs, underlining the absence of a bathroom. Ipswich Museums.

Facing page: **The east front of Queen Mary's doll's house, which was designed by Sir Edwin Lutyens and presented to the Queen in 1924. This photograph shows how the outer walls are raised in order to view the interior. Reproduced by gracious permission of Her Majesty Queen Elizabeth II.**

period. The tradition of estate-made houses was also maintained throughout the 19th century and several examples are encountered that were especially constructed for an individual child.

The number of commercially made houses increased steadily throughout the 19th century, as the ever widening middle classes were eager to provide their children with good toys. These later houses are often sturdily made and are extremely decorative, with their balconies, columns and neatly curtained windows. The effect of the interiors was much improved as specially made papers were now available, so that a good scaled appearance could be created. Furniture was available from both France and Germany, as there was only a limited production in Britain. While it was uneconomical for the Germans to export houses, the small tin and wooden furnishings could be packed tightly together for shipping and these were so cheap that there was little point in the British manufacturers attempting to compete.

Occasionally, a specially constructed house made as an adult toy still appeared, such as that in

the Bethnal Green Museum created to the specifications of Miss Bryant in 1860 and furnished with the heavily buttoned mahogany furniture which exactly characterises the period. The house is an obvious adult's conceit, as it contains some good miniature pieces such as Chinese jars, a Doulton water filter and correctly stitched carpets. The whole arrangement was kept under lock and key and has the perfect, untampered-with air seen in the earlier Continental houses.

Although the idea of a cabinet house does not seem to have appealed to the British in the 18th century, there are several 19th century examples in a similar vein, though usually contained in a very functional cupboard. One such construction was that created between 1835 and 1838 by the wife and daughters of a Manchester doctor who placed their miniature furnishings in a well-made lacquer cabinet. This is an idea which many modern collectors have followed, as a closed cupboard looks quite appropriate in any room.

One of the few known manufacturers of doll's houses was Lines Brothers, who sold many of their strongly made houses through Gamage's, the department store in London. Gamage's catalogue for the year before the First World War is now reprinted and some of the Lines houses can be identified by comparison with the drawings. Many of these houses look completely Victorian in design and indicate the difficulty of dating doll's houses purely on appearance.

Bathrooms occasionally appear in doll's houses from 1838, though they did not become common fixtures until the early 20th century and some very elegant Edwardian doll's houses were completely without any washing facilities, except for a tin bath in front of the bedroom fire, protected by a metal bamboo or decalomania screen. One very expensive house made in 1907, however, contained a bathroom with hot water that was supplied from a cistern heated by a spirit lamp. German firms such as Märklin supplied many small baths and lavatories that could be filled with water and made to fill and flush correctly, but as these were such successful toys they are now rarely found without a disfiguring amount of rust.

The concept of folding houses absorbed the attentions of several designers before the First World War, and their specifications were registered at the patent office, though whether any were actually produced is questionable. One firm, trading as Benda & Hipauf in 1910, designed a 'Toy room or house of the collapsible kind, to be erected upon the box containing it'. It was supplied with windows and a door and sides and roof slotted into position. The illustrated house was given printed windows with curtains and any furniture was to be fixed to the card from which the whole construction was made. Another firm devised a system for houses based upon separate boxes which could be linked together by press-button fastenings so that a structure of several floors could be assembled. The fronts of the rooms were all provided with hinged flaps. A doll's flat, registered by L. G. Slocum in 1912, consisted of boards, suitably ornamented to form the outside or inside of rooms and hinged together at their vertical edges. Each wall was decorated with an arched top and when not in use they could be folded together. Efforts to create folding furniture were also made, but these were mainly of paper or card and once cut from the sheets have only rarely survived.

Adult interest in doll's houses was reawakened in 1924, when Queen Mary was given a perfectly equipped house as a gift. The structure was far more complete than any of the early cabinet

Printed folding houses provided a cheap alternative to the traditional wooden doll's houses, and had the virtue of providing a variety of different scenes in a compact format. This example in the form of a book is 'The Doll's House', published by Raphael Tuck, 'Publishers to Her Majesty the Queen'. Late 19th century. Betty Harvey-Jones Collection.

houses, as it was consciously created as 'A house of the Twentieth Century, which should be fitted up with perfect fidelity, down to the smallest details, so as to closely represent a genuine and complete example of a domestic interior with all the household arrangements characteristic of daily life of the present time'. The house was designed by Sir Edwin Lutyens and it was three years before all the details could be assembled; miniatures were specially commissioned from famous manufacturers, and even the jars of jam were properly made and labelled. Though few women could hope to own such a perfect model, the publicity given to the Queen's house encouraged many families to embark on similar projects, with the men taking charge of the woodwork and the women the soft furnishings. Considerable ingenuity is seen in several of these houses, and all sorts of card containers and pieces of household junk were utilised in the making of items such as longcase clocks, or stools and tables from broken chess pieces. The author once retrieved a fine 18th century cameo from a house of this vintage, which had been glued to the wall as a

picture because the pin had broken. These home-crafted houses are very difficult to evaluate, but they are often more evocative as period pieces than those which are completely commercial.

Lines, trading as Triang, made some very large houses with small rooms in the 1930s which are characterised by gold paper sundials glued to one of the gables. The same basic units were used for houses made to the size required by the customer so that some stretched for about six feet while others were of very modest size. Firms such as William Britain made metal furnishings for houses on this small scale, and the author recently found a marked Meccano doll's-house lamp, though this is an unusual product for that firm.

Though the houses in which children lived were becoming lighter in the second quarter of the 20th century, for some reason doll's houses became narrower and meaner and the furniture was often so small that only the most basic detail could be added. However, there were a few interesting miniatures, such as crystal sets with earphones, telephones and curiously designed electric fires, which make these years not completely without interest for the collector.

Houses in original condition are obviously preferred, but as some were repainted and redecorated several times, even during the childhood of the original owner, this is not as important as with most of the other toys discussed, and an example with sensitive restoration is worth buying. There are now several small firms making very well constructed reproductions and it is also possible to furnish these with elegant but recently made pieces in 18th century style.

American doll's houses

During the 18th century, the doll's houses with which American children played were mainly imported from Europe, and as the shipping costs would have been high, they must have formed part of the nursery equipment of only the most fortunate of girls. Miniature furniture was manufactured at this time, particularly in Western Pennsylvania and Philadelphia, but there appears to have been no production of pieces suitable for baby houses. The earliest known doll's house of certain American manufacture was made in 1744, and is now in the Van Cortlandt Museum in New York. It was specially made for a member of the Homans family of Boston, and carries the dates 1744 and 1774, possibly the dates of birth of the first two generations of owners. The Dutch influence on the design of the house is strong, and indicates that it was probably made by a new immigrant. It also illustrates the difficulty of attributing early houses made in America, as they are obviously reminiscent of the craftsman's country of origin. Collectors are therefore very wary of claiming American manufacture unless there is some positive record, though it seems unlikely that many were produced until conditions became really settled.

German doll's-house furniture was so cheap in the early 19th century that there was little native production, despite the fact that miniatures of fine quality for the amusement of adults were made. Another fairly early American house is that in the Independence National Park Collection, which was made in 1810 for Sarah Emlen Cresson, who was born in 1806. In this house, as in the Van Cortlandt example, the floor coverings and the hearth rugs are painted directly onto the wood. This house is of great interest to doll's house enthusiasts, as it carries a miniature Green Tree Fire Mark, an indication in a full-sized house that it is covered by an insurance policy. It also boasts a Captain's Walk, a form of balcony running around part of the roof that was popular on houses of American construction, but only rarely seen in Europe. A house in the Shelburne Museum in Vermont, again dating from the early 19th century, has windows, a fanlight, curtains and even chimney-pieces all painted in position, and indicates a style of construction that was later used by firms such as Bliss and Converse.

One of the most impressive mid 19th century houses was that created by the Rev. Dr. Phillip Brett between 1838 and 1840 for his daughters and now displayed in the Museum of the City of New York. The house is fairly complex in structure

and obviously a model rather than a child's toy to be moved regularly about a house. The opening drawing-room doors are particularly effective and are completed by elegant six-paned fanlights in the Georgian style. The contents are also highly impressive and occupied some seventy boxes when transported to the museum. In the dining room hangs the Brett coat of arms, while a portrait of Brett himself is in the drawing room. The basic furnishings are mainly commercial and include pieces of Sèvres and Bristol blue glass, and as the house can be so accurately dated, the contents are a source of useful information about the range of pieces available at the time.

Despite the obvious attractiveness of the Brett house, the furnishings of the house owned by the Chester County Historical Society are a great deal finer, being the work of a Philadelphia

This house, which shows obvious Dutch influence, is interesting as it is the earliest known American doll's house, constructed in 1744 for a member of the Homans family of Boston and equipped with useful drawers in the base for the storage of furnishings and toys. Height 48 inches. Van Cortland House Museum, New York City.

firms such as Turner's of Meriden, Connecticut, while the manufacturing areas in New York and Philadelphia were also active. In Pennsylvania brightly painted wares decorated with bold flowers and leaves were produced, while the Pattersons of Berlin, Connecticut, were also making tin toys. Francis, Field & Francis, otherwise known as the Philadelphia Toy Manufactory, also began production in 1847, and their products included tin chairs, clocks, bureaus, and other doll's house furnishings. Brown & Co. of Forestville made sets of tin furniture in imitation rosewood or oak, for the equipping of parlours and bedrooms, some of which were further embellished with 'velvet' upholstery. Iron furnishings were made by J. S. Stevens of Cromwell, Connecticut, and appeared in their 1868 catalogue both in full size for adults and in miniature for doll's houses. Washstands, rocking chairs and even dust pans were included. Pewter furniture was made by firms such as Peter F. Pia of New York, established in 1848, who made filigree-type furniture, similar in construction to that made at the time in soft white metal in Germany. A silversmith, Benjamin H. Chamberlain, made an intricately detailed house as an extravagant present for his daughters, which bore an engraved silver nameplate on the door. Many of the furnishings in this house originated in Europe and it is probably far more typical of the equipment owned by the majority of American children of the time.

The American doll's houses most popular with modern collectors are those made by the Bliss Manufacturing Company of Pawtucket, Rhode Island, a firm that was established in 1832 and incorporated in 1893. Their characteristic lithographed houses were introduced in 1895 and were made of brightly printed paper that was glued to wood. The houses are memorable because of the inventiveness of the designs and the abundance of decoration. Fortunately many carry the maker's mark, so that the few unmarked examples can be authenticated by comparison with an identical model of known provenance. Despite the delightfully complex exteriors, the houses are slightly disappointing inside, as they are frequently composed of only one room up and down. This company produced stables, mansions and skyscrapers as well as the idiosyncratic houses with their bobbin-turned pillars and printed 'wrought iron' verandas. In larger houses, the windows are made of mica, but in smaller versions they are also printed. Though originally produced quite cheaply and in commercial quantities, the houses are a

Above and facing page: **These two wooden doll's houses with lithographed paper decorations are typical products of the Bliss Manufacturing Company, dating from the period between 1890 and 1910. Both are marked 'R. Bliss', and the example above is 21½ inches wide, while that on the facing page measures 25½ inches from ground to chimney top. Both Margaret Woodbury Strong Museum, Rochester, New York.**

cabinet maker by the name of Vogler. The scale is much larger than that usually found in play houses, as the structure stands some eight feet high and this size was necessary in order that the beautifully made craftsman's pieces could be adequately displayed. Some of the important furniture was made of mahogany veneered with pine, and there is a fine longcase clock by an English Quaker clockmaker, Thomas Wagstaff, who sold clocks to American families of the same faith. This house is of importance as it illustrates very accurately the appearance of a middle class American house of the 1830s. Its creator would of course have normally been engaged in making full scale furniture for such homes.

Although wooden furniture was still imported in the 1850s, metal pieces were available from

delight because of their gingerbread richness and fairytale effect. It was claimed by the firm that they were made to 'American designs to suit the taste of American children'. In earlier versions, the interior walls were also decorated by lithography, but ordinary wallpapers were later used. The company also supplied its own furniture though the variety does not appear to have been large.

Folding rooms and doll's houses are also more typical of American than European makers and among the surviving examples is one made by Stirn & Lyon of New York who patented a 'Combination Doll House' in 1881. It was contained in a large box decorated with a decidedly idealised impression of the contents. The box itself served as the foundation of the house while the lid formed the roof, the two being joined by simple prefabricated sections. The designs were painted and embossed directly onto the wood. Grimm & Leeds of New Jersey also marketed a folding house, but theirs included isinglass windows. The most popular of the American folding rooms were produced by McLoughlin Brothers of New York, who marketed the 'New Folding Doll's House' that was patented on 23 January 1894. The sections were contained in a boldly lettered box and when erected represented four rooms with printed floor coverings, wall decoration, vases and some furniture. The house was 'Designed to be played with on a table,' so that 'A number of little girls may thus get around it to the best advantage.' In 1903, McLoughlin introduced the 'Dolly's Play House', in which the rooms were also printed with fine mirrors and

Left: **A folding house produced by McLoughlin Brothers of New York, with a front garden.** *Circa* **1911. Margaret Woodbury Strong Museum, Rochester, New York.** *Below:* **Another McLoughlin Brothers product, 'The New Folding Doll's House, Patented Jan. 23rd 1894'. The room and furniture are printed in rich colours. Museum of the City of New York.**

elegant sofas. These lithographed furnishings were so splendid that even the better three-dimensional furniture must have looked mean in comparison. Another, simpler house made by this firm has a front that is lowered to form the front garden.

Morton E. Converse of Winchendon, Massachusetts, was another great producer of houses, whose home town became known as the Nuremberg of America as a result of his activities. He helped found the firm of Mason & Converse, which changed its name several times, becoming the Converse Toy and Woodware Company in 1883. Their early houses are lithographed directly onto the wood and are much less fanciful than those created by Bliss. Their houses are often characterised by details such as a printed cat staring from a window. The most basic of their houses had a hinged façade with two columns, a veranda and printed windows, while the interiors were also printed with items such as a fireplace and curtained windows. In 1913 'Perfect models printed directly on wood by our new three-dimensional process' were available in five different sizes. They are often found marked 'Converse'. In 1931 the firm marketed its 'Realy Truly Doll House' (*sic*), which was made of fibre-board and wood. This model was also provided with furniture made by the company and included such items as miniature packaged food for the refrigerator. The firm went out of business in the 1930s.

American houses of the early 20th century were almost invariably more lavishly equipped than those made in Europe, which was depressed by the austerity of the First World War and its aftermath. In the early years of the century, Schwarz were offering houses lit by electricity at their Fifth Avenue shop. Other pre-First World War houses were provided with a water tank in the roof that supplied both the kitchen and bathroom, while a splendid 1920s house boasted a 'magic floor' that moved the doll occupants around.

Albert Schoenhut was another producer of doll's houses and in 1917 advertised 'Artistic high class doll's houses and bungalows, New styles and Modern Architecture'. The houses were made of fibre-board, glass and wood embossed to resemble stone walls and roofs, and opened at the sides. Inside were unusual lithographed doors showing perspective views of the rooms within; the fireplaces were also printed. These houses were made in a variety of sizes from eight-roomed mansions to single-roomed bungalows. After 1927, they ceased to use the attractive perspective

interiors and ordinary wallpapers were used, though the gardens could now be equipped both with shrubberies and a garage. Schoenhut produced their own furniture after 1928 and were then able to offer completely furnished residences.

Tootsietoy houses, produced after 1925, are also well known to American collectors and included a fine Spanish house and a washable mansion in heavy book board. Tootsietoy furniture – 'All the strength of metal, all the beauty of wood' – was also produced by this company, which was owned by Dowst Brothers of Chicago.

Facing page: **An extremely complex American house constructed in 1893 for the daughter of the Vogel family. It was used as a toy until the 1930s and several generations added to its contents. Height 5 feet 6 inches. Milwaukee Public Museum.**

Shops and shopping

A model grocer's shop with bisque headed figures, and an interesting metal scale on the counter. The contents were added to by several generations. All the drawers have china labels. English, *circa* 1895-1900; Width 30 inches. Author's Collection.

It is surprising that, despite the fact that shopping was becoming an enjoyable social activity in the 18th century, there are so few surviving toys in the form of shops and early references are usually to market stalls or booths of various kinds rather than actual buildings in miniature. The sole recorded example of an 18th century shop is the model antique seller's in the Staatliches Museum für Volkskunst, Dresden. In the 18th and very early 19th centuries market places and fairs in miniature seem to have filled the place that was later taken by model shops. As early as 1696 an inventory of the Dauphin's possessions mentioned nine shops of the market place filled with enamelled figures. The Bestelmeier catalogues from around 1800 offer a variety of market stalls made completely of wood, though a few made at this time were supplied with wares of gum tragacanth, which when painted resembles plaster or composition. The Erzgebirge sample books also offer both fair and market sets in wood, while the makers of tin flats produced entrancingly painted figures on the same themes, such as the fair made by Allgeyer in the mid 19th century. When Princess Augusta of Prussia sent Queen Victoria's eldest daughter a gift, it was in the form of four small

shops with fruit and vegetables 'Like those in the Berlin markets' and it appears that the commercially produced doll's shop as we think of it today is mainly post-1850.

The surviving early 19th century shops are often rather gloomy in appearance, with dark stained or mahogany woodwork and merchandise that is placed discreetly on shelves rather than colourfully displayed as in later examples. The two splendid shops at the Germanisches National-museum in Nuremberg, with their perfectly made contents, seem more in the manner of the British pedlar dolls of the same period, as both exhibit a standard of construction that appears aimed at an adult rather than a child. The back of the Nuremberg milliner's shop is fitted with glass-fronted doors, behind which hang finely made model frocks of the period, while correctly assembled bonnets with lace and feathers are displayed on stands. A haberdasher's shop in the same museum is also adequately supplied with stock and fitted with wall mirrors. The stock of another includes straw hats and bonnets and miniature lace work.

It seems possible that the arrangement of many of the commercially produced toy shops developed

from the 18th century German dressers, with doors that open to reveal a large number of shelves and small drawers. Certainly this became an accepted layout for shops, though it probably bore little resemblance to actual designs. It was superseded in the 1870s by a three-sided form, without a roof, standing on a wooden base. Both types of construction were invariably provided with a solid counter running along the front and on this, in earlier examples, stood a scale of the hanging type. An early date is also often indicated by the handwritten labels on the drawers that are nearly always found at the back, whereas later versions were supplied with commercially printed labels of enamel or tin. Well stocked shops are not easy to find, and as it is very difficult to restock an empty one with contemporary pieces any good models are worthwhile acquisitions. They only rarely carry a maker's mark, and even the labelling of goods is not always a help in assessing the country of manufacture. Shops intended for the British or American markets, for instance, bore labels in the language of those countries regardless of their place of manufacture.

Generally the German shops are heavier and more sturdily constructed, while those made in

Above: **Two very small German cardboard market stalls contained in the two halves of a box, dating from the 18th century. The crudely made, painted wares on the shelves are scarcely identifiable. The stall-holders are made of plaster.** *Left:* **A particularly fine milliner's shop made in Germany, with glazed display cases containing accurately sewn garments. The shop's stock also includes items such as prayer books, tapers and shoes. On the counter lie an accurate miniature yardstick and pieces of toy money.** *Circa* **1835. Both Germanisches National-museum, Nuremberg.**

France, especially at the end of the 19th century, are attractive despite their often tawdry construction, because of their wealth of printed decoration and colour. Au Paradis des Enfants, Paris, in catalogue of 1897, offered a 'Boutique d' Epicerie' which was composed of two rooms packed with colourful packages and jars. The London catalogue of Charles Morell produced in 1896 shows a similar range of French shops, including a grocer's and a confectioner's. Cut-out shops for pasting on cardboard were also available in France in the form of the Pellerin 'Imagerie d'Epinal' sheets (see Craft and Constructional Toys), which also included customers.

Similar establishments were sold partly as an advertisement by Pascall's, the confectionery and chocolate manufacturer, with the title 'Pascall's Original Parlour' on the top and a range of sweets

that the firm produced neatly packed in glass jars. Rather surprisingly, they also sold a model butcher's shop.

Several of the well modelled or carved butcher's shops that are displayed in toy collections were not in fact intended as playthings but were made or commissioned by butchers themselves, sometimes as models of their own shops and possibly to use as a decoration in an empty window. Genuine toy butchers are fairly easily recognised, as all the joints unhook and there is a simplification of detail not seen in the more accurate models. Though butcher's shops are mainly associated with Britain, they were also made in Germany, an example being the 'Bull Butcher' shown in a catalogue of around 1848. The effectively carved figure of the butcher stands outside his shop, which has living quarters above and joints of meat hanging outside

The construction of bazaar stalls and shops under domes was popular in the mid 19th century. This example is particularly well stocked and was probably assembled at home. English. Ipswich Museums.

Left: **One of the haber-dasher's shops in the Germanisches National-museum, Nuremberg. Though very well equipped it is obviously intended as a toy. The assistant and customer both have porcelain heads. German,** *circa* **1840.** *Below:* **An interesting model of a carriage builder's shop constructed on the large scale usually reserved for doll's houses. Probably made in Norfolk. Ipswich Museums.**

from hooks. A poulterer's shop appears in the same catalogue using the identical man and building, only the stock being different. The simplest model in this range was the fishmonger's, which was no more than a booth.

Some shops were sold without fittings, while others passed into the hands of a merchant to be stocked before they were sold. Items for the equipping of stores were sold in Germany by J. J. Landermann of Nuremberg, a specialist in clock-work trains and mechanical toys, who supplied packets of China tea, Chylong ginger and bottles of scent. Kindler & Briel of Bobblingen, Württem-berg, made child-sized shops and counters, and these also required appropriate stock. One Ameri-can grocer's shop, described as the 'Choice Family Grocers', contains American-made boxes labelled '½ gross David's Prize Soap – No mistake' and 'Rising Sun Stove Polish'.

The Pets Grocery stores that were widely sold in Britain were also manufactured in America and contained packets of Uneeda Biscuits, Wheatena, Fels Naphtha Soap and Van Camps Pork and Beans. Kitchen-type cabinets that were free standing and filled with miniatures of com-modities available from actual stores were pecu-liarly American, though their manufacturer, Mason & Parker, also made toy shops, doll's houses and furniture.

Although model butchers and grocers are the most frequently found and are universally popular, there are also some very well made tobacconists, milliners and cake shops, sometimes produced to the special order of a particular family and stocked with a mixture of commercial and home-made

This mid 19th century English butcher's shop is very similar in both decoration and construction to one in the Bethnal Green Museum in London, suggesting that they are both of commercial manufacture. The flat above the shop is purely decorative and does not open. Height 18 inches. Bedford Museum.

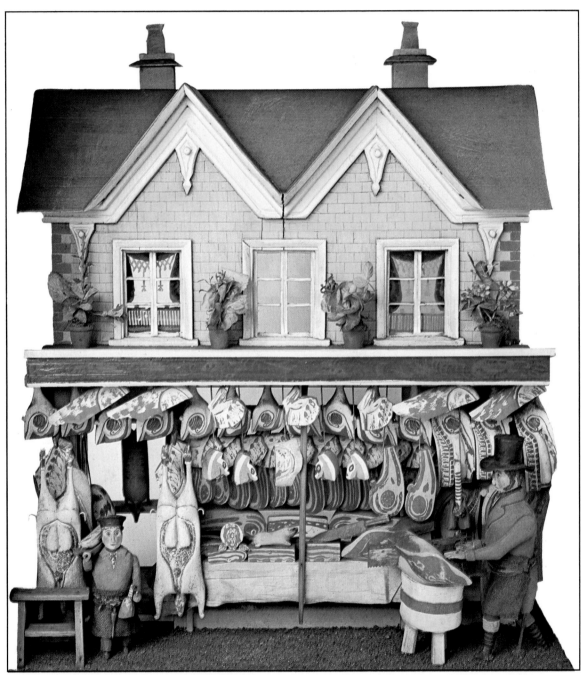

pieces. Model shops in the form of boxed table games were also widely available after 1885, and the Pets 'Emporium' made in 1908 contained a counter with opening drawers, bolts of cloth, scissors and cottons, while the Pets 'Post Office' was complete even to telegraph forms. Pets products were manufactured by Ralph Dunn of the Barbican, London. The Glevum Works of Gloucester produced a similar range known as the 'Tiny Tots' series, 'Replete with all the items sold in a grocer's shop'. The box lids of these models were adapted to form a realistic shop, aided by the

wing attachments which were provided with nearly all editions. Another firm, Gage's of Liverpool, established in 1869, made 'Cash Stores', 'Come to Tea' and 'Let's play School'. Peacock & Co., whose trademark was a peacock with the words 'Toys to Teach' in a scroll, include some child-sized shops in their 1922 range. An example nearly 5 feet high retailed at £9 without stock. After 1930 the standard of model shops declined rapidly and only occasionally are craftsman-made examples found. These, however, are naturally of some interest to the collector.

Play housekeeping

The fascination of miniature kitchenware is almost universal and even the children of kings played with models of this type. Though model rooms have survived from the late 17th century, the majority of available examples are of 19th century manufacture, though many have a deceptively ancient appearance. Few toys of this domestic type are marked in any way and they have to be dated and valued on their style and quality. It is sometimes even difficult to be certain of the country of origin, as the basic methods of making, for instance, a simple tin plate, are the same in most areas of manufacture.

The most collectable toys of this type are the kitchens contained in a three-sided construction, usually without a roof. They are described as Nuremberg kitchens, as merchants in that town assembled the work of various craftsmen and organised the export of the fully equipped toys. They contain model kitchenware in copper, tin, pewter, brass, wood and, occasionally, silver. Both pewter and silver are sometimes marked, so that it is possible to date individual pieces precisely. Earlier examples are supplied with the flat-topped stoves seen in the German cabinet houses, with a storage area beneath for dry wood and charcoal. The actual cooking took place over charcoal piled on the surface bricks, and the smoke was carried away under large canopies, sometimes decorated with painted flowers. From the mid 19th century, these kitchens were supplied with cooking ranges of iron or tin, though the general arrangement of the room remained the same.

Although the model kitchens are particularly associated with Germany, they were also made in other countries. In 'Wonders of a Toy Shop' dating from around 1835, a toy seller proudly shows his young customers a kitchen which is obviously of English manufacture as the fireplace is exactly that found in so many baby house kitchens, as is the built-in dresser. The equipment is also sparse and quite unlike the overwhelming accumulation of skillets, meat cleavers, graters, knives and skimmers that hang from every available inch of wall space in those of Nuremberg origin. The early American kitchens have obvious affinities with those made in Germany, but are on a much more modest scale and often constructed completely of tin; they are three-sided, and mock tiles are sometimes stencilled on the walls. Occasionally they were supplied with a pump that was fed by a tank fitted to an outer wall, though some German firms, such as Märklin, produced similar kitchens in japanned tin.

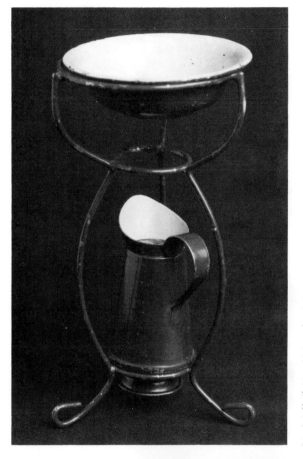

This metal doll's house washstand set was made by the German firm of Märklin around 1895. Author's Collection. *Below:* An illustration from *The Wonders of a Toyshop*, published around 1835, showing a range of toys including a large model kitchen and a wheeled hobby horse. Victoria and Albert Museum, London.

This painting by an unknown Viennese master, entitled *The Christmas Gift Table,* **shows an assortment of presents likely to have been given to a girl of the period and mostly of a domestic nature.** *Circa* **1840; Germanisches Nationalmuseum, Nuremberg.**

The complete identification of girls with mock housekeeping is seen particularly in *The Christmas Gift Table*, painted by an unknown Viennese artist around 1840. Here, with the exception of a few pieces of fruit and a superb Grodnertal wooden doll, all the girl's toys, including a chest of drawers, a toy broom, coffee pot, brass pestle and mortar a model room, and a doll's bed are of a purely domestic nature.

From 1800 Bestelmeier was offering in his catalogues not only wooden kitchens but also very well equipped laundries with drying areas. Stoves and cooking ranges of all types were also produced in great number, some being so effectively made and ornamented with copper and brass that they appear as fine miniatures rather than toys. The firm of Märklin in particular made a wide assortment, some with as many as six working burners. This firm, from 1859, was selling toy kitchenware, pumps and doll's baths, as well as cooking stoves. Their range was considerable, as they produced all this equipment in a variety of materials including tin, German silver, japanned tin, iron and brass, all very correctly made in several different qualities. These smaller pieces were not marked, though they can sometimes be identified by reference to the reprinted catalogues which are

now appearing. Their wooden kitchens, constructed at the end of the 19th century, were very well equipped and made with either straight or oblique wooden sides. It was customary for German children to add pieces to their kitchens, so cards of cleaning and cooking wares were sold as well as more expensive boxed sets. Märklin's book, *Püppen und Kinder-Kochbuch*, produced in a miniature format, was another necessity for the young housekeeper. Shelves supplied with a candle at each side which could be hung in a kitchen were also produced, and these were so laden with equipment that the removal of even a single piece must have presented a problem. Neither Carette or Bing were as interested in the production of toy kitchenware as Märklin though both, around 1900, made some good quality working models of dairy machines and even a complete butter manufactory worked by a hot air engine and claimed to be also suitable for adult use. Another firm produced a very functional washing machine, also for attaching to a stationary engine.

Although the main suppliers of domestic toys to both British and American children were German, there was some native manufacture of fairly simple tin and brass equipment. In Britain, this was centred in particular in Birmingham, while in the first few years of the 20th century the Reka Company of London, who specialised in light metal castings, made a variety of kitchen toys in their penny range. These included stove kettles in imitation tin with black or coppered bottoms, toilet jugs and basins, saucepans and tea pots. Some of the penny toys were boxed and for this small sum the child would receive a jug, basin and chamber pot in gilt finish enamelled in art colours. William Britain, better known for soldiers, also sold sets of saucepans, kettles and other small pieces for the kitchen.

American makers excelled in the creation of cast iron stoves, often with names such as 'Jewel Range' or 'The O.K. No 1' on the doors. Some of the simplest were only 4 inches long but even these had four boiling holes, a dumping grate, a large fire box with door, draught damper openings, a length of pipe and a lifter as well as a kettle, spider and baking pan. The Jewel Range, made apparently by Wood and advertised in the 1892 Marshall Field Toy catalogue was described in the following terms: 'Undoubtedly the best and most handsome range made. In its mechanical construction it embraces all the practical features found in the larger ranges, being complete in all its working parts. Nickel plated doors, panels and

These items of toy housekeeping equipment date from the 19th century. *Above* is a small pressed tin doll's house range of German origin. *Circa* 1860; height 5 inches. *Left* is a group of cookery equipment including earthenware moulds and wooden boards and utensils. Both Author's Collection.

Kitchens and kitchen equipment were a necessary part of toy housekeeping. *Above*: a typical 18th century Nuremberg kitchen with an interesting assortment of cooking utensils, 1 foot 4 inches high. Bethnal Green Museum of Childhood, London. *Below*: A late 19th century model kitchen range with brass decoration marked 'D.R.G.M. 74586'. The attention lavished by the manufacturers on such pieces was great and they now form fine decorative pieces. Betty Harvey-Jones Collection.

edges, nickel plated legs, frame and ornamental high shelf. Cooking can be done upon this range. Each stove packed in a wooden box with kettle, spider and cake griddle'. These well made American stoves epitomise the possibilities of ornamental cast iron work at the time and are highly impressive.

Pastry sets including rolling pins, pastry board and cake tins have remained popular to the present time, though few children of today can cook on their own toy range. The Pets 'Pastry Maker' was offered by Ralph Dunn of London in the early 20th century and several firms produced children's cookery books. One of the earliest known is that printed in Nuremberg in 1858 and described as 'A Little Cook Book for the Doll's Kitchen'. It was intended for the instruction of girls between

the ages of eight and fourteen. The cover illustration shows a standing girl who is reading the instructions from the book to a seated friend. They are playing with a typical Nuremberg kitchen with the usual flat-topped brick stove but in the foreground is also a much more up-to-date kitchen range of the metal type, which is wood-fired and fitted with a chimney.

Doll's washing day is another game which, though intended as a preparation for adult life, was in fact played by children from the highest social backgrounds. Specially made toys were certainly available from the late 18th century, though it is the mangles in particular that have survived in some quantity, as they were so strongly made. Those dating from the mid 19th century are usually of heavy cast iron, but those made nearer 1900 tend to be made completely of painted light metal. Occasionally a rare box mangle is found. In Britain, many of the cast iron examples are discovered with the 'Holdfast' mark on the side which was used by Cartwright Ltd. of Birmingham. This firm was established in 1880 but in the 1920s was still producing mangles in the traditional idiom which were claimed to be unbreakable and true to scale. Chad Valley of Birmingham also sold some attractively boxed sets containing mangles entitled 'Dolly's Washing Day', and including a tin bath, clothes line and the usual pegs. Some of Chad Valley's washday sets were particularly good models with well made wooden tables that held the bath with a shelf beneath for a bucket. A scrubbing board, a soap dish hooked to the side and a wire soap shaker provided a girl with a useful occupation on her mother's wash day. In Germany, Kindler & Briel of Böblingen, Württemberg, produced a number of kitchen, washing and toilet sets, washstands, pumps and baths, all in child rather than doll's house size.

As bathrooms became commonplace in the home, the toy-makers produced miniature versions, some of them of unrealistic splendour and others with ugly and untidy copper water tanks and very rudimentary equipment. A few with fringed curtains and highly decorated walls seem almost certainly of French manufacture. Some more advanced examples such as a bathroom with a shower bath and heated running water appear to be American.

With the exception of the kitchen ranges and the Nuremberg kitchens, few of the toys of a purely domestic nature are highly priced, and consequently they form a promising field for the new enthusiast.

Toy china

There was little manufacture of miniature china purely for the amusement of children until the late 18th century, with the possible exception of a few British Whieldon ware sets with their characteristic cream and brown mottled decoration. Earthenware pieces of small size are found in the remains of both the Egyptian and the Greek civilizations, but it is impossible at present to assess whether they are toys or models made as burial ornaments. The London Museum has some miniature bronze and pewter pieces which date to the 14th century. These were almost certainly toys, and similar earthenware miniatures were probably made. The Dauphin, in the early 17th century, is recorded as having played with 'little earthenware toys' and his sisters owned 'un petit ménage' which included a doll's dinner set complete even to the spoons. Many small sets that were described as 'toy' were in fact trifles for the amusement of adults, and it is often difficult, with pieces of good quality, to decide on the maker's intention.

The majority of late 17th and early 18th century miniature Oriental pieces were made exclusively for adults, in particular for the Dutch burghers, who collected pieces of the K'ang Hsi period in some numbers. The Dutch East India Company began to trade with China in 1600 and with Japan a little later, and miniatures from these countries were used in equipping the miniature rooms and cabinets of which they were so fond. The cabinet house at the Hague has a particularly fine porcelain room of this type. A few of the Oriental sets were purchased for children and a Captain Randall was instructed 'to buy a child's set' in Canton in 1779. Mrs. Delaney, that very talented English gentlewoman, was asked to look at her seven-year-old grand niece's set of 'Young Nankeen China' in the same year, and described it as follows: 'Not quite so small as for baby things nor large enough for grown ladies. The set was composed of twelve tea cups and saucers, six coffee cups and teapot, sugar dish, milk jug, two bread and butter plates.' The composition of this set is interesting as it makes clear that only one set of saucers was shared between tea and coffee cups, an arrangement that can be seen in the few surviving sets of this period.

Miniature china made for children's play is often decorated with appropriately childish motifs. *Above* is a lustre decorated and transfer printed porcelain coffee set made in the late 19th century, unmarked but of German origin. Height of coffee pot 7 inches. *Left:* A blue transfer printed earthenware tea set marked 'Punch. C. Allerton & Sons, England'. *Circa* 1900; height of teapot 5½ inches. Both Author's Collection.

Nankin wares were so popular that they were imitated by several British potteries, such as Caughley, who produced some of the finest toy sets, usually of twelve settings. Their coffee cans often have a completely different pattern to the tea bowls, and the shade of blue is sometimes the only unifying factor. One set, at the Victoria and Albert Museum, includes meat plates and an oil or essence bottle, indicating that matching tea and dinner services were sometimes sold. The 'Fisherman Pattern', with the pieces marked with an 'S', was often used, and the 'Island' pattern showing a hut perched at the end of an island was also popular. Collectors once thought such sets too fine to have been used as toys and suggested that they were traveller's samples, used in lieu of full-sized pieces to show shopkeepers new patterns. In fact, the great majority of such sets were sold expressly for children and appear in early catalogues and bills.

Joseph Lygo, writing to William Duesbury at the Derby factory in 1788 complained that the 'two toy sets in white and gold are very much wanted'. If the Derby factory was unable to supply them he would be forced to obtain the matching coffee pots from the Salopian warehouse. Little wonder, if this mixing of the work of various factories took place before sale, that attribution of many of the 18th century sets is difficult. In the same

firm's records, another set of toy ware was criticised as being too small, presumably the children found them so, a complaint that again suggests a play rather than a cabinet intention. Full sized Caughley and Worcester sets only occasionally included a coffee pot, but this piece appears to have been common in miniature. The 'Pleasure Boat' service was included in the Chamberlain accounts at a cost of 2/4d. Several such sets are displayed at the Victoria and Albert Museum, but the collector of today has usually to be content with a few individual pieces of these early services.

The Staffordshire potteries made a number of services in salt glazed stoneware. One very attractive specimen, with pieces under two inches high, was intricately decorated with shells, leaves and flowers. Another salt glazed stoneware set includes a tea caddy with a somewhat Chinese inspired decoration in crude colours. Leeds also made a variety of play items, ranging from pierced-work baskets to dishes with moulded food attached, such as a fish garnished with lemon or a cauliflower in white sauce. Such pieces are often found in baby houses, though the scale is sometimes over large. The spirit of 18th century England is particularly reflected in the Bow sets, with their chintz-like polychrome flower decoration. These are particularly important as they stand at the beginning

A blue transfer printed earthenware tea set marked 'Ridgways W.R.S. & Co.' It is one of the 'Humphrey's Clock' pattern, decorated with scenes from Charles Dickens' *The Old Curiosity Shop.* **Mid 19th century; height of teapot 5 inches. Author's Collection.**

of a purely native style of decoration, when other makers, such as Longton Hall and Lowestoft were working mainly in the Chinoiserie manner.

Many potteries were making creamware by the end of the 18th century, though it is mainly associated with the Wedgwood factory, from which the royal family ordered two toy sets in 1765. The Bethnal Green Museum in London has a good miniature soup tureen made in the typical Wedgwood urn shape with reeding and simple blue band decoration. Unmarked sets of creamware plates are often found, but are usually completely plain and virtually unattributable.

The European factories of note appear, in the 18th century, to have concentrated on cabinet pieces rather than toys. Around 1730, Meissen created some small bottles in Japanese and Chinoiserie styles and both Sèvres and Vincennes made fine quality miniatures for display. Some of the small Paris mugs, decorated with scenes such as a child leading a goat, were possibly intended for children, but the green and blue earthenware pieces seen for instance in the Nuremberg rooms and cabinets were mainly intended for adults. The intention of the makers of miniatures changes completely in the early 19th century and the majority of sets were made purely for play. Spode's 1850 shape book still offered a variety of pieces intended for adults, such as a 'bow handled china bucket and Déjeuner Paris toys'. However, their transfer printed sets such as the 'Milkmaid' and 'Tower' patterns were intended exclusively for children. Much cheaper play services were made by Spode at the end of the 19th century, some with prints that appear to be cut down sections of larger patterns. Willow pattern china was made in great number by almost all the potteries, as were white sets with simple banding.

American children played in the main with toy china that was imported from England and Germany, though there was some manufacture of simple stoneware and slipware in New England, Ohio and Pennsylvania. There is often difficulty in the attribution of these simple pieces. Many immigrants worked in the traditions of their own country and, unless a piece bears some mark or inscription, collectors may be unsure of its origin.

Parian ware, said to resemble statuary marble, became popular in the late 1840s and the makers of miniature pieces both in Britain and Germany quickly imitated its fine quality in cheaper unglazed bisque, which was used in particular for the small ornamental items made for doll's houses.

The firm of Doulton made toy hot water bottles, as well as harvest jugs, water filters and a whole range of small mugs that were originally intended as ornaments, but soon found their way into doll's houses and toy boxes. Most of the British factories marked their work so there is little problem in attribution; some firms such as Davenport even marked the year of manufacture. The mid-Victorian dinner services are often astonishingly complete, with china ladles and decorative pieces such as fruit comports. They became smaller and much less ornate by the end of the century; Edwardian sets are often intended for only six place settings and are equipped only with a pair of tureens and a single gravy boat. Japanese sets were imported in considerable quantity in the early 20th century and though a few of these are of acceptable quality, they are not popular with collectors. Complete services, if they are to be effectively displayed, often take too much room in small flats and houses, so that many collectors now buy only individual pieces from the better marked sets. These are not difficult to find, though miniature blue and white transfer printed wares in particular are now quite expensive as they are so heavily collected.

Much sought-after by collectors are the blue and white transfer printed wares such as these plates from an earthenware dinner service (*top*), **decorated with various English scenes such as the 'Entrance to Blaize Castle' and 'Kenilworth Priory'. Probably made by Stevenson's; first half of the 19th century.** *Bottom:* **A delicately painted German porcelain dinner service decorated in red and pink with lustre finish. Mid 19th century; height of soup tureen 2½ inches. Both Author's Collection.**

PRODUCERS OF TOY CHINA

Allerton, Charles & Sons – Longton, Staffordshire, 1859 to 1942. Pottery. Taken over by Cauldon Potteries in 1912; made a number of fairly large scale toy sets including a 'Punch & Judy' pattern.

Bennington Pottery – USA, 1820 to 1890. Made miniature pitchers and jugs, also vases in stoneware and bisque.

Bow – Stratford, London, *circa* 1747 to 1776. Porcelain. Made flower-decorated sets often in underglaze blue, also some known sets in polychrome. Marks include a crescent and an anchor.

Caughley or Salopian Ware – Made by Thomas Turner, Shropshire, from 1775 to 1799. Many Chinoiserie sets were produced, mainly decorated in underglaze blue, particularly the 'Fisherman' and 'Pleasure Boat' patterns. Toy sets were featured in the firm's closing-down as 'Toy table and tea sets'. Impressed marks are rare. Some pieces are marked 'S' and there are also crescent and 'C' marks in the underglaze blue. Some have Chinese symbols. Some rare pieces are marked with an 'H'.

Chelsea Porcelain – London, *circa* 1745 to 1769. Soft paste porcelain. There are a few very rare recorded miniature pieces. William Duesbury of Derby bought the factory in 1769 and the term 'Chelsea Derby' is used for pieces produced from then until 1784.

Chinese Export Wares – Imported in the 18th century when European porcelain was still very expensive. Many pieces were made to European designs. After the American Revolution and during the Federal era much of the ware destined for the USA was decorated with American motifs.

Coalport – Shropshire, 1795 to present day. Early pieces are unmarked, but some porcelain flower-decorated sets are usually attributed to this firm.

Copeland, W. T., & Sons Ltd – Stoke-on-Trent, Staffordshire, 1847 to present day. Marked 'Copeland Late Spode' from 1847 to 1867. The mark always includes the word Copeland. Some pieces are also year-marked. A wide variety of tea and dinner ware was produced.

Davenport – Longport, Staffordshire, 1793 to 1887. Marked 'Davenport' with an anchor. Some porcelain pieces dating from the 1820s are marked only with an anchor. Doll's tea and dinner services were produced, some with hand-coloured transfer decoration. Most earthenware pieces carry a date mark. Some blue and white transfer-printed wares.

Derby Porcelain Works – Derby, 1750 to 1848. The majority of 18th century pieces are unmarked and were intended mainly for cabinet display. Toy sets however were certainly made during the period from 1769 to 1775 when the factory was run by William Duesbury.

Derby, Royal Crown – 1856 to present day. Made a large number of porcelain sets and miniature pieces, mainly for display, the majority of which have characteristically gaudy colouring. Miniature watering cans, tea sets etc. were made particularly between 1910 and 1920. Though intended for adults, many pieces such as small candlesticks are found in doll's houses.

Doulton & Co Ltd – Lambeth, London, *circa* 1858 to 1956. Earthenwares and stonewares. Impressed marks 'Doulton, Lambeth'. Produced large numbers of adult type vases, harvest jugs and bottles. The factory has continued at Burslem to the present day. Made a bone china set for Queen Mary's doll's house.

Hackwood – Shelton and Hanley, Staffordshire, 19th century. Several different members of the Hackwood family produced transfer-printed earthenware services which can be recognised by their impressed or printed marks.

Doulton Lambeth miniatures such as these were originally sold for the amusement of adults, but are frequently found in doll's houses. Mainly stoneware, late 19th century; 1½ to 2 inches. Author's Collection.

Facing page: A completely original French doll's luncheon set contained in a blue leathercloth-covered case with the title 'Dinette'. Early 20th century; width 14 inches. Author's Collection.

This Leeds creamware toy dinner service made in the 18th century is identifiable by its very light weight. Note the characteristic feathered edging of the plates and tureens and the pierced work dishes. Ipswich Museums.

Leeds – Yorkshire, 1758 to 1840. Various owners. Made earthenwares, basalt and creamwares, though the miniature pieces are mainly creamware. There are few marked pieces. Surviving examples are usually recognised by their unusually light weight. Feather-type moulded edges were very popular and dishes with moulded food were made. The important soup tureens are often very ornamented. Complete services were made in sizes small enough for baby houses, as well as in the usual child size. Some of the pierced work dishes have added transfer-printed decoration.

Limoges – France. Term for the work of several factories working in hard paste porcelain in this area. Miniature pieces are mainly 19th and 20th century and they are still made. Often marked 'L'· Numbers of doll's house size vases were made in the late 19th and early 20th centuries.

Longton Hall – Staffordshire, *circa* 1749 to 1760. Porcelain. The majority of pieces are unmarked but some have crosses in underglaze blue. Miniatures are mainly in Chinoiserie patterns.

Lowestoft – Suffolk, 1759 to 1802. Porcelain. No recognised marks, but early pieces are often in Chinoiserie style, while later examples tend to have sprigged patterns. Made dinnerwares and teasets.

Mason, Charles James – Fenton Works, Staffordshire, *circa* 1845 to 1848, at Longton from 1851 to 1854. Pieces marked 'Masons' or 'Masons Patent Ironstone'. Produced a large number of miniature jug and basin sets decorated with flower patterns in colours. Some miniature chimney pieces were also made at this pottery.

Minton – Stoke-on-Trent, Staffordshire, 1793 to the present day. Porcelains and earthenwares. From 1842 year marks were added. Toy sets are mentioned in the estimate books dating from 1831 to 1842. Transfer printed earthenware sets were produced in a variety of patterns, including many with subjects of interest to children.

Moorcroft – Burslem, Staffordshire, 1913 to the present day. Mainly art-type miniatures of larger pieces intended for cabinet or display use but also suitable for doll's houses.

Mortlock's Ltd – Oxford Street, London, 1746 to 1930. This retailer was associated with several factories, and the shop's name is often found on toy sets, including plates probably made as gifts with the firm's name incorporated in the design. Good quality creamware sets are also found decorated in black, which can be indentified by the Mortlock's monogram.

Ridgway, John and William – Hanley, Staffordshire, 1814 to 1830. This firm had a thriving export trade with America and was one of the best known importers. It produced blue transfer-printed wares in particular.

Ridgway, William, Son & Co – After 1843 made toy services decorated with the 'Humphrey's Clock' pattern, derived from a magazine called *Master Humphrey's Clock* written by Charles Dickens and illustrated by Hablot Browne (Phiz). Some of the plates used for printing the china were based on Phiz originals.

Rogers – This impressed mark was used by John and George Rogers of Longport between 1784 and 1814, and by others to 1836. The miniature sets are unmarked but Rogers are known to have used the 'Monoptoris' design showing the remains of an ancient building near Firoz Shah's Cotilla in Delhi, derived from a book of views published between 1795 and 1807. Miniature sets were made in two distinct sizes, one for doll's houses and another, such as that illustrated, in usual child size.

Staffordshire – General term for large numbers of unattributable white glazed earthenware sets made in the 18th century.

Stevenson, Andrew – Cobridge, Staffordshire, *circa* 1806 to 1830. Made good quality transfer printed earthenwares, exporting mainly to the USA after 1818.

Tuckerware – Philadelphia, USA, 1826 to 1838. Porcelain. A few very rare miniature pieces are found. This firm were imitators of Sèvres wares.

Wedgwood, Josiah & Sons Ltd – Staffordshire: Burslem 1759, Etruria *circa* 1769, to the present day. Made earthenwares, basalts, jaspers etc. Early pieces are unmarked. Miniature sets were made in perforated creamware, and some in caneware with classical designs and vertical engine turning. Wedgwood's pink lustre was introduced between 1805 and 1810, and some toy sets of this are found. Cabinet pieces were made in black basalt and blue and white Jasper ware. Black painted creamware services were produced in child size. Pieces are year dated after 1860. Some of the early 20th century sets are very crude; one existing set is poorly printed with submarines, battleships etc. and marked 'Etruria'.

Whieldon, Thomas (circa 1719 to 1795?) – Fenton Low, Staffordshire. Whieldon made some small teapots 2 to 3 ins. in diameter and is associated with agate and tortoiseshell wares.

A Copeland Spode china tea set with transfer prints in blue of birds and animals. Registered between 1891 and 1892; height of teapot 5 inches. Author's Collection.

Miniature furniture

The pedigree of much miniature furniture is impeccable, for it was collected by princes and wealthy merchants from the 17th century and has continued to attract affluent collectors who are fascinated by these small scale exhibitions of the craftsman's skill. The term miniature is usually applied to objects that are too large in scale for a conventional doll's house and too small to be used by a child as a utilitarian item. These pieces, which were sometimes made as toys and sometimes purely for display, are also occasionally defined as 'second size miniatures'. It was once fashionable to describe them as apprentice pieces, the suggestion being that the apprentice furniture maker finally proved his skill by the creation of a small sample piece. This romantic explanation is now largely discredited, as it was not based on any evidence, and it seems more likely that they were created in the normal course of work by craftsmen such as Richard Groff of Newfoundland, who, around

1800, made a miniature chest of drawers. His stamped-on trademark indicated that he manufactured 'Every description of plain and fancy furniture. Also turning and carving of every description'. Miniatures formed an ideal vehicle for the display of a craftsman's skill, and another interesting example is a sideboard in the Winterthur Museum in Delaware, USA. The drawers are marked 'Made by J. Curtis on Dec. 24th 1823', the front inside edges of each being decorated with an inlay of seven lines of different woods in a rectangle. Curtis underlined his skill by decorating the sides of the drawers with inlaid rectangles and triangles.

Miniatures were also sometimes created purely for trade display. A dress shop, for instance, might require an elegant piece to complement a small model figure, or a furniture maker or upholsterer might wish to indicate the variety of his work in the confined space of a window. A few items may have been made as traveller's samples, though

English makers of miniature furniture produced some particularly fine chairs. This pair of carved beech and elmwood armchairs with leaf carved toprails and turned supports, legs and stretchers, are used to seat the famous dolls of Lord and Lady Clapham in the Victoria and Albert Museum, London. 17th century; height 21 inches.

The variety of skills involved in the production of miniature furniture is demonstrated by these three chairs of markedly different type. *Far left:* **An elaborately carved beechwood chair with cane back and seat which was probably made as an expensive toy, though it may have been intended purely as a miniature. English, late 17th century. Bethnal Green Museum of Childhood, London.** *Left:* **A very fine miniature chair covered in flocked and gilded 'Spanish' leather. English,** *circa* **1690; height 20 inches. Saffron Walden Museum, Essex.** *Below:* **A beech chair made for Maud Victoria Johnston of Edinburgh by a local craftsman as a Christening gift when she was three months old in 1879. Height 5½ inches. Author's Collection.**

the availability of pattern books in the 18th century makes it unlikely that there was any general use of this kind. The quality of the 17th and 18th century pieces has made collectors reluctant to accept the very real possibility that many were intended purely as children's toys. However, 18th century London trade cards indicate that turners such as Willerton and Roberts were also makers of children's toys and Gough in 1772 claimed to make 'mahogany toys such as chairs, buroes (*sic*), commodes, basin stands, looking glasses, chests of drawers'. A good standard of workmanship might therefore be expected of such craftsmen.

The finest early pieces were created by the Dutch, who were the first to succumb to the charm of miniatures carefully displayed in cabinets and room settings. Items were sometimes specially commissioned regardless of expense, and made exclusively for the enjoyment of adults. German activity in this field does not appear to have been as intense and the standard of surviving pieces, usually in a much heavier style, is not as immediately impressive. The Germans seem to have put more energy into small furnishings and equipment such as pewter and silver. They did however construct some model rooms of a very high standard. A pair of rooms displayed in the Germanisches Nationalmuseum, Nuremberg, which date from the second half of the 17th century, exhibit some particularly fine panelling.

The French also became interested in miniatures, and several makers are recorded, such as Biennais, who was working in the late 18th and early 19th

Above: **A wide variety of miniature furnishings, including an interesting straw-work chest of drawers surmounted by a handsome toilet mirror, is shown in this model room which once formed part of a larger setting. English, 18th century; width 2 feet 2½ inches.**
Right: **Another toilet mirror, finished in black and gold lacquer.** *Circa* **1720; height 22½ inches. Both Victoria and Albert Museum, London.**

centuries and a certain Lobjoy who worked in Paris in the early 19th century. The French furniture is very ornate, with serpentine fronted cabinets and richly brocaded Rococo sofas and armchairs. Many pieces made in the Louis XV and XVI periods are of mahogany or fruitwood, sometimes completed by a marble top, while later pieces made great use of walnut, often inlaid with coloured woods such as holly or tulip. The French miniatures are not all mannered and elegant, and include some fine robust provincial pieces.

British interest in miniatures appears to have developed after the Restoration, possibly because Charles II had admired the Dutch work when in exile. The early pieces are carved mainly from oak, elm, beech and walnut and there is sometimes an engaging avoidance of the true miniature scale. A late 17th century beech day bed at the Bethnal Green Museum in London has an elegantly carved and caned seat and back rest on disproportionately massive legs. The skill of British makers is perhaps more fairly seen in the exquisitely carved chairs, again with caned seats, which were made in some numbers. Examples are to be seen in several museums, though collectors are probably most familiar with those that accompany the world famous dolls, Lord and Lady Clapham, at the Victoria and Albert Museum. In the same museum there is a large scale folding room, obviously made purely for the display of its well made furnishings and dolls. In creating miniatures, the craftsmen copied the whole variety of furniture that was available in full size. Dumb waiters, longcase clocks, dressers and low boys were faithfully copied, though the most popular subjects were

coffers and chests of drawers as these made useful and amusing trinket boxes.

Despite the fact that a considerable amount of 'children's furniture' was imported into America in the mid 18th century, the craftsmen in that country seem to have developed an interest in the creation of miniatures before there was any general concern with the manufacture of toys. In certain areas such as Philadelphia, the Connecticut valley and Western Pennsylvania, large numbers of good quality pieces were produced. The principal woods used were elm, walnut, oak, ash, maple, some red cedar and, obviously, pine. The latter was decorated with distinctly Alpine flower patterns or painted scenes, or even painted in simulation of marble, as on a fine highboy at the Essex Institute, Salem. The carved coffers which were produced are often embellished with the initials of the recipient and a date, and are thought to relate to the Pennsylvanian Dutch dower chests. Both types of furniture are characterised by the fact that the dovetailed joints at the sides are often used as part of the decoration. A few good quality pieces, intended as children's toys, were made between 1830 and 1850 by members of the Tower Guild, a group of craftsmen who formed a guild in South Hingham, Mass., with the aim of producing fine toys. At the Old Ordinary, Hingham, can be seen a fall-front desk 9¼ inches (23.5 cm) high made by Loring Cushing, one of the best known members of the guild, as well as a simple pine settle which was also his work. The guild unfortunately marked its work with labels, and few positively attributable pieces are now to be found.

The finest quality miniature furniture is mainly associated with 18th century craftsmen, but some very effective pieces continued to be made even into the early 20th century. Half tester beds, complete with meticulously made hangings, deep buttoned chaise longues, mirrored chiffonniers, dressers and correctly made country chairs are among the 19th century products that are in demand, both as interesting pieces in their own right and as a foil for miniature china, glass or dolls. As so few miniatures are marked in any way, it is almost impossible to attribute them precisely. It should be remembered that fine quality work does not necessarily indicate age, as modern reproductions are often finer than the antiques, though without much of the appeal of the old.

A simple but attractive example of miniature work is provided by an oak flap table with an 8½ inch circular top, dating from the 18th century (*top left*)**. The late 18th century dresser** (*bottom*) **is very correctly made, and utilises commercially produced brass fittings. Both English; Bethnal Green Museum of Childhood, London.** *Top right:* **The sideboard in the Henry Francis Dupont Winterthur Museum, Delware, signed by its maker James Curtis and dated 'Dec. 24th 1823'.**

Doll's beds and cradles

It is unusual to find either a doll's bed or a cradle that bears a maker's name, unless it is that of a local cabinet-maker or carpenter who has produced an individual example to special order. These toys, essential to every girl who owned a doll, were commercially made in large numbers in the late 19th century, and were also carved and colourfully painted by home workers in areas such as Berchtesgaden in Germany and parts of Russia. The earliest recorded toy cradles of European origin appear to be those seen in 16th century woodcuts. One, dating from 1540, shows a girl holding a wooden cradle with flat sloping sides, and slots – presumably for ease in carrying – cut along the upper edge. Another woodcut from the cycle *Die Lebensalter des Menschen* shows in the background a small cradle of unusual construction for the period, with a high head and foot board and deep, box-like sides.

The depth of some of the early cradles might suggest that the doll occupant would be quite lost at the bottom but, as in full-sized versions, the depth was largely taken up by a thick mattress and layers of padding, so that the doll lay almost on a level with the top and the blankets could rest on the sides of the cradle itself. Pine, oak, fruitwoods, elm and beech were all used in the manufacture of cradles, which closely followed the local styles of the places where they were made. American examples, often painted in green, with thick pine bottoms and dowel sides reminiscent of the work seen on the backs of Windsor chairs in Britain, are connected particularly with New England. Heavily carved dark oak cradles with Renaissance style hoods, made in the early 19th century, are often described as German. The British cradles are usually fairly simple in construction and their effectiveness depends on the quality of the wood and the carpenter's skilled exploitation of that quality. Miniature cradles, like their full-sized counterparts, often have large turned or carved knobs at the corners. In real life the nurse could tie a length of string or a scarf to one of these and rock the baby without using her foot – a method illustrated in many prints and woodcuts.

The basketwork cradle probably has a longer history than the wooden type. Its method of construction was particularly suitable for a toy, as it was light enough for a child to move about easily. Unfortunately the basketwork was also easily damaged, so that few early examples are known except in prints. Dating of existing examples is also difficult unless some of the original lining fabric is still in place, as the shape changed little over some two hundred years and they are of course still made today. Some very fine but fragile specimens were made in large numbers in France in the late 19th and early 20th centuries, since some of the leading French dollmakers sold their elegantly costumed baby dolls lying in draped and be-frilled cradles of this type.

Of a much more substantial nature are the splendid mahogany half tester beds whose perfection of construction has often caused them to be described as 'traveller's samples', though the vast majority were, of course, toys. When complete with the original covers and hangings they are frequently of documentary interest, showing precisely how sheets and blankets were sewn and how the curtains were hung. It is this type of bed that can sometimes be identified by a cabinet-maker's or supplier's label, made of bone or light wood and nailed or glued in place. The high backs of the half testers were sometimes inlaid with lighter woods, while others are painted or even ornamented with applied silk or brocade padding.

Empire day beds, carved four posters and American Field beds were all made in doll's sizes

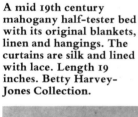

A mid 19th century mahogany half-tester bed with its original blankets, linen and hangings. The curtains are silk and lined with lace. Length 19 inches. Betty Harvey-Jones Collection.

Left: **An effectively made American field bed dating from the early 19th century and complete with miniature patchwork quilt. The American Museum in Britain, Bath.**
Bottom: **Not strictly intended as toys, glazed earthenware cradles such as these were often given as Christening gifts in 18th and 19th century England. One is Staffordshire,** *circa* **1800, and the other, with an occupant, is Whieldon ware,** *circa* **1780. Length of both about 5 inches. Saffron Walden Museum, Essex.**

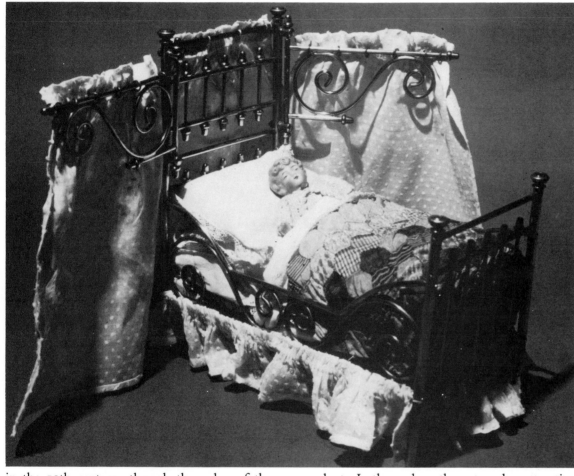

This 19th century doll's bed is unusually made of brass, with swing wings and high, cot-like sides. Probably British; height 9 inches. Betty Harvey-Jones Collection.

in the 19th century, though the value of those made for the bigger dolls is often disappointingly low in comparison with the work involved in their construction, mainly because toy collectors do not have sufficient room for their display. Those made in lengths up to some 14 or 15 inches, however, are always in demand if in good condition.

Cast and wrought iron was used in the 19th and early 20th centuries to make some of the most decorative of toy beds and cradles. The manufacturers by this time were becoming more aware of the problems involved in storing toys, so they were frequently made to fold away. Bases of swinging cradles were often embellished with leaves and flowers highlighted in gold with the pattern repeated on the upper border. Popular adult styles of beds were all copied in miniature and often supplied with an additional lace canopy. A few of these low beds were as long as 4 feet, but were easily moved because of the castors. They were manufactured not only by the toymakers but also by factories specialising in wrought and cast ironwork, though again few marked their

products. In the early 20th century less attractive but more convenient cradles that folded away completely when not in use were made from strips of metal. When draped and decorated, these can look extremely attractive, but they are not popular with collectors as they are again of a type that is still made today. Matching cradles and standing baskets of this type smothered with broderie anglaise were offered by Gamage's just before the First World War. The baskets were equipped with powders and brushes for the doll, just as in the baby-sized versions.

Printed sheet metal, though occasionally used for smaller beds and cradles before the First World War, did not become really popular until the 1920s. Unfortunately, the paint used for the decoration of these toys was often of poor quality and many examples are so scratched that they are not worth including in collections. When in nice condition, some examples are attractive as they are decorated with scenes of children at play. Moreover, as by this time it was important that toys should be completely modern they can be quite accurately dated by the children's clothes.

Facing page: **A particularly well shaped four poster doll's bed with its original clothes and hangings, including a well made patchwork quilt.** *Circa* 1840; **height 18 inches. Bedford Museum.**

Arks, farms and zoos

With the exception of some farms and an ark made in the 20th century by William Britain, very few manufacturers of these frequently complex toys are known and even the country of origin of certain examples is debatable. Their value and interest to collectors therefore depends to a great extent upon the workmanship of particular examples, and as few can be well displayed in the space of a modern house, buyers tend to be choosy about their purchases. Both the ark itself and the farm house often served as a convenient box in which the animals could be transported, and the dozens of occupants could be utilised for a wide variety of games.

Animals were often carved in the 17th and 18th century crèche settings which were used to illustrate biblical scenes for the illiterate, and it is thought that the first model arks might have formed part of such arrangements. A Scandinavian example dating from the early 17th century survives, but as it is carved from solid wood it is doubtful whether it was intended as a toy. Individual craftsmen in both Europe and America have fashioned a variety of models of this type, but the greatest area of production was in Germany, particularly in the Berchtesgaden, Erzgebirge Sonneberg and Oberammergau regions. The products of peasant craftsmen in these areas were sent to Nuremberg for distribution and are often termed 'Nuremberg Ware'. The merchants were producing their own catalogues by the end of the 18th century and the workers were expected to copy the designs of the most popular lines so that the individuality of specific areas became stifled. Families frequently undertook the carving of a very small range of animal types, so that they were able to work at great speed. In 1879, a traveller visited an elderly German woman who had been taught by her mother to carve only a goat, elephant, dog, cat, wolf and sheep, and who had instructed her daughter and granddaughter to do the same. Other families, he reported, 'paint nothing but grey horses with red spots, another only red horses with white spots'. These animals were turned into an outline shape on a lathe and then sliced into sections before the detailed carving of separate legs, ears and facial features was attempted. The same traveller, visiting St. Ulrich, saw bins filled with wooden animals, and Noah's arks both full and empty which were being assembled for export. Georg Lang at Oberammergau had begun organising the work of local carvers as early as 1750 and had gradually closed down the agencies manned by his own employees in other countries so that they could be run by local men, who were aware of the tastes and requirements of their own localities.

For a short period, the work of the traditional carvers was threatened by the introduction of a composition substance which meant that figures could be moulded, and it was in reply to this threat that the ring method of cutting was introduced by, it is believed, a turner in Seiffen. In the Groden valley the animals were sent away for painting, as decoration was not a traditional craft. Before the middle of the 19th century all the animals were

A toy which makes effective use of animals is this fretwork menagerie on wheels, made around 1905. The man is articulated and the cage opens and the wheel moves, creating a toy which is very much in the spirit of the earlier German arks and zoos. Betty Harvey-Jones Collection.

painted before sale, but it became normal in Oberammergau after this time to leave the figures completely plain, though workers in other parts of Germany continued to decorate the animals traditionally. These small animals, which absorbed the attention of so many families, were known as 'penny beasts' by their purchasers but as 'misery beasts' by the peasants who worked long hours on them for a pittance. It is not unusual to find as many as four hundred figures contained in a German ark, all carved with specific characteristics but with no regard to scale, so that a lion will be as large as an elephant and a ladybird as large as a sheep. The animals usually stand on thin and easily damaged legs, but those made in the Oberammergau area were sometimes given rectangular bases for extra stability.

There was a greater demand for realism in toys after the mid 19th century, and this is particularly reflected in the moulded composition figures.

The latter are often effective individual models, showing the temperament of various species in a way that could not be attempted in the so-called 'penny beasts'.

The improved characterisation of the composition figures is particularly seen in the rendering of Noah and his family. The Elastolin figures produced by the Hausser company in particular show great, if somewhat over-dramatic, realism. An example is the figure of Noah's wife, who kneels with hands clasped and the drapery of her robe carefully disposed to suggest agitation. The sons, Japhet, Ham and Shem are also given individuality and are painted with great attention to the detail of the figures.

The ark as a toy continued to be popular until the 1930s and the animals and family were made in the various new materials introduced, so that a few made of rubber and celluloid have survived. Several firms made printed paper figures for arks

An attractive ark decorated with straw work which is probably of German origin, though similar examples are sometimes described as 'prisoner of war' work. *Circa* 1840. Bethnal Green Museum of Childhood, London.

A late 19th century German
toy farm of the most basic
type, which relied for its
effect on the painted decoration. Welsh Folk Museum,
St Fagan's, Cardiff.

A late 19th century German
toy farm of the most basic
type, which relied for its
effect on the painted decoration. Welsh Folk Museum,
St Fagan's, Cardiff.

Facing page, top: **A mid 19th
century straw-work ark
with a sliding lid at the
front. Probably German;
length 12 inches. Luton
Museum and Art Gallery,
Bedfordshire.** *Bottom:* **A
group of animals and
buildings from a farm
made in the Erzgebirge
region of Germany and
purchased between 1880
and 1919. Height of house
4 inches. Betty Harvey-
Jones Collection.**

and farms, particularly the French firm of Pellerin.
These printed figures were sometimes used commercially and glued to heavy board or wood, but
the majority were assembled by children and
because of their poor colouring and often untidy
cutting have no real value to the collector, who
would prefer an uncut sheet.

The arks themselves were made in a much
greater variety than the animals they contained,
though the same basic shape was frequently used
and simply decorated with bright colours, borders
of flowers or geometric patterns to give a different
appearance. At Halbach, near Olbernhau, traditionally a centre for the manufacture of chipwood boxes, some twenty-four firms by the mid
19th century were making nothing but arks in a
wide variety of sizes. These were sent from the
small factories to home decorators, who returned
the work to the towns in large baskets. The design
of arks has remained similar until the present time;
a porch is always necessary, as is a dove, either
painted or carved on the roof; there is only rarely
any attempt to organise the interior in any way
and it is considered purely as a container.

The catalogue issued by Georg Hieronymus
Bestelmeier of Nuremberg in 1793 offered a
variety of arks. The larger, besides holding a very
large number of animals, also contained several
rooms as well as kitchens and stables and must
have resembled the German cabinet houses of the
period. Certainly they are closer to the Biblical
description of the vessel than the hut on a raft-
like base which was the usual representation. No
examples of these grand arks are known to have
survived, but the manufacturer was aware of the
hazards facing a toy that a child would quite
probably attempt to sail and in the same catalogue
provided smaller examples which were very
heavily varnished so that they could float. Even
these contained as many as a hundred figures.

Very large arks sometimes have two storeys
painted on the sides, while smaller versions might
be decorated with stencilled Chinoiserie or
Gothick style windows. Bavarian examples often
have a removable panel at the back for entry, but
this is very frequently lost, which may explain
why the hinged roof had become so popular by
the end of the 19th century. Some approximation
of the region of Germany in which the toy was
made can sometimes be given by similarities in
architecture to the traditional farmhouses and
cottages of the area, though this method is not
always reliable. At Oberammergau, for instance,
where locally made arks might be expected to be
very heavily decorated, those which survive are
of the very simplest and undecorated type.

After the introduction of colour lithography,
patterned paper was sometimes applied to the
wooden exterior, though the traditional animals
continued to be used as occupants. In the early 20th
century, both ark and occupants were sometimes
made of lithographed board and the surviving
examples, when found in good condition, are
extremely attractive, despite the fact that the boat-
shaped base has usually been replaced by a flat raft.
The most splendid arks are those whose complete
surface is decorated with coloured straw, giving a
mosaic-like effect which is evidently the result of

hours of patient labour. This technique was particularly favoured in the Erzgebirge region of Germany, where the method was to glue straw that was stained in rich natural colours to a pine-wood construction. It is examples of this type that are the most highly regarded by collectors, as they are obviously works of fine craftsmanship.

Various small American firms also made arks, and as many of the craftsmen had emigrated from Germany, collectors often find difficulty in being sure of the origin of traditionally made pieces. Arks were imported so cheaply into Britain from Germany in the 19th century that there was little native manufacture, except for a few which were craftsman-made to individual requirements. The pattern changed in the early 20th century when several firms, such as Chad Valley, began to make simplified toys of this type. Native manufacture was encouraged by the halting of supplies during the First World War and arks were among the items chosen to occupy disabled ex-servicemen and Belgian refugees. The carving of model farms and zoos also held little general appeal for manu-facturers outside Germany before the 20th century, since the German figures made for arks could also be utilised in this context. As a result, menageries and farms could be produced at a very low cost with which it was impossible to compete.

A few German farms were supplied with the animals packed into the farmhouse itself, but a greater number were contained in the traditional oval or round chipwood boxes and so carefully packed among woodshavings that not another piece could be included. In these boxed sets, the

A group of exquisitely modelled and painted figures of apes made at the end of the 18th century by the Hilpert family of Nuremberg, best known for their production of model soldiers. Germanisches Nationalmuseum, Nuremberg.

farmhouses and farm buildings were suggested very simply and were not intended to be opened. The scale of objects, as in arks, was completely ignored and a farmer might stand as high as a mansion-like farmhouse. A Bestelmeier catalogue, *circa* 1800, showed a large scene which could be assembled from separate boxed sets and included a sheep farm and a herd of cows for a pasture. A few trees were usually included in these sets, so that the child could assemble the scene realistically, within the fences and walls that were also supplied. There is considerable variation in the size of these scenes; those on a very small scale were the most popular exports because of their low shipping costs. As so many of the figures are fragile, few have survived outside Germany in relation to the number that were made and it is rare to see a farm complete with several hundred pieces. A great number of the trees and buildings are considered to be the work of craftsmen in the Seiffen region, where matchwood box making was also a traditional skill.

The popularity of travelling menageries in the 19th century encouraged the wooden toy makers to create charming zoological garden scenes with the animals neatly chained up outside decorative cages. The sets, like the farms, were supplied together with appropriate fences, trees and even pieces of statuary. An illustration in a Waldkirchen catalogue shows a smartly dressed keeper, stick in hand, leading a chained monkey in a most elegant setting of arched animal houses and tall trees. Less complex figures made in the traditional manner can still be purchased, though their colouring does not compare well with those of the 19th century.

Papier mâché and composition figures were also supplied in some numbers for animal scenes. A group displayed at the Germanisches National-museum at Nuremberg and made around 1865 shows characters and animals from a circus. The horses are balanced on a small wire spring so that they move when touched and the clowns which are balanced in grotesque positions on their backs seem about to fall. A few of the horses are ridden by monkeys and the group as a whole must have formed an arresting toy when completed.

The energetic German craftsmen did not confine their production of such scenes to wood and composition, but were quick to take advantage of the mass-production potential of cast metal. The Hilperts of Nuremberg in the 18th century made a particularly lively series of monkeys on shaped bases, as well as reindeer, horses and a leopard. All of these bore their Latin names on the base, providing a simple means of instruction. The fine modelling and artistic colouring almost raise these figures above the level of toys. Close attention to detail is a characteristic of the Hilpert family's work and is particularly evident in scenes such as their Boar Hunt.

A variety of similar scenes were made by other firms in the Nuremberg area, but they are difficult to attribute because the modellers worked for several companies and did not identify their designs. As a result, unless a set is contained in its original box showing the factory name, it is almost impossible to be sure of its origin.

In Lüneburg, a town with several master pewterers, Johann Heinrich Friedrich Ram sold a menagerie, performing monkeys, dogs, hunting scenes, a poultry yard and a Noah's Ark with thirty-two pairs of animals. In the 1840s Ernst Heinrichsen of Nuremberg also marketed a farm, a menagerie, a circus and a Garden of Eden occupied by a decidedly under-fed Adam and Eve. As was the case with the wooden settings, fences, trees and other accessories in metal were provided for the flats. The production of these scenes was encouraged by public interest in the unusual animals displayed in zoos and by the exploits of travellers who brought back exciting tales of those encountered in distant lands. The desire to instruct the young had been the original inspiration for many of the flats made in the very early years of the 19th century, and had inspired sets such as those made at Hildesheim, representing various species of birds and fish.

Metal figures, like the wooden ones, were sold in matchwood boxes, though they more frequently carry the name of the maker, together with details of the medals won at the various trade exhibitions. Like the lead soldiers, they were sold by weight rather than by number.

The German producers appear to have lost much of their impetus in the creation of animal-based scenes after 1900, mainly because small boys were now becoming much more interested in contemporary transport. The effectiveness of the exported scenes was also diminished because the poor economic situation of the world, combined with protective import duties, meant that the settings became much smaller in scale and less complete. In America, the gap was filled to some extent by the 'Humpty Dumpty Circus', a name that was registered as a trademark by its manufacturer, Albert Schoenhut, in 1903. It was originally composed of some twenty figures and animals, which were very strongly made and provided with six joints each so that they could assume many positions. The clowns had slits in their wooden hands and feet so that they could balance on a chair-back or on the rung of a ladder. The circus was so popular that it became one of the few American-made toys to be exported in considerable quantity and appears in many European collections. In 1913 thirty-three animals and figures were included as well as pedestal tables, weights and wheelbarrows. All the figures could be purchased separately, but the sets that were boxed were accompanied by a book of illustrations and rhymes with photographs of the various tricks that the toys could perform. Existing sets are often found in almost perfect condition – a tribute to the strength of the animals and the quality of their decoration.

In England, William Britain produced his 'Model Home Farm', which became surprisingly popular in view of the mechanical interests of most 20th century boys. Like the Humpty Dumpty Circus, the farm could be purchased a piece at a time. The smaller figures were well within the range of children's pocket money, while the larger boxed settings made ideal Christmas or birthday gifts. Trees and hedgerows were supplied as in the wooden German farms, but as Britain's prided themselves on their realistic approach, different species such as oaks and cedars were modelled. Fences, gates, styles and flint and stone walling could be combined to create an organised layout. The farm house and farm buildings were made of wood and were traditional in design, though the farmer was provided with some modern equipment. In the farm included in Britain's catalogue for 1940 one finds, surprisingly, that the plough is still horse-drawn and the vehicle provided for the farmer is a gig. No motor cars appear in this setting and, with the exception of a few lorries, the mood is very much that of an earlier decade.

Judging by the number of surviving pieces, Britain's zoo characters were nothing like as popular as the farms, though the animals were again modelled with great realism and their appearance and habits were fully described in the firm's catalogue. Railings that were joined by interlocking posts, date and coconut palms, keepers and visitors to the zoo, all contributed to the effect of completeness. Boxed sets were also available, as well as pools and animal houses which were large enough to contain particular species.

The Britain's circus was a much smaller arrangement, though some of the pieces such as the white prancing horse were extremely attractive. The equestriennes were specially made to stand on the backs of either the horses or the elephants.

After suffering an almost complete lack of interest among collectors, the Britain's animal-based settings are now becoming more popular, especially among newer collectors, as they are among the few relatively old toys that can still be purchased cheaply.

The Hilpert family made these finely painted deer *(top)* **at the end of the 18th century. Also German in origin, dating from around 1870, are the papier mâché circus figures, which are mounted on springs for movement. Both Germanisches Nationalmuseum, Nuremberg.**

2

TOYS
PURELY
FOR
PLEASURE

Soft toys

Rag dolls were made for children from the earliest times. There is an Egypto–Roman example, dating from the 3rd to 4th century AD, which together with other simple toys was found in a child's grave. Early playthings of this type are very rare as they soon became damaged and discoloured and being of little monetary value were discarded. It was only the more costly toys which were sometimes passed down to the next generation. When toys are depicted in prints and paintings, it is often difficult to be sure of the substance from which an item is made, though it would seem unlikely that soft toys representing a favourite dog or horse were not made. It is not until the 18th century that actual examples are known, and even then they are very few. In Ann Sharp's baby house, dating from around 1700, there is a charming horse on a stand, and in the house at Nostell Priory there is a poorly made and rather bedraggled dog that stands in the kitchen. The horse is made of most effectively ruched linen and is of a decorative quality that would not immediately be associated with the period. It appears to be of commercial manufacture, whereas the dog is fairly obviously home made.

The collector's interest in soft toys really begins with those of the late 19th century, when such pieces began to be made on a commercial scale. They were eventually made to represent a whole variety of stage and screen characters as well as the more conventional animals and dolls. One of the strangest soft toys is the somewhat frightening golliwog, thought to have been first made by Florence Upton (1873 to 1922), who introduced him in a series of books begun in 1895, which included *The Golliwogs' Bicycle Club* and *The Golliwog in War* (1899). This toy was almost a necessity in British nurseries until some adults decided that his design embodied the worst aspects of colour prejudice in the 1960s, and its manufacture was almost completely discontinued.

Condition is extremely important when soft toys are collected, as the majority obviously left the nursery in a state quite unacceptable to the majority of collectors. In general, prices in this area are still reasonably low, mainly because of the problems involved in maintaining such pieces in a clean state and free from moth. Consequently there are still bargains around for those prepared to buy the curious or the socially interesting objects as well as the beautiful.

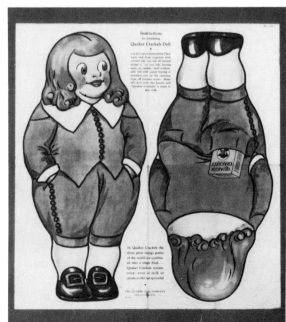

PRODUCERS OF SOFT TOYS

Alexander, Madame–New York. This firm was founded in 1923 by Beatrice Behrman. Their first dolls were made of rag with pressed mask-type faces. The costumes were always particularly well made. The toys included characters from *Little Women, Alice in Wonderland* and the works of Charles Dickens.

Arnold Print Works–North Adams, Mass., USA, 1876 to 1919. This firm was one of the largest manufacturers of prints and dress fabrics in the country and was quick to see the potential of figures printed on cotton and sold by the yard for home assembly. Patents for printed cloth dolls and animals had been granted to Celia M. Smith of Ithaca, New York in July and October of 1892 and these were bought by the print works. The dolls and toys were printed in 'natural colours', and it was suggested that cardboard should be put in the bottom so they would stand securely. All genuine figures carried the trademark 'Arnold Print Works. North Adams, Mass. Incorporated 1876'. In 1892 Little Tabbies and Tabby Cat, Tatters and Little Tatters, Little Red Riding Hood, Topsy, Little Jocko, Little Bow-Wow, Our Soldier Boys, Bunny, Jocko, Floss (a sleeping dog), Hen and Chicks, Rooster and Owl were made. Most of these were printed on a complete yard of cloth but the smaller figures were four to a half yard. The company also worked with Palmer Cox, who had created the well known Brownies

and these also appeared in 1892. The twelve small figures were printed on a yard of cloth and were to be stuffed with bran or sawdust. They were all about seven inches high and were marked on the right foot 'Copyright 1892 by Palmer Cox'. The set included John Bull, Canadian, Chinaman, Dude, German, Highlander, Indian, Irishman, Policeman, Sailor, Soldier and of course, Uncle Sam. A large number of these were made and with patience it is possible to assemble the whole set.

Art Fabric Mills–New York, USA, 1899 to 1910. Manufactured printed fabric toys. Selchow and Righter were their main distributors. President

This home-made rag doll was produced in Philadelphia around 1810. Its method of construction indicates how little such figures change through the centuries. Height 15 inches. Atwater Kent Museum, Philadelphia, Pennsylvania. *Below, left:* A pair of Hungarian costume dolls wearing red and black costumes. The faces are of the pressed mask type with stockinette stretched over the surface. Soft toys of this type were made from 1900 to 1935 in most European countries. *Circa* 1930. *Right:* A First World War Teddy bear with several changes of uniform. The clothes were made by Helen Roy Lister between the ages of seven and eleven. Height of bear 11 inches. Both Pollock's Toy Museum, London.

The set of 'Brownies'
drawn and copyrighted by
Palmer Cox and made by
the Arnold Print Works of
North Adams, Mass. Two
sheets of six Brownies
each were produced. The
uncut sheet *(right)* shows
the front and back of one
group and the second
illustration shows the
other six in made up
form. Margaret Wood-
bury Strong Museum,
Rochester, New York.

of the firm was Edgar G. Newell and in 1900
he patented a 'Life Size Doll' that could be dressed
in the cast-off clothes of real children. 'Life Size'
was registered as a trademark. The legend 'Pat
Feb 13th 1900' appears on one foot of the doll and
'Art Fabric Mills New York' on the other. At this
time they also sold a 'Cry Baby' pincushion and
smaller figures known as 'Topsy Dolls' that were
sold in white and black versions. In 1904 Foxy
Grandpa and Buster Brown were produced.
Diana, Bridget, Uncle, Billy and Newly Wed
Kid were all in production by 1907. A number
were also sold in Europe and in 1908 the firm's
British branch in Queen Victoria Street, London,
were offering a life-size dog and cat, kittens,
puppies, Punch and Judy, noiseless skittles, Buster
Brown, and the remainder of characters already
mentioned in the lists for home sales.

Beecher, Mrs T. K.–New York, USA. Mrs
Beecher produced her 'Missionary Rag Babies'
between 1893 and 1910. The features were stitch-
moulded and hand-painted and the dolls were
given woollen hair. Both black and white baby
dolls were made from old silk jersey underwear,
which gave the toys a much softer feel than, for
instance, the printed cut-out figures which were
produced by many manufacturers.

Bell & Francis–Bread Street, London. Manufactured printed dolls and toys sold on sheets for
cutting out and home assembly. In 1910 their
characters included Duck, Chantecler Hen, Tabby
Cat, Bunny Rabbit and a Toy Spaniel. All the
toys were of the simple two-part type, which had
to be sewn together and stuffed.

THE "BAMBINA" DOLLS (UNBREAKABLE)
(Trade Mark Registered. Patent Nos. 235424, 237520 and 255184)
An exquisite Range of Models in assorted Art shades.

Made in 3 sizes, "0" Approximately 14½ ins. high
"1" 16 ins. "
"2" 18½ ins. "

Made in 3 sizes, "0" Approximately 14½ ins. high
"1" 16 ins. "
"2" 18½ ins. "

THE "BAMBINA" DOLLS (UNBREAKABLE)
(Trade Mark Registered. Patent Nos. 235424, 237520 and 255184)
An exquisite Range of Models in assorted Art shades.

No. 793   No. 794   No. 795   No. 796   No. 805   No. 806   No. 807   No. 811

No. 797   No. 799   No. 800   No. 804   No. 813   No. 785   No. 815   No. 816

Each Doll packed in patent "Bye-Bye" Bed-box (see Page 29)

Each Doll packed in patent "Bye-Bye" Bed-Box (see Page 29)

HYGIENIC TOYS   HYGIENIC TOYS

Bing, Gebrüder–Nuremberg (see also Tin Toys). Manufactured soft toys in fur fabric, velvet and felt including some models on wheels. A considerable amount of the firm's production in this area was assembled by outworkers and the dolls were also costumed in this way. In 1920 a spaniel type dog made of plush was produced and given the name Bello; this was a wheeled toy, but was rather better constructed than usual with swivelling front wheels. The dolls made at the same time included some with painted fabric faces, cloth arms and legs and mohair wigs.

Bruckner, Albert–New Jersey, USA. The firm was founded in 1901 and in the same year a pressed and stiffened mask-face doll was patented. The features were printed on the fabric face before it was pressed into shape. The heads were modelled nearly to shoulder level and marked 'Pat'd July 9th 1901' along the lower edge. A topsy turvy doll in black and white, with a skirt covering the unwanted face, was made with the patented heads.

Butten & Loening–Frankfurt a.M., Germany. This firm were producing printed fabric figures around 1900, including a purple and pink Struwelpeter (Shock-headed Peter) with the unusual addition for a rag doll of long paper fingernails. The figure appears to have been assembled by the factory before sale and was marked with a patent notice which reads 'Gesetzlich Geschützt. Register Nummer 318m'.

Carvaillo, Adrien–France. Was producing rag dolls with the trade name of 'La Venus' between 1923 and 1925.

The cover and two internal pages from the Chad Valley catalogue of 1927, illustrating the 'Bambina' dolls introduced in that year.

Caspar, Bertha–Berlin. In the early 20th century was among the largest producers in Germany of fur and velvet animals, barking, hopping and running dogs as well as the usual fluffy toys.

Ceresota Flour–USA. The North Western Consolidated Milling Company produced a figure of a farmer's boy to advertise this flour around 1895 to 1900. The words 'Ceresota Flour' appear on the front of the printed shirt. The Farmer's Boy trademark was registered by this company in 1895.

Chad Valley–Harborne, Birmingham. (See under Constructional Toys for early history.) The

One of the soft toys made by Dean's Rag Book Company, this Mickey Mouse is made of printed plush velvet with felt hands and is marked 'Reg. No. 750611'. Height 12 inches. Author's Collection.

firm was established in the 1820s and the Chad Valley Factory was opened in 1897. A few toys made around 1900 are found with a Chad Valley mark though this trade name seems to have been officially registered in the 1920s. Mascots and grotesque animals in soft velveteens were made from 1920 and included figures such as The Padre, Bobby Penguin, Grotesque Cat, and Dame Quack. Several of these figures were provided with felt hats. In 1923 the Aerolite range of hygienic down-stuffed rag dolls was introduced. These were printed figures but assembled at the factory and included Pixie, Beaver and Peter Pan. The 'ISA' range of animals, which walked, hopped, skipped and jumped and were provided with growlers and grunters, were also made in the same year. A Peter Pan dressed in velvet cloth was made in 1926, and the same year saw the introduction of the 'La Petite Caresse' series of dolls. In 1927 the 'Bambina' dolls and the Mabel Lucie Attwell figures appeared. Bonzo, the 'Famous Study Dog with a variety of expressions and poses' was first sold in 1929. Automobile Association and Royal Automobile Club mascots, wearing the uniforms of the two organisations, were marketed in 1930, together with Buster Bunny, Cockatoo and Parrot and the Chad Valley Niggers, which are very reminiscent of those made by Nora Wellings. The 'Carina' dolls, dressed in fashionable costumes,

were introduced in 1931. Fortunately Chad Valley products are usually clearly marked with sewn-on labels, which often give the name of the toy series in which it appears also, so that dating should be possible from this list, though obviously once introduced a particular doll or toy appeared for many years. The doll-like figures were usually provided with plush velvet limbs, but in 1933–34 calico began to be used instead of plush. In this year some 'Carnival Dolls' were created, set in alluring poses rather in the manner of boudoir figures and costumed mainly in parti-coloured suits. Similar figures known as 'Sofa Dolls' were made in 1935 and aimed very much at the young adult market, while 'Nursery Rhyme Character Dolls' were provided for the young. 'Walk Away' was registered as a trade mark by Chad Valley for toys in 1936. In 1938 their new toys included gnomes and, with the war looming near, soldiers and sailors. The firm still produces soft toys (see also Tin Toys and Teddy Bears).

Chase, Martha – Pawtucket, Rhode Island, USA. Established in the 1880s. Made mask-faced dolls over which stockinette was stretched. The heads were then sized and painted. Both the ears and thumbs were separately applied. Early dolls have sateen bodies but white cotton was later used. In 1921 characters from *Alice in Wonderland* including the Frog Footman were advertised and also some characters from Dickens.

Columbian Dolls – Oswego, New York, USA, established in 1891. These were hand-painted rag dolls that were stuffed with cotton wool over a sawdust core. The dolls made before 1900 were stamped in ink on the bodies 'Columbian Doll, Emma E. Adams, Oswego Centre, NY.' The costumes were particularly well constructed.

Dean's Rag Book Company – Rye, England. Established in 1903 to make rag books for children who 'wear their food and eat their clothes'. The company is still very much in production and makes a good range of quality soft toys. This firm had produced covers for scrap albums as early as 1900 before they became toy makers. There is a tradition that their first rag doll was made in book form, but as no examples have survived it is impossible to be sure of the authenticity of the story, which goes on to say that as parents disliked cutting up these books to assemble the printed rag dolls, they were eventually printed on sheets. The firm employed well known artists

such as John Hassell, Harry Rowntree and Hilda Cowham to design their toys, which were sold all over Europe and, to a smaller extent, in America. Their printed rag dolls appeared before the First World War, but were still sold in 1936. The early dolls and toys were mechanically printed from hand-engraved rollers. As many as eight colours were employed in the printing and the tonal quality of the firm's early work was excellent. The qualities of 'Indestructibility, Washability and Hygienic Merit' were claimed very loudly and wood wool or granulated cork were used as a filling. Various unusual characters such as Mr Puck and his Family from *A Midsummer Night's Dream* were issued before the First World War as well as golliwogs and the characters from *Alice in Wonderland* that were popular with so many toymakers. From 1913 a soft woolly cloth was used for printed toys as well as plain cotton, and 'Tru-to-Life' dolls were made in printed felt, cotton, plush and velvet.

Two groups of soft toys made by the German firm of Schuco. *Above:* **Three dogs, all with their original labels and lever operated head movements, 1925–1930; height of largest dog 10½ inches.** *Below:* **A group dating from 1930–1937, including a clockwork mouse and clown which perform somersaults when wound up. Height of clown 5 inches. By courtesy of Sotheby's Belgravia, London.**

This unusual Christmas stocking was patented by S.H. Howe of New York State in 1889. The uncut cloth bears instructions on how to make up the stocking, which is 26 inches long. Margaret Woodbury Strong Museum, Rochester, New York.

Facing page: **This group of soft toys is arranged on a doll's convertible high chair, 26 inches high. The plush covered Teddy bear is made by Merrythought, and is 21 inches high. The two smiling Polynesian dolls, in brown plush velvet with fixed glass eyes, are marked with Nora Wellings labels and are 13 inches high. By courtesy of Christie's South Kensington, London.**

It is thought that soft toys were produced before the rag books were marketed. In the 1912–1913 catalogue appear the Humpty Dumpty and Ponchinello rattles, an Owl, Dog Toby, Bunny, Pussy Cat, Life-size Profile Cat and Dog, and Punch and Judy glove puppets. The glove toys were mainly sold in 'Knockabout' sheet form to be assembled at home. In 1914 Grenadier guards in the form of soft ninepins were made. Doll and toy making was very limited during the First World War and it was not until 1920 that really inventive toys again began to be made in some numbers. One of the 1920 toys was Gilbert the Filbert the Nursery Knut, a grotesque figure with a pointed head wearing an eyeglass and carrying a walking stick. 'Buy Gilbert and take Happiness home with you', the advertisements said. In 1923 clown figures and Dancing Darkies were added, followed in 1926 by Ole Bill, a walrus, and some plush King Charles spaniels, and in 1927 by Dickie Blob the Inkwell fairy, who was dressed 'in velvet from head to foot and taken from a popular series

of gramophone discs'. The year 1928 saw the appearance of Wabbly Willy, a British legion mascot in dog form to be dangled from a string, and Tatters the Hospital Pup. Wooliwogs made of bunches of ringed wool and decorated with tinkling bells also appeared in 1928, and were described as 'quaint little figures of the wog tribe'. The year 1933 saw the introduction of Mickey and Minnie Mouse, made with 'Everipoze' jointing so that the limbs could be bent in any direction. Woodsey Mickey was produced in several colours. Mimie and Shah, two elegantly costumed cats from the 'Vicompte de Maudit's' book of the same title, were marketed in 1935. In 1936 several new models were introduced including Donald Duck, Flossibunn Rabbits in pink and blue, and a nice Pluto whose head turned when his tail was moved. Ma and Pa Coney were rather anthropomorphic rabbits wearing spectacles. Dismal Desmond, who had appeared a few years earlier, was supplemented in 1936 by Cheerful Desmond and Tiddley Winks, the dog made famous in the song hit of the season. Nero the News Hound was issued by permission of the *Daily Mirror* and had a black body with a golden face and paws. A pair of Aberdeen terriers, Mac and Jack, added to the impressive range of these pre-war years. After the Second World War, the range of toys was limited and the firm now concentrates mainly on the traditional soft fluffy toys that have always remained popular.

Finsbury, Samuel & Co – London. Made printed rag dolls to be cut out and assembled at home in the early 20th century including a British Tommy.

Horsman, Edward I. – New York City, USA, established in 1865. A distributor and maker of dolls who employed the Horsman trademark from 1897. 'Babyland' rag dolls were made with painted faces from 1904 until 1907, when they were given 'life-like faces printed in colour'. From 1910 painted and printed dolls and white and coloured babies were made.

Hughes, Henry J. – Tottenham Rd, Kingsland, London. In the early 20th century this firm were producing well-made rag dolls, soft toys and wool rattles.

Ideal Novelty and Toy Company – Brooklyn, New York. Founded by Morris Michton in 1907 and best known for its teddy bears, which were the first on the market.

A group of fur fabric covered birds representing a crane, an owl and a duck, made by Shuco. *Circa* 1935; height of crane 17 inches. By courtesy of Sotheby's Belgravia, London.

Lenci–Trade name of Enrico Scavini of Turin, Italy. The firm was founded in 1920 and the trade name was in fact Scavini's pet name for his wife. Their well constructed toys were made 'in the Artistic Manner for sale to parents of good taste and discrimination'. It was claimed that the figures were designed by Italian artists and all painted by hand. The dolls had felt faces which were pressed in moulds so that there were no disfiguring seams. By 1921 a hundred different character dolls were being sold, including policemen, milkmaids, pierrots and harlequins. Those representing either children or babies were given real hair, and the majority of the dolls have sideways glancing eyes. They were marked with labels and/or a button, and on the foot. The clothes were usually of felt, and were interestingly idiosyncratic in design, with applied cut-out flowers and abstract shapes. When woollen garments were worn, they were correctly knitted.

Lindler & Sons–Sonneberg. This firm was operating in the very early 20th century and specialised in skin-covered animals in large and miniature sizes; various soft animals and circus toys were also made.

McMillan, Adelaide–Workington, England. In 1915 patented a rag doll that was marketed as a 'Mac Doll'. The head and trunk were made in a very simplified manner from four sections of cloth. The hands were made of wood. The filling was cork and the features were painted. These dolls were completely assembled before sale and were marked with the patent number 10533 on both front and back of the torso.

Merrythought Toys – Dale End, Ironbridge, Shropshire. Established in 1930, the main founders being members of the local Holmes family. In 1932 the firm registered Movietoys as a trademark. Soft toys of fur fabric and felt have been in continual production ever since. Their range of whimsical felt-costumed toys and figures made in the early years are liked by collectors and can be identified by sewn-on labels and sometimes tags. In 1931, a patent was registered for a metal armature for soft toys with wire loops on the end of various sections.

Pedigree Soft Toys Ltd–Triang Works, Merton Surrey. Registered as a trade name in 1942. Since that time the firm has produced a large number of soft toys. It still operates in Canterbury, Kent.

Saalfield Publishing Company–Akron, Ohio, USA. Made lithographed muslin toys including some inspired by the drawings of Kate Greenaway in 1907. In 1908 the firm made a Delft Girl, Papoose, Santa Claus, Little Red Riding Hood, baby dolls and a Japanese doll; in 1909, Goldenlocks, Topsy Turvey and Dottie Dimple.

Schuco–Germany. This firm was founded in 1912 by a Herr Schreyer and Heinrich Müller, and traded under the name of Schreyer and Company with Schuco as its trademark. The first toys were clockwork animals and some of these were wound by turning an arm or tail instead of a key. In the 1920s and 1930s, products included a Dancing Mouse, a Trotting Dog wearing a cape, a 'Pick-Pick' bird of brilliant plumage and a comical clockwork mouse.

Steiff—Giengen an der Brenz, Germany. Established by Margarete Steiff (1847 to 1909). She had begun to make dolls for local children in 1879, and these were so popular that she took on extra help and utilised scraps of felt from a local factory.

In 1893 the firm was entered in the Trade Register under the names of Margarete Steiff and her brother Fritz Steiff. Fritz had nine children and all were involved in specialised sections of the firm, two of the daughters managing the outworkers, one son becoming a textile engineer and another managing the technical development. The firm's first catalogue was issued in 1894, and the characteristic trademark of a hexagonal metal button in the ear of the toy was used after 1905. In 1906 the firm became an incorporated company with Margarete Steiff and her nephews Paul, Richard and Franz being entered as associates. In 1908 dolls with the characteristic seam running down the centre of the face were advertised. This method of manufacture ceased after 1922. The firm mounted a display at the 1909 Leipzig Toy Fair which consisted of huge set pieces, including part of a zoo complete with houses lit by electricity and lively water chutes etc. In another part of the fair was a complete village school with appropriate figures. To show off the polar bears and dolls in winter sports outfits, there was a snow scene. A rabbit hutch contained 'bunnies of almost every variety'. New lines for the year included chimpanzees and tumbling elephants and for the zoological collection a fine kangaroo. A report on the fair commented that it was eight years since the firm had introduced this type of toy. They were recorded as employing nearly 3,000 hands. Their soft toys were appreciated because they 'get as near the real living object as possible and where the living object is parodied, this is done in a really clever and amusing yet dignified manner'.

Margarete Steiff died in 1909 and the firm was carried on by her two nephews Paul and Richard. In 1910, they showed a complete parade ground of felt-faced soldiers at the Leipzig Fair and were marketing kelly-like figures and their latest novelty, Krackjack, a fat creature with a large pointed head. Their 'Marionetten' were also described as new, as were the foxes, seals and lion cubs. In 1913, the firm was advertising soft toys with real animal voices, including bleating lambs, mewing cats and grunting pigs. The plush toys included a jointed and a crouching cat, a realistic model of a Welsh terrier in imitation of the Prince of Wales's dog, 'Gwen', a Cat Baby and Cat Lady, and Humpty Dumpty with a 'felt skin'. There were also 'Popular Grotesque and Character' dolls which could stand without support on very large feet and these included Gaston and Alfons, 'the two polite Frenchmen', Captain and Mrs Captain, and an Eskimo doll. All these figures were marked by the button in the ear and had the characteristic seam down the felt faces.

The company is still in operation today, and all the shares are still owned by members of the Steiff family.

Terry, William J.—Kingsland, London. One of the largest British manufacturers of soft toys in felt, plush, cloth and soft fur in the early 20th century. Unfortunately few of their toys were permanently marked.

One of the largest and most famous manufacturers of soft toys was the firm started by Margarete Steiff in Germany, which is still in production today. This advertisement from *The Toy and Fancy Goods Trader* of January 1910 shows some novelty dolls with the seam down the face which was characteristic of the firm's products in the early 20th century, and refers to the Steiff 'button in ear' trade mark.

Right: **A group of clock-work marching soft toys which move on wheels concealed under the feet. The faces are strongly reminiscent of Steiff products, although these examples were marketed by Schuco. Height of black figure 10½ inches. Photo: Sotheby's Belgravia, London.** *Below:* **A glass-eyed spider monkey with velvet hands and feet, made on a soft wire armature so that it could be moved into a variety of poses. Marked 'Made in England. Nora Wellings'; height 15 inches. Author's Collection.**

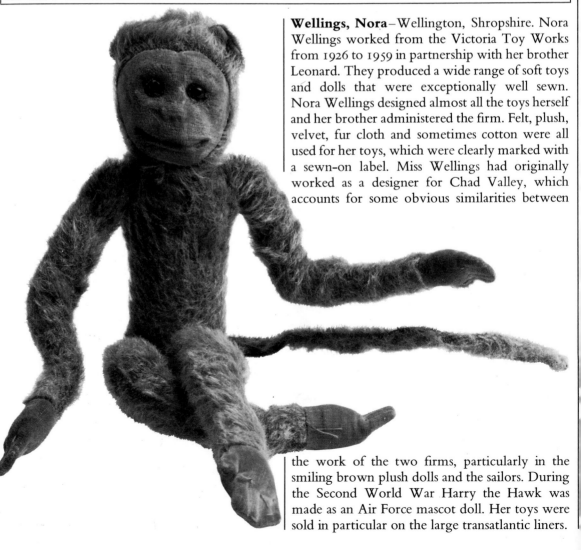

Wellings, Nora – Wellington, Shropshire. Nora Wellings worked from the Victoria Toy Works from 1926 to 1959 in partnership with her brother Leonard. They produced a wide range of soft toys and dolls that were exceptionally well sewn. Nora Wellings designed almost all the toys herself and her brother administered the firm. Felt, plush, velvet, fur cloth and sometimes cotton were all used for her toys, which were clearly marked with a sewn-on label. Miss Wellings had originally worked as a designer for Chad Valley, which accounts for some obvious similarities between the work of the two firms, particularly in the smiling brown plush dolls and the sailors. During the Second World War Harry the Hawk was made as an Air Force mascot doll. Her toys were sold in particular on the large transatlantic liners.

Teddy bears

Though originally hailed simply as an amusing novelty, the Teddy bear has maintained its popularity for some seventy-five years. It has been produced not only in the basic plush and woollen fabrics but also in rubber, china, plastic and metal. It has provided the subject for items as diverse as nursery candlesticks and women's scent bottles, and though popular with succeeding generations, has only undergone very minor changes in construction. Many people who have little general interest in antique toys treasure their Teddy bears and while they are quite willing to sell, for instance, their old dolls they will not part with these bedfellows of their childhood.

As relatively few bears are marked, their collecting is based on their condition and interest. Though a large number of bear makers are mentioned in trade papers and general advertisements, it is impossible, except with makers such as Steiff, to attribute unlabelled examples to them, so that the value of a bear depends very much upon the appeal of a particular toy. An early bear with a musical movement contained in the torso or one whose eyes light up from a battery-powered light is obviously of greater interest than the most basic type of animal.

The bear itself was popular as a children's toy throughout the 19th century. The bear Mishka, for instance, is a traditional Russian folk toy. In Victorian England the figure of Bruin was regarded with great affection, and automata, growling bears with fierce expressions and bared teeth, and realistic chained bears covered with fur were made. In 1903 the form of the bear changed completely and the Teddy as we know it today emerged.

German and American makers both lay claim to the original design, though it is now felt that the American claim is the stronger, as it is based on more factual documentation. A cartoon which appeared in the *Washington Post* in 1903, drawn

Toy bears of a realistic nature were popular long before the advent of the Teddy. This rather ferocious looking mechanical example was made in France around 1880. Bethnal Green Museum of Childhood, London.

Above: **A much loved English bear with the pointed nose and hump back typical of early versions.** *Circa* **1910; height 14 inches. Owned by Miss N. Smith.** *Top right:* **A pair of bears made by Gebrüder Sussenguth of Neustadt near Coburg, Thuringia, around 1926. The top bear is grey and growls when tilted forwards. The other is brown. Both have eyes and tongues which move from side to side and tags round their necks with the name 'Peter'. Author's Collection.**

by Clifford Berryman, showed President 'Teddy' Roosevelt with a small bear cub at his feet which he had refused to shoot, not out of sentimentality but for political reasons. This drawing inspired Morris Michtom, founder of the Ideal Toy Corporation of America, to produce a series of bears with button eyes for his toy shop. He obtained official permission to entitle them 'Teddy's Bears', a name that was later modified. The success of the animals was instant, and their production quickly accelerated. In Germany, and in the same year, Margaret Steiff also made bears. There is a tradition that a traveller visiting her factory showed her the same American cartoon and suggested that she should make a jointed doll-like figure of plush

with a bear's head. The evolution of the firm's bears is said to have been influenced by Richard Steiff, who supposedly studied the behaviour of real bears in the Stuttgart zoo.

The Steiff bears were shown at the Leipzig Fair in 1904 and the firm was overwhelmed with orders. Toy-trade papers of the years before 1910 contain continual complaints from retailers that they are unable to meet the public demand for the toy. The Steiff production figures are interesting, as they indicate clearly how the interest in bears grew. The numbers produced after 1904 rose to a peak of 974,000 in 1907 and then fell rapidly in 1913. After this the level remained almost static until 1953, when the number rose to

A Teddy bear in
particularly good
condition that was bought
for the present owner at
Hamleys toy store in
London in 1908. Un-
marked; height 22 inches.
Owned by Mrs M.
Eccles-Holmes.

Facing page, right centre:
**An early 20th century
Teddy bear with the early
long straight arms, on
a yellow swing rocking
horse. Rides on the horse
were given as rewards for
good work at an elemen-
tary school in Luton.
Luton Museum and Art
Gallery, Bedfordshire.**

An appealing unmarked Teddy bear in sailor's uniform, made around 1911. Bethnal Green Museum of Childhood, London.

bodies were filled with kapok and the heads with a type of wood wool. If a growler was used in the torso, that part of the body was also filled with wood wool. The growler which sounds when the bear is tipped backwards was first introduced in 1908, but it was later replaced with a cheaper press squeaker. Between 1903 and 1909 the range of sizes was continually increased and puppets, kelly-like figures, containers and musical boxes were all produced as Teddy bears. These early versions are characterised by their long noses and hump backs, but these details gradually altered, and by the 1920s, a much flatter faced bear of an extremely friendly appearance had evolved.

In Britain, firms such as the Bear Pit of St Peter's Road, London, and William J. Terry, who claimed to be the largest manufacturer, struggled to keep up with the demand. A printed cotton flannelette bear which could be cut out and assembled at home, was made as a cheap alternative by Samuel Finsberg & Co, together with a miniature version printed on the same sheet. Ralph Dunn & Co of the Barbican supplied the biscuit makers Peak Frean with 36-inch bears in 1909 to promote the sale of their newly introduced Teddy Bear biscuits. In 1910 some effort was made to introduce a rival, and a white Barbara Bear was made, though this toy never became popular. In the same year Decamps of Paris registered a patent for a tumbling bear that worked by turning the arms around to wind up a simple motor. Other firms such as Fleischmann & Bloedel adopted the popular toy as part of their trademark, as did Deuerlan, while even the doll-makers began to produce figures with the bodies of bears but with the china faces of ordinary dolls. Elegant young women parading on the seashore carried specially made mascot bears, while motorists and cyclists fixed the toys to their machines. The bear appeared at fashionable parties and in drawing rooms and adults were not in the least shy about including this novelty figure in carefully posed photographs.

One of Britain's largest producers of bears to the present day is the firm of Chad Valley, who in the early 1920s were proud of their exclusive use of hygienic British materials. Their largest bear at this time stood 28 inches high and could be obtained in a variety of materials from 'long beaver brown' to 'best long golden' fur. The cheapest was the upright 'golden'. Six qualities and thirteen sizes were made by this one firm, and the limited ranges now produced even by the leading firms are a witness to the stifling economies of design imposed by modern mass-production.

258,000 a year. The Steiff bears were marked with the firm's button in the ear, though this was often removed by the child owners. The very successful years of the factory are known as the *Bärenjahre* ('the bear years') and at one of the Leipzig toy fairs there was a Bear Pit, set out with great ingenuity and occupied by tumbling, growling, swinging and climbing versions of the Steiff toy.

The plush which the German makers used for their bears is thought to have come from Yorkshire and, thwarted in their efforts to obtain sufficient Teddies from Germany, the British toymakers began to create their own. The British bear was given a much plumper body than the German and more shaping was given to the limbs. The

Musical toys

Toys that emit sound are usually the first to be enjoyed by a baby, and examples of simple clappers, rattles, bells, and balls containing seeds that sound when thrown, are among the traditional playthings to be found in the remains of early civilisation. In ancient Greece, spoked hoops were made to clank and jingle as they rolled along, by threading them with discs of metal. The earliest musical toys still available to collectors are the rattles and whistles which often formed a child's Christening gift and were therefore treasured throughout life. In the Victoria and Albert Museum is an earthenware rattle in the form of a knight's head which dates from the late medieval period. Other examples are the engaging agate ware whistles made in Staffordshire from the 18th century, which often took the form of birds. The bodies of some of these birds could be filled with water so that a warbling sound was emitted when the whistle was blown, the mouthpiece being formed by the tail. Switzerland produced bird whistles carved in wood, and these cuckooed when blown, while their beaks opened and closed and their tails moved up and down.

Among the finest Christening gifts were silver and gold rattles, sometimes ornamented with hanging bells, and often provided with a teething coral that is unfortunately, but almost inevitably, damaged, so that the balance of the item is spoiled. Many of the silver rattles are of complex structure and some even have the bells enclosed within the central section with delicately formed arched supports. The most exquisite examples were rarely played with and were often attached to the mother's chatelaine; one of these is worn by a fine Grödnertal lady doll in the Stranger's Hall, Norwich. Ivory and bone were also used for carved rattles, while the poorer children were given wooden or even basketwork versions. Unless there is a hallmark, rattles have to be dated by their style and while it is usually possible to be fairly accurate regarding those made for wealthy children, the problem is much more difficult with regard to those made of base materials.

The musical toys of play warfare, such as trumpets and drums, are also traditional toys of childhood and formed an essential part of every young nobleman's toy box from the medieval period. Tin trumpets were among the toys that were produced in vast quantities in Nuremberg from the 16th century and contemporary paintings and prints show children with a variety of similar well made, but basically simple toys. The German craftsmen were also particularly skilled in the creation of musical instruments and these formed a large percentage of the early toy production in the towns of Sonneberg and Grünhainichen. By the late Victorian period, the turners of Pobershau had become completely specialised in the manufacture of pipes, while other areas concentrated on the manufacture of accordians and mouth organs. In the Erzgebirge, scenic musical toys were constructed with great skill; some examples consisted of couples dancing on a small stage to the sound of a simple musical box in the base. In other examples, the figures might daintily revolve on an extravagantly carved roundabout. Tinkling toys were made in particular at Marburg in Hesse, and included items such as go-carts, organs, and pianos, as well as dancing figures moved by the turning of a handle. Few of these folk-type musical toys are attributable but they are often bought by collectors because of their decorative charm.

Many of the firms producing musical instruments for adults also made small child-size versions and these fall on the borderline of toys but are sometimes included in collections. Among such firms was Kohnstam of Fürth who specialised in

The rattle is the earliest and most primitive form of musical toy. This extremely interesting child's rattle was made in England in the 14th century. The eyes are incised and the moustache is cleverly textured. It is made of brown earthenware and glazed in tones of yellow, orange and green. Height 3 inches. Victoria and Albert Museum, London.

Facing page: **This late 19th century musical toy is made of fabric over a wire frame. The rabbit rises from the lettuce as the music plays. By courtesy of Phillips, New Bond Street, London.**

This painting by Paul Van Somer (*circa* 1576–1621) represents Elizabeth, daughter of James I. She carries a fine rattle, shown in detail *below*, with an ivory biting section instead of the more usual coral. At one end is a whistle. Leeds City Art Gallery.

the manufacture of children's instruments and used among their trade names, 'Zingara', 'Muskateer' and 'Revotina'. Math. Hohner of Trossingen in Germany produced harmonicas and accordians in vast quantities which, though they were stocked by toy shops, were bought for use by adults as much as by children. This Württemberg firm was run by several generations of the same family, and they were the largest manufacturer in the world of small musical instruments, producing hundreds of standard brands that were continually added to. In 1910 they were the first in the market with their mouth organs sold under the brand 'King George Harp' and decorated with portraits of King George and Queen Mary and a bright Union Jack. Another brand made especially for the British market was the 'Prince of Wales Harp' which showed the young prince between the blue and white ensigns. Among the other Hohner brand-names were the 'Mavis' and the 'Scout', the latter decorated with a representation of a group of scouts at work. The firm's products were very highly thought of by toy sellers and considered unrivalled both for quality and power of tone. A similar range of accordians, concertinas and mouth organs were produced on a much smaller scale by Meinel of Untersachsenberg, Saxony, while much cheaper musical toys simply made of paper and tin were produced in Berlin by Felix Schlunper.

In America one of the great toy-making factories was founded on the manufacture of toy pianos. Albert Schoenhut, a German immigrant working for the toy importers John Deiser & Sons of Philadelphia, became aware of the shortcomings of imported German pianos and in 1872 set up his own company for their manufacture. These toy pianos had sounding pieces of metal plate and were later joined by other instruments such as glockenspiels, xylophones and metallophones – though the firm's name is primarily associated by collectors with the 'Humpty Dumpty Circus' which it produced.

The oldest American manufacturer of proper toy drums with skin heads was Noble and Cooley of Granville, Massachusetts. This company looked like obtaining a complete monopoly of the market after the last of their competitors went out of business in 1890 and they were able to buy up all their assets. Morton Converse, who was already manufacturing tin and wooden drums, decided to compete with this important firm and the two fought a battle for the control of this fairly lucrative market for many years. Converse

A simple toy polyphon or musical box with interchangeable discs to play six different tunes. The box is of varnished birchwood. Late 19th century. Welsh Folk Museum, Cardiff.

This simple Swiss-made musical box with applied paper decoration plays 'Santa Lucia' and has the alphabet printed around the base. *Circa* **1925; diameter 2½ inches. Author's Collection.**

offered an astonishing range of sixty different styles and could produce 7,000 drums in a single day. The majority were at first given sheepskin heads but in an attempt to lower prices Converse began to use parchment instead and found that besides being cheaper this material was also well suited to the American climate as it was less affected by heat and cold.

The number of attributable toys suddenly increases in the late 19th century when musical pieces were included among the products of the great tin-toy makers. Bing, Carette and Märklin all produced toys with a musical movement in the base and Bing's 1912 English catalogue shows lightweight model roundabouts, including some with galloping horses. They were hand cranked at the side and produced a fairly basic tinkling sound. Miniature tin gramophones were soon included and were provided with some specially recorded discs. Carette's 1911 catalogue illustrated phonographs of 'surprising resonance', claiming that 'the reproduction of a record is clear and distinct'. Their gramophones were intended in many cases for adult use and were provided with cast iron bases and japanned flower horns. The Bing Werke range of model gramophones was good and though of very simple construction they were usually provided with three distinct speeds, whereas most tin gramophones of the horn type have infinitely variable speeds. Among the interesting American contributions was a 'Carillon' produced by Milton Bradley which was an 'automatic music box in which the hammers of a metalophone are operated by the passage of a keyboard through the machine by the turning of a crank'.

Among the most attractive musical toys are the marottes, whose musical movement is usually concealed by a doll's skirt, though sometimes the complete figure stands on a platform with the musical movement hidden under a layer of fringed silk. When the stick on which the figure was mounted was swung slowly around, the music played. Other, much simpler versions were known as folies and consisted of a whistle or stick surmounted by a doll's head with a frock. The latter sometimes concealed a simple squeaker that sounded as the figure was shaken. The effect was heightened by the sound of the bells that were sewn to the costumes and to ribbons that hung round the neck. Such figures were made by both German and French toymakers and were again often given as Christening gifts.

In the USA, bell toys were made by most of the tin and iron toy makers and included subjects

BELL TOYS.

No. 24.   Bellringers; half size cut........................per doz., $3 75

No. 4.   Chime, with horse; 6½ inches, ½ dozen in package, per dozen $1 75

No. 15.   Half size cut; ⅓ dozen in package...........per doz., $1 85

No. 39.   Half size cut; horse swings on pedestal and rings the bell...per doz., $4 00

No. 37.   Half size cut; girl with doll on sled, with chimes, per dozen $4 00

No. 23.   Half size cut; jumping horse and monkey rider, per doz., $3 75

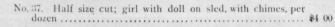

READ THE PREFACE BEFORE ORDERING.

Among the most attractive musical toys are the doll-like figures known as marottes. This bisque-headed example is dressed in a red and white costume. The musical box is activated when the toy is swung. Late 19th century; height 12 inches. By courtesy of Christies South Kensington, London.

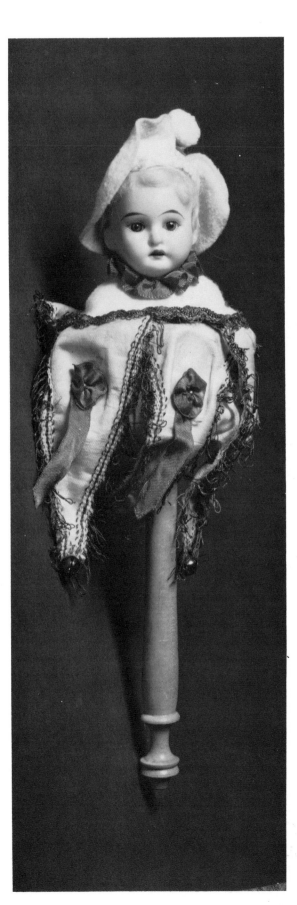

Previous page: **A page showing a variety of bell toys from the 1892 catalogue of the American mail order firm of Marshall Field.**

such as Cinderella's chariot and a cat and dog fight, both of which were made to be pulled along while a bell rang underneath. Another iron toy was a horse which activated a bell by swinging on a pedestal. Another represented a pair of bellringers sitting opposite one another on a see-saw. As they moved up and down, they pulled the ropes of the large bell that hung between them. One of the most amusing American bell toys, however, is a model of a father reading 'The Evening News baby quieter' and bouncing his baby upon his knee. As the toy was pulled along, each revolution of the wheel rang the bell and bounced the baby. Though such iron bell toys are particularly American, plainer tin versions were also made in Germany.

A number of games involving music were produced in the 19th century, including one created in 1801 and dedicated to Princess Charlotte of Wales. Known as 'The Newly Invented Musical Game', it was contained in a mahogany box that opened flat to represent a keyboard and had ivory and bone pieces that were engraved with musical notation. The game is of such complexity that the rules and method of playing it are no longer known. On a much less elevated plane are the games such as that made by L. Saussine of Paris in 1888, in which a pond revolved under a bridge to the accompaniment of a musical box, and cardboard fish with brass rings were caught by magnets attached to fishing rods.

After Goodyear's discovery of the vulcanization process and improvements in moulding techniques made in the 1850s, rubber was used by most of the leading dollmakers in the production of simple figures, usually provided with a squeaker or whistle. Every conceivable type of animal and character was made in this way, though good examples are not very easily located as the substance tended to crack and shrink with age and the whistles rapidly failed. The Marshall Field catalogue for 1892 to 1893 gives some idea of the range, as their stock varied from figures moulded as gnomes to others that were quite Napoleonic. Some wore knitted frocks while the rattle dolls were also supplied with bells. The well modelled dogs, sheep and cats, all provided with whistles, were sold either painted or with a plain finish.

Many musical toys such as xylophones, trumpets and the various varieties of penny whistles are still very cheap, as they fall outside the scope of the main collecting fields, but marottes and all the metal type toys are expensive as they are included in collections of dolls and tin toys.

Automata

Automata were only occasionally created as children's playthings, even those of the simpler kind being necessarily expensive and primarily intended for adult amusement. A few of the most basic forms, made of pressed cardboard and having only one or two simple movements, were obviously nursery toys, but the main development of the subject has to be linked firmly to adult taste, whether it was for romantic and extravagant figures in the grottoes of St Germain-en-Laye or for parodies of contemporary fashions and manners. Monkeys in particular were popular subjects; they were richly costumed in silks and velvets and bowed or elegantly took a pinch of snuff in a grotesque parody of contemporary fops. France, Austria, Germany and Switzerland were the main producers of automata and both America and Britain depended in the main upon imports.

Even the simplest of the adult-inspired automata are now expensive, especially those incorporating a doll-like figure, which command prices out of all relation to the fairly basic movements, which they perform. Many contain a musical movement or are mounted on a musical box base and their development is therefore closely linked with that of mechanically produced sound.

Figures which imitated the basic movements of the human figure fascinated the Greeks, and attempts to create mechanical music are recorded in the 3rd century BC. Moving statues of gods made by Daedalus were described by Plato, and Aristotle claimed that they were activated by quicksilver, though Bishop Wilkins in his *Mechanical Magick* of 1648 thought that weights and wheels were a more likely form of motive power. The greatest advances were undoubtedly made by Hero of Alexandria, whose moving models relied on pneumatic and hydraulic power. One of his groups, operated by water pressure, involved four singing birds who became suddenly silent when an owl turned to confront them. Another tableau of a priest and priestess at an altar, with

This fine monkey automaton forms the top part of a 20-note barrel organ which is contained in a mahogany case. The monkey magician in the conical hat performs a conjuring trick with the two cups held in his hand and the musicians move their heads and eyes while playing their instruments. French, mid 19th century; overall height 36 inches. By courtesy of Sotheby's Belgravia, London.

arms that moved to pour libations on a sacrifice, was moved by heat. After the death of Hero, there was little real advance until his works were re-discovered in 1573, though individual examples of automata are known. Around 835, the Byzantine Emperor Theophilus, for instance, owned a throne whose steps were flanked by roaring lions and trees containing mechanical singing birds.

The earliest creators of commercially viable automata were the clockmakers who incorporated moving figures as striking Jacks. Several of the finest examples of their work still survive, one of them having given its name to the village of Abinger Hammer in Surrey, England. Groups of figures were later added to smaller clocks and the skills acquired in such mechanical creations were later utilized by the makers of automata and clock-work toys. Even in the 15th century the town of Nuremberg began to be associated with contrived mechanical movement and there is a reference to an eagle that could fly.

The barrel organ was the first means of repro-ducing music mechanically and some fine speci-mens were made in the early 16th century. The carillon type of movement was a later improve-ment, while the musical box is thought to have been invented in 1796 by Antoine Favre, who made a simple device for use on snuff boxes. From around 1810, the industrial manufacture of musical boxes in Geneva developed, while larger boxes were made at Ste Croix. Their structure and ornamentation became more complex as the century advanced and the peak of quality pro-duction was attained in the 1870s when many were so detailed that they were protected by glass shades. Some examples intended for public display were supplied with a penny in the slot device to operate them.

Probably the greatest maker of automata was Vaucason, who exhibited his work in the early 18th century to the amazement of a credulous public. His most famous creations were a flute player, a Moorish bellringer with a hammer and, possibly his most fascinating, a duck which he described as 'An artificial Duck made of gilded copper who drinks, eats, splashes about on the water and digests his food like a living duck!' It was realistically feathered and is thought to have worked by a system of cams, while the food was acted upon by chemicals. The duck was still exhibited as late as 1847, when a reporter com-plained that the smell given off by the figure was almost unbearable. Vaucason's ideas were de-veloped by Jaquet Droz and Leschot, who created a particularly fine lady with moving fingers that played an organ and, later, a similarly constructed figure which played a harpsichord or clavecin. The latter is illustrated on page 94.

The impression of a walking figure was at first created by concealed wheels or rollers hidden under a wide skirt. The earliest surviving dancing figures are a cavalier and his lady, which were once contained in the Art Cabinet given to King Gustavus Adolphus by the town of Augsburg in 1632. Attempts to create a lifelike moving figure were continually made and in 1815 Charles Abram Brugier created a doll that moved by placing one foot in front of the other and also turned its head. Less adventurous dolls that moved on wheels were patented by Theroude of Paris in 1853 and 1854, while in 1855 Steiner also patented a 'walking' doll. Theroude also created figures that dropped chocolates as they moved along, including a chicken that laid eggs and a rabbit that left chocolate droppings. Generally, however, the makers of automata catered for a less robust

Above: **Monkeys were among the most popular subjects used for automata. This scene of two monkey musicians is a sand toy. When the box is tilted, sand runs through hoppers inside it, activating the scene. Marked 'J.D.' possibly for J. Debertrand, Paris;** *circa* **1900. Ipswich Museums.** *Left:* **A pair of clockwork clown acrobats with composition heads and metal hands and feet. French, late 19th century; height of figures 11 inches. By courtesy of Christies's South Kensington, London.**

Facing page: **This hand-operated automaton consists of a fur-covered bear playing the piano, a bisque-headed fiddler and a composition-headed monkey cymbalist. As the music plays the figures make the appropriate movements. Probably German or Swiss,** *circa* **1900; height 17½ inches. By courtesy of Christie's South Kensington, London.**

One of the highly
sophisticated automata
made by Pierre Jaquet
Droz, this figure is known
as the Musician, and was
first shown to the public
in 1774. Not only do the
young woman's fingers
move as she plays the
clavecin, but her head and
eyes also move, she bows
slightly over the instru-
ment, and her bosom
rises and falls in imitation
of breathing. The figure
has been re-dressed and
given a new wig. *Inset:*
The complex mechanism of
the Musician. Musée d'Art
et d'Histoire, Neuchâtel.

taste and attractively costumed figures were the most popular.

Animals were nevertheless a popular subject for automata, and fur-covered cats and rabbits in particular were made to appear from boxes, riding boots or bunches of flowers. One group that was contained in a glass shade consists of some monkeys sitting at a card table surrounded by mirrors and rich upholstery. One holds a cigar that is lifted to its mouth while another holds a box containing dice which it throws on to the table. This group cost eleven guineas in 1884. Vienna, where the finest musical boxes were made, is particularly associated with monkey automata, though makers both in France and Germany often used musical boxes manufactured in Austria or Bohemia, and it is often difficult to be precise about the origin of an unmarked piece.

Figures of black men were also highly popular, an example being a satin-costumed fruit seller with a companion lady flower seller, both very lavishly supplied with gold jewellery. Other black dolls were dressed as dandies or flute players, while those holding meerschaum cigarette holders were specially recommended as display pieces for tobacconist's shops. Magicians and illusionists were also popular subjects and were used in particular by the firm of Decamps. One of their mechanical conjurers which has survived is the figure of a girl in front of whom, on a table, stand three heads concealed under covers. When the mechanism is operated she lifts the covers in turn to show that the heads have disappeared. The bisque heads used on these figures were obtained from the makers of conventional dolls and are frequently found to have been made by such firms as Jumeau or Simon and Halbig, which accounts for the frequent inclusion of automata in toy collections.

A group of automata showing the diverse and sometimes bizarre figures which were produced. *Above:* **An allegorical papier mâché toy in the form of a British guard which devours an enemy soldier when the handle is turned. Sonneberg, Germany, late 19th century; height 7 inches. Ipswich Museums.** *Far left:* **The division between tin toy and automaton becomes indistinct in this clockwork rowing boat made by Edward Riley Ives around 1875. Length 12 inches. Bill Holland Collection.** *Left:* **A variety of scenes with moving parts and figures illustrated in the 1884 catalogue of the London firm of Silber and Fleming. Victoria and Albert Museum, London.**

A spectacular silver swan made in the late 18th century by James Cox. When set in motion, the bird appears to catch a fish and swallow it. It is operated by chains and cams. Bowes Museum, Barnard Castle, Co. Durham.

THE MAKERS OF AUTOMATA

Bontem(p)s, Lucien–Late 19th century. Produced figures of humans and monkeys often on square bases and also monkey or human smokers. Also made flower sellers and mandolin players. Pieces marked 'LB' are usually attributed to this maker.

Bertran, Charles–Paris, 1878. Manufacturer of swimming dolls.

Brown, George–Forestville, Connecticut, USA, *circa* 1856. (See also American Metal Toys.) Apprenticed as a clockmaker, Brown patented various mechanisms, including a doll pushing a double hoop containing a bell.

Brugier, Charles (1788 to 1862)–Geneva. Founder of a firm that made automata and, later, singing birds of good quality. Worked with his brother Jacques.

Cox, James (d. 1788)–London. A clockmaker and jeweller who employed Zoffany to design some of his automata. His work included a group of very expensive figures intended for sale to Indian princes, including an eight-foot elephant that moved its eyes. He made the silver swan that is in the Bowes Museum, County Durham.

Decamps, Henri Ernest (1847 to 1909)–The son-in-law of Jean Roullet (see below), with whom he worked in the firm known as Roullet et E. Decamps. Their catalogues show automated fur-covered cats, foxes, dogs, elephants and smoking and drinking figures. They patented a walking doll in 1893 and made an amusing elephant that sucked up water and blew it out again.

Decamps, Gaston (1882 to 1972) – Paris. Followed in his family tradition and made automata and robot-like figures. Also elegantly dressed girls ironing and washing, as well as organ grinders etc. Some of his automata were operated by electricity.

A composition-headed clown with brown glass eyes and a protruding tongue mounted on a musical box. Made by Lucien Bontemps, late 19th century; height 26 inches. By courtesy of Christies South Kensington, London.

One of the most famous automata is the **Writer** made by Pierre Jaquet Droz and first exhibited in 1774. It can inscribe any phrase of under forty letters by means of a preset mechanism, and the figure's eyes follow the pen as he writes. The inscription in the photograph reads 'Les androides Jaquet Droz à Neuchâtel'. A similar piece, but with a simpler mechanism, is the **Draughtsman** made by Pierre's son **Henri Louis Droz** (*facing page*). The cams shown in the view of the mechanism are interchangeable, enabling the figure to draw four different pictures. Both Musée d'Art et d'Histoire, Neuchâtel.

Droz, Pierre Jaquet (1721 to 1790) – Switzerland. Made automated figures with his son and J. F. Leschot (see below). Made the famous Writer, a 28 inch boy who dips a quill in ink, shakes it twice and begins to write at the top of the page, removing the pen from the paper between words. Sentences are finished with a stop and the figures can produce both light and heavy strokes of the pen. Droz sometimes engraved his name on the musical movement of his figures.

Droz, Henri Louis (1752 to 1791) – The son of Pierre Jaquet Droz. Worked with J. F. Leschot and Henri Maillardet (see below). Made a draughtsman that was simpler in construction than the Writer but was able to draw four different figures. This figure can be seen at the Neuchâtel Museum. It is thought possible that he made the peacock now in the Leningrad Museum.

Edison, Thomas Alva (1847 to 1931) – Worked in Orange, New Jersey, USA. Patented a phonograph doll in 1878. The original design was unsatisfactory and the model actually produced in 1889 was very much more sophisticated, with a metal torso and bisque head. The doll recited nursery rhymes, the sound being emitted through perforations in the torso. The factory is thought to have made 500 dolls a day.

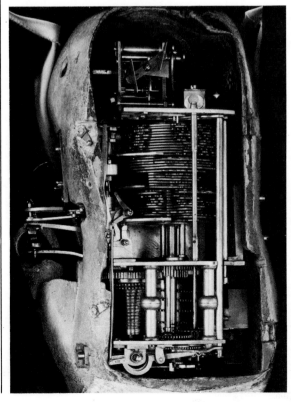

Frisard, Jacob – Born at Villaret, France, in 1753, Frisard specialised in fitting singing bird mechanisms into scent bottles etc. He worked in Vienna, London, Geneva, and was with Leschot to 1800.

Hero of Alexandria (285 to 222 BC) – Hero used hydraulic and pneumatic power and left records of his inventions that were rediscovered in the Renaissance.

Horsdorfer, Georg Philipp – Nuremberg, early 17th century. Made automata representing various tradesmen.

Ives, Edward Riley (b. 1839) – Bridgeport, Connecticut. Ives set up a factory in Bridgeport in 1870; in 1872 the firm became Ives and Blakeslee. They made mechanical figures for window display and automata originally designed by Robert J. Clay and Jerome Secor. Also the walking men with heavily weighted feet such as Uncle Tom, the Heathen Chinee and General Francis Butler, originally patented by Arthur Hotchkiss.

Kintzing, Pierre, & Roentgen – Germany, 1746 to 1816. Made the tympanon at the Conservatoire des Arts et Métiers in Paris, which plays music by Gluck. Dressed in fabrics from Marie Antoinette's dress and hair from her wig, it was originally bought by her but soon sold.

Knauss, Friedrich von (1724 to 1789) – Court mechanic and inventor of four writing automata. Three of these consisted of a hand that wrote with a pen on top of a metal globe.

Lecoultre Frères – Geneva. Made automata and musical boxes after 1850, which are identified by the mark 'Lf Gve' or just possibly 'LB'.

Leschot, Jean Frederic (1746 to 1827) – La Chaux de Fonds, Switzerland. Leschot worked with Jaquet Droz, who was his adoptive father, and until Droz's death in 1791 all his work carried the latter's name. Made singing birds.

Maillardet, Henri (b. 1745) – Coming from a family of clockmakers, Maillardet was apprenticed to Jaquet Droz and worked with both him and Leschot. He set up his own business around 1791.

Maillardet, Jean David (1748 to 1808) – Younger brother and associate to the above. Their automata were shown at the Spring Gardens, Charing Cross,

Probably the best known American producer of automata was Edward Riley Ives. *Left* is a clockwork figure of General Grant smoking a cigarette which was patented on October 30th 1877 by Albert H. Dean of Bridgeport, Connecticut, and manufactured by Ives and Blakeslee. *Below* are three examples of the clockwork walking doll patented by Arthur E. Hotchkiss on September 21st 1875. The cast iron feet move on rollers. Shown here are the Heathen Chinee, General Francis Butler and Santa Claus. All Margaret Woodbury Strong Museum, Rochester, New York. *Facing page:* An automaton representing the spectators at a race meeting with horses which move in a circle. Made by William Tansley of Coventry, *circa* 1870; height including metal stand 37 inches. By courtesy of Christie's South Kensington, London.

London, in 1802, and included a musical lady who played the pianoforte by finger pressure, also a magician and a trapeze artist. The Maillardets also made a bird that performed for four minutes with one winding and a lizard that ran around a table, shot out its tongue and hissed. Other automata included monkeys, clowns and acrobats, and also the Great Magician Clock in which the figures foretold the future.

Morrison, Enoch Rice – New York. Patented a walking doll in England and America in 1862 that was produced by various firms and known as the Autoperipatetikos. It has clockwork movement with feet that move in imitation of steps.

Rochat, Frères (Ami, Napoleon and Louis) – Geneva, 1810 to 1825. Makers of luxury automata whose father had worked for Jaquet Droz. They made birds on snuffboxes, cages and parasol handles, and marked their work with the initials 'FR' in a diamond shape.

Roullet, Jean (1832? to 1907) – Founded the firm of Roullet et E. Decamps, Paris.

Secor, Jerome B. – Bridgeport, Connecticut, USA. Made mechanical toys and birds in cages with musical movements in the 1880s.

Theroude, Alexandre Nicholas – Paris. Theroude patented a number of automata in the mid 19th century including a mechanical rabbit (1844), a chicken that laid sweet eggs (1846), a tumbler (1848), a talking doll (1852), dolls that moved on wheels (1853 to 1854) and a monkey violin player (1862).

Torre, Gianello della – Cremona, Italy. Inventor of mechanical devices for the Emperor Charles V, including flying birds and figures on horseback which blew trumpets. The Lute Player in the Kunsthistorisches Museum, Vienna, carved from wood and dated around 1600, is thought to be his work. The mechanism is hidden under the figure's skirt, and it moves on wheels, turning its head from side to side while its hand plucks the lute.

Vaucason, Jacques de (1709 to 1782) – Grenoble. Vaucason showed the figures he had created, such as a flute player and a duck, at fairs. He sold his automata in 1743 and later became inspector of mechanical inventions at the Académie Royale des Sciences.

The Lute Player in the
Kunsthistorisches
Museum, Vienna, thought
to have been made by
Gianello della Torre. The
carved wooden figure
moves forward with her
head turning from side to
side and her hand plucking
at the lute. *Circa* 1600.

Facing page: A bisque-
headed Autoperipatetikos
with leather arms,
patented in Britain and
America by Enoch Rice
Morrison on July 15th
1862. The mechanism is
clockwork. Height 10
inches. By courtesy of
Christie's South Ken-
sington, London.

3

WHEELED TOYS
AND
CHILDREN'S
TRANSPORT

Prams and pushchairs

**Early British
perambulators had
three wheels, since four-
wheeled vehicles were not
allowed on the pavement,
and this trend is reflected
in the miniature versions
produced at the time.**
Facing page: **A doll's
pushchair with deep-
buttoned upholstery.
English, *circa* 1875.
Ipswich Museums.** *Below:*
**A doll's perambulator of
similar design with an
unusual framed hood. It is
painted green with red
wheels. British, *circa* 1860;
height 25 inches. Welsh
Folk Museum, Cardiff.**

Babies and children were transported in simple wheeled vehicles from the earliest times and there is a 14th century reference to the fact that they were carried in 'waynes'. These cart-like items, pulled by a single shaft that terminated with a plain wooden handle, were also made in miniature for play and in several early prints they are seen as toys, used either in the nursery or out of doors. Basket-like cribs on wheels are also seen in prints of children playing with their dolls in the late 18th and early 19th centuries and these were obviously intended to be pulled along by a cord or strap. The earliest recorded full size baby carriage made in Britain was that purchased by the Duke of Devonshire in 1730 with a scallop-shaped body and an undercarriage depicting snakes, the latter being a reference to the Cavendish family crest. Though no miniature versions of such carriages are known to have survived, it seems likely that they were copied as toys in common with most adult equipment of the time.

Wagon-like vehicles of a less splendid type, often referred to in contemporary descriptions as 'chaises', were made throughout the 19th century. Though sometimes large enough to accommodate several children these were often made with the handles set so low that they could not possibly have been intended for use by an adult. In a water-colour dating from 1840, a boy is shown pulling his two brothers in a low, flat, box-like wagon with brightly painted blue woodwork and wooden spoked wheels. This toy was obviously intended for indoor use but other, larger versions, with refinements such as hand brakes, were made by firms such as Hugo Roithner of Schweidnitz, Germany, well into the 20th century. They were obviously delightful toys and consequently have rarely survived.

The first perambulator, made of wood and with three wooden wheels, is thought to have appeared in 1840 and its originator is unknown. It differed from earlier baby carriages in that it was pushed rather than pulled, and the handle, often of china or later even of celluloid, became an integral part of the design. Three wheeled upright prams, very similar to bathchairs, remained popular until the 1880s, as any four wheeled carriage was classed as a road vehicle in Britain and not allowed on pavements. The basic shapes of the toy prams of this era are very effective for displaying dolls, and are therefore much liked by collectors.

By 1856 there were four shops in London that sold perambulators and some twenty makers. Many of these makers, by tradition, also made toy versions, possibly considering them as a form of advertising. Pram springs were first patented in 1855, while curved steel springs were introduced by Johnson in 1856, and these were of course imitated in the toy versions. One of the first prams to be produced in a factory is probably that made at Frampton's in Trinity Street, London, in 1862. The owner had it specially made for his daughter, but considered that there 'was no business to be done in such nonsense'.

Joel A. H. Ellis, in America, had patented a more traditional type of child's carriage and set up the company of Ellis, Britain and Eaton in 1856. Various carts with spoked wheels and a pole, painted in bright colours, were made before the manufacture of the carriages began, but it was as 'Cab Ellis' that the owner was known, in reference to his new invention. A descendant, Herbert Ellis, later described the type of wood used in manufacture; maple, bass and oak were regularly combined in a single piece.

In 1880, four-wheeled prams were first allowed on the streets of Britain. The earliest examples took the form of a bassinet – a flat-bottomed wicker cradle – which was mounted on a chassis and

given wheels. The cradles themselves were mainly imported from France. Canework bassinets in toy size have survived in some numbers, though the full-size versions were soon worn out. They were sometimes found even in the 1880s with four wheels of the same size, though generally two large and two small wheels were used on perambulators until the First World War.

The 'mail cart', usually with two long shafts, is considered to have originated at the factory of Simpson, Fawcett & Co in Leeds. Initially intended as a toy, it was later made for nursery use. The majority of toy versions have seats made from wooden slats or dowel rods and large steel-rimmed wheels. A few upholstered versions are found but the majority are completely functional though sometimes brightly painted. Even the toy mail carts were made in a variety of sizes, some large enough for children to ride in, while others were made for dolls. They were cheap to make, and are often seen in old photographs being pushed by the most poorly dressed children.

Prams, wagons and mail carts were all produced in the late 19th century by a number of makers,

Above: **An effective mail cart made of a combination of basketwork, wood and metal. The hood is lined with cotton fabric. British,** *circa* **1905. Welsh Folk Museum, Cardiff.** *Right:* **A fully adjustable blue painted mail cart of Scandinavian origin.** *Circa* **1895; overall length 38 inches. Seated in the cart is a German jointed doll made by Kestner. Author's Collection.**

Left: **Two early three-wheeled toy prams dating from the late 1860s. With them are a 'Parian' headed German doll (*left*) and an English wax doll. Betty Harvey-Jones Collection.** *Bottom:* **A black painted doll's pram with a china handle and brass decoration. Unmarked;** *circa* **1905. Seated in the pram is a 'dream baby' doll made by Armand Marseille. Author's Collection.**

Over page: **An advertisement from** *The Toy Trader* **of October 1908 showing a typical range of toy perambulators available from an English manufacturer.**

SIMMONS and CO.,

WHOLESALE AND EXPORT MANUFACTURERS,

DOLLS' CARRIAGES

AND CARTS.

SELECTION FROM CATALOGUE.

THE "TOY "WEST-END."
Patented.

THE "POPULAR."

Wooden body nicely stained and lined; fitted with strap, apron, brass-jointed hood and 14-in. rubber-tyred wheels, **17/3**; finished in white or light blue, **21/3**.

THE "AVENUE."
(Varnished Wood.)

THE "ELYSIAN."
(Painted Wood.)

Mounted on strong bow springs and 12 and 8 inch wheels and fitted with straps and brass-jointed reversible hoods. A, with iron-tyred wheels, **18/-**; B, with rubber-tyred wheels, **19/6**; C, in art finish, tan, brown, electric blue, &c., **20/9**; and D, in white, cream, or other light art shades, **23/-**; also made with bodies 25 ins. long, mounted upon 14 in. wheels in the C quality, **24/9**; D at **28/6**.

High-class miniature of children's cart of same name. Interior upholstered, fitted with waist strap, detachable cushions and apron, body handsomely beaded, coach painted, with steam-bent ash shafts and patent bed, brass-jointed hood, leather-hung springs, 14-in. wheels and rubber-tyred tilt wheels, **46/6**.

THE "LADY."

Doll's Carriage of pretty design and best finish. Body 25 ins. long; cee springs; wheels 14 ins.: rubber tyres; apron; **31/6**: if with specially handsome colour striping, **3/6** extra.

THE "ELEGANCE."

Pretty canoe-shaped body, 25 ins. long, with raised and rounded side-panels; cee springs; 14 in. wheels; apron, **33/9**.
The "Babyboat." Same shape, but with side-panels divided, **33/9**.

THE "CORACLE."

Simple but tasteful design with body 25 ins. long; cee springs; 14 in. wheels, with plain painted side-panels, **33/9**.
Or with imitation canework panels, **10/6** extra.

Extras upon either of these Carriages:—Leather-hung springs, **4/6**. Nickel-plated, tangent-spoke wheels, **15/9**. Light art colours, pure white, cream, pale blue, &c., **3/9**.

3, 5, and 7, Tanner St., Bermondsey St., LONDON, S.E.

Telephone No. 980 HOP.   Telegrams: "QUADRICYCLES."

Discount off above prices, 33⅓ per cent.   Send for complete Catalogue.

Advertisers will appreciate your mentioning "The Toy Trader" when writing them.   A 2

among them being the Gendron Wheel Company of Toledo, Ohio, which was established in 1872. In Germany, Louis Schmetzer & Cie of Rothenburg and Chr. Nemmert of Nuremberg, who made doll's and children's perambulators as well as invalid carriages, in wickerwork and basketwork, were among the larger manufacturers providing the child with a close imitation of her mother's pram. In Britain, J. Green & Co Ltd of Nottingham, one of the largest Midland manufacturers of baby carriages, mail carts and toy prams, offered in 1910 a wooden mail cart with wings and beaded sides, and 14 and 10 inch rubber tyred wheels. This model was described as 'well fitted and upholstered, with brass-jointed hood and celluloid handle'. Green's also produced wooden toy pushchairs on four wheels and a doll's barouche described as being 'of excellent workmanship with oval sides and hidden well. Painted in best motor style, well upholstered, with brass jointed hood and celluloid handle'. Their most expensive barouche was decorated with beaded panels.

Early 20th century prams were given highly evocative names such as the Promenade, Mayfair, Victoria, Empress and Belgravia. Those made in America often had colourful fringed and tasselled canopies, in contrast to their more sombre European counterparts.

Patterson Edwards of the Old Kent Road, London, was among the greatest producers of prams, pram horses, galloping gigs, pole carts and cane-work pushchairs. Folding wooden pushchairs with carpet or American cloth seats were also made by this firm in the early 20th century. In 1909 a visitor to their factory watched all the stages in the manufacture of a toy pram and marvelled that an object requiring the skill of so many people could still be sold for 7/6d. The firm was supplied with wood from its own yard on the Surrey Canal, and this was planed and cut in their workshops. From the planing machine, the boards passed to a patterning block, a type of press which stamped out the shape of the sides and the body sections as a guide for the detailed fretsawing which followed and, in the same operation, drilled holes for nails. The pieces then passed from the sandpapering and end-graining machines to the carpenter, in this case a woman, who drove nails through the ready-drilled holes. The bodies of the prams were then undercoated, painted twice, lined and varnished before entering the upholstery department, where girls trimmed the bodies with American cloth and sewed hoods. The

Left: **An Edwardian folding doll's pushchair made of wood with a carpet seat. Unmarked but probably English. Author's Collection.**
Bottom: **This unusual boat-shaped pram was made by George Munson, a boatbuilder of Wivenhoe, Essex, for his eldest child in 1890. Colchester and Essex Museum.**

This English doll's pushchair is made of leathercloth and wicker on an iron frame. It has iron wheels and is painted brown and cream. *Circa* 1905; height 25½ inches. Ipswich Museums.

completed top was then sent to the fitters for mounting on the sprung wheel base.

The range of colours in which doll's prams were supplied was large. The Star Manufacturing Company of Davis Street, Manchester Road, London, for instance, offered them in dark tan, bronze, claret, dark blue, peacock and sage green. The framework of the bodies was available in glossy cane, cane, American reed or wood. As some companies charged extra for light colours, doll's prams in darker tints are more frequently found.

Another British manufacturer was W. Bottomly of Leeds, who made both prams and pushchairs. Their 1930s range included a pram with four small matching wheels which had an occasional seat for an additional doll. A wide range was made by Simmons and Company of Bermondsey, London, in the Edwardian period. It included 'The Toy West End, A high class miniature of the children's cart of the same name . . . coach painted, with steam bent ash shafts . . . patent bed and leather hung springs'. This toy cost 46/6; it was of the flat type, without a foot well, and was provided with a large pair of wheels at the back and two small ones at the front. Simmons's cheaper prams were varnished, while others were decorated with canework panels. At Zeitz in Germany, both E. A. Nather and Wunsch Pretzch made doll's carriages around 1900, and among these were some which had folding seats.

Probably the most effective of doll's carriages are those with swinging, pivoted horses attached to the front, which are known as 'galloping gigs'. The full-sized versions were made so that the child could play at driving as he was pushed along. Some have as many as four horses, and the toy versions were constructed as correct miniatures. Sometimes, in both the child and the toy versions, cheaper models were made with fixed horses, screwed to a rigid platform base. Patterson Edwards and the Midland Tent and Strong Toy Company of Birmingham made galloping horse gigs, the latter also producing pole wagons and perambulators, in common with the other well known firm of Lines Brothers.

Less attractively shaped prams with deep bodies and four matching small wheels became common after the First World War and were still made in the late 1930s. Tin was not widely used for doll's prams until the mid 1920s, though corrugated metal was sometimes used earlier for the sides. The Lloyd Loom Manufacturing Company in the USA made matching doll- and child-sized prams in the 1920s, which were described in their catalogue as 'almost perfect miniatures . . . made on the same graceful lines, finished with the same rich, lasting enamels and upholstered with the identical corduroy'. They also advertised a deep, boat-shaped pram which had a rigid pivoting hood. The latter was made on the Lloyd looms, which wove a smooth, endless strand of wicker.

Facing page: **This English doll's pram made around 1905 has a swivel hood which can be placed at the head or foot as required. Seated in the pram are two jointed bisque-headed dolls of the same period. Betty Harvey-Jones Collection.**

Pullalong and pushalong toys

The earliest surviving wheeled toys show as wide a divergence in quality as those produced in the late 19th century, when the available variety was greatest. A simple outline-cut wooden horse from Greece, dating from around 400 BC, which was pulled along by a string threaded through its nose, is completely rudimentary in design. In comparison, a limestone porcupine and lion from Persia, dated 1100 BC, are modelled with great assurance and realism, indicating the work of a fine craftsman. War chariots were obviously popular toys in the ancient world and in one clay example from Athens both the horses and the driver are modelled together on a platform that is mounted on a wheeled base. The variety of materials thought suitable for toys of this type is a feature of a more adventurous toy-making period, and the child of today is, in comparison, very poorly served with plastic, nylon fur and, very occasionally, wood.

Early prints show children playing with simple toys of this type, and from the 16th century bronze knights some five inches high were produced in Germany, where the wooden toy industry was also becoming established. Actual examples are extremely rare before the 17th century, but small carved wooden animals in the German cabinet houses of the period give some indication of the high quality that was available. One of the most interesting early pull-along toys is that which can be seen in Ann Sharp's baby house, assembled around 1700. The toy is in the form of a small scene showing a well dressed man in knee-breeches sitting, together with his dog, in a rocky landscape beside a pool. In the same baby house is a linen horse mounted on a wheeled base with a decoratively treated surface and woollen mane, a figure made with great ingenuity and unlikely to have survived without the protection of the doll's house. The group in a rocky landscape is probably of German origin, as it has definite similarities to those seen in early catalogues. German toys of this type were mostly made by peasants, especially in Thuringia, and one charming example from this region represents a woman and geese riding in a farm cart; as it moved along, the geese bobbed up and down on the wire springs which connected them to the wheeled base.

A new material that was eminently suitable for toys of this type was developed around 1740. This was a composition made from dark flour and glue that was quite easy to model and could be used in moulds as well, so that detailed carving could be dispensed with. Wooden models made in very

basic detail were sometimes completed by parts moulded in this substance, which is known as brotteig. Though it was common in small workshops, it was not so suitable for the individual worker as moulds were needed, and its use was mainly confined to the more basic commercial undertakings. The production of carved wooden figures continued unabated well into the second half of the 19th century.

Coaches and horse-drawn transport of all kinds were obviously of primary interest to 18th century children and it is models of this type that are most frequently seen, sometimes provided with fringed curtains and correctly made luggage. The amount of detail which was lavished on the more expensive examples indicates that the more discriminating children were as eager to obtain completely correct models as were the boys of the 1930s, who insisted that their metal cars should have all the most recent additions. One fine early 19th century coach from Sonneberg is drawn by horses with very delicate, realistic legs and occupied by a correctly dressed lady and gentleman. The catalogues of Georg Hieronymus Bestelmeier of Nuremberg show a wide variety of such toys, including a number of genre subjects indicating how almost any scene was thought suitable for

mounting on a wheeled base. The genre subjects include a flower-seller with her baskets, two agricultural workers, a woman kneading dough and a man with a windmill, the sails of which revolved as the toy was moved along. Their horses were often sold separately and sometimes mounted two to a single platform, so that if a four-in-hand was required, they could be simply joined by the harness. Bellow toys also appeared in some number, with small birds or animals fixed to the top that appeared to cry as the object was pulled along; a vast number of these effective toys appear to have been exported to the United States and can now be found more easily there than on the continent of Europe.

Some of the larger animals carved at Oberammergau are so exquisite that they approach the quality of ornamental items rather than toys. Camels, elephants, wolves and donkeys, bison and cows were made in sizes up to three feet high to be mounted on wheels, and all were carved to represent the skin of the particular animal. The balance achieved in some of these figures is remarkable and only in the most complex is the device of standing the figure against a prop of some kind resorted to. Some of these wheeled toys were only a few inches high, yet the quality of the execution was maintained. A very large collection can still be seen at the Folk Museum in Oberammergau, though they are mainly in an unpainted state. The folk basis of the industry is clearly

Toys representing a coach and horses were inevitably popular with 18th and 19th century children. This mid 19th century example is made of wood painted in yellow and black, with porcelain-headed passengers. English. Bethnal Green Museum of Childhood, London.

indicated by the hundreds of drivers and passengers representing people of all types and all ages which were carved by peasant woodcarvers in seated positions, and placed as required in the horse-drawn transport by the commissioning merchants.

By the mid 19th century, the influence of horse-drawn transport on wheeled toys was growing less, and the skill of the craftsmen was to some extent in decline. The inventiveness of the models, on the other hand, increased, and this can be seen in figures such as a composition Irishman, who pivots on a rod as though dancing a jig when pulled along. Another effective toy of this period was a papier-mâché cat, whose head nodded as it moved, and a similar mother cat with a group of kittens. The kittens in the second toy were in the form of skittles and a soft ball was provided to bowl at them. Complete boats with sailors standing on the decks and, of course, Noah's Arks, were considered completely appropriate for a wheeled base, though in some cases the wheels were secreted under the hull. Waldkirchen sample books illustrate a clever arrangement in which a bird perches on a wheel that is mounted on a crossbar;

as the toy is pulled the bird whirls around, sometimes accompanied by the sound of a simple tinkle box. In other examples, bells ring as the toy is moved or figures bounce up and down on a simple bellows. The illustrated wax baby in a bassinet works on this principle, and the last owner remembered how fast it had been necessary for her to run in order to turn the wheels fast enough to work the bellows.

The French were particularly skilled in the creation of the more unusual pieces and the 1879 catalogue of Au Printemps shows several toys on coloured metal wheels that played a tune as they moved, including a group of card players seated at a table, 'Le Galant Cordonnier' who appeared to play an instrument, and a large Polichinelle costumed richly in gaudy satin who played the cymbals and beat a drum. A doll in a baby walker was also an ever popular subject, and in some versions the doll is mounted on a wire pivot so that it swings when pulled. Many basic dolls were also fixed to wheeled bases by the French manu-facturers, some remaining in fixed positions and depending on their splendid costumes for their

A pull-along toy of a poured wax baby in a wicker basinette. As the wheels move the doll is raised on a bellows and utters a squeaking noise, while the upper part of the torso turns from side to side. Several variations on this basic toy are found. *Circa* **1855; length 15 inches. Author's Collection.**

Facing page, bottom: **Two examples of late 19th century pullalong animals with a wheel attached to each foot. A goat with glass eyes (***left***), probably German. Height 14 inches. And a horse wearing a red checked blanket, also with glass eyes. Height 9¾ inches. Both Ipswich Museums.**

appeal, while others perform simple movements.

Elephants, camels and even pigs were frequently finished in thin leather for greater realism, and were sometimes given voice boxes activated either by the toy's movement or by pulling a wire or string. Barking bulldogs with small wooden wheels neatly concealed under their feet seem to have first appeared around 1870 but are still made in a simplified version today. Some French and English bulldogs were made which growl alarmingly when the chain running into the body is pulled. Early versions can usually be distinguished by the very precise detail of the ribs and the almost bare appearance caused by the rubbing away of the flocked surface. They are always great favourites, as their appeal is not limited to toy collectors.

Changes in transportation were quickly reflected in the style of pull-alongs and by 1900 there was a vast range of buses, trams and trains, not only in wood but also in metal, pressed cardboard and even wickerwork. Most of these toys were marked with tie-on labels, or with cheap metal plates which where they have survived have often rusted so badly that they cannot be read. As a

Two flock-covered papier mâché dogs which bark when their leads are pulled. Both made in France. The French bulldog (*left*) is early 20th century, the English bulldog *circa* 1880. Length of both 18 inches. Author's collection.

result, attribution is usually of the loosest kind and based mainly on the resemblance of an item to those illustrated in catalogues. Frequently firms are described as 'the largest producers', yet not a single known example of their work is in existence. The collector therefore has to evaluate toys of this type purely on quality and interest.

One of the most prolific manufacturers of pull-alongs and push-alongs was Lines Brothers, whose toys were marketed in particular by Gamage's, the London department store. Some of their models are found with the original brass trademarks and a sufficient number of examples are known to identify many of the toys they produced. In 1913, their range included a VV Bread cart and horse with a large wicker basket, a Great Western Railway van with an adjustable tail board that was supplied with or without sacks, and Pickford's lorries with opening packing cases. Lines Brothers also manufactured a variety of child-size push-along vending barrows, and these included baker's and confectioner's carts and a GPO barrow. Their transport models, made completely of wood, included the 'Rapid Motor Bus', an 'LCC Double Deck Electric Tram' and 'Motor Lorries Loaded with Goods'. In common with all the other makers of strong toys, they of course produced horses in a variety of different qualities.

Barrel-shaped beech-wood horses were the

basic product of most firms, as they sold very cheaply and looked quite effective when their paper saddles and harness were glued in place. Stool horses, whose wheels were concealed under the legs and which were provided with flat backs upholstered as seats were also an almost basic line. The Joiboy range of such toys was augmented in 1908 by 'Bumpo', a horse that moved along when the saddle was bumped up and down. This company also made express trains of wood in above average quality, with polished brass hub caps and fine model hay wagons. In 1910 the Star Manufacturing Company of Davis Street, London, was offering horses with china handles that are so similar to those made by Lines and those sold by Hamleys that identification is impossible if the item is unmarked. Patterson Edwards also made a similar range including all varieties of farm carts and such peculiarly Edwardian vehicles as water wagons which sprinkled water on the streets to keep down the dust.

Strong toys of this type have often survived in good condition, and are liked by collectors with enough space for their display. The fur-covered toys have generally fared much worse, tending to suffer from split seams, moth and dirt which is often difficult to remove. Consequently it is only the pieces in the very finest state that are purchased and the sadder nursery relics have virtually no interest value. The finest toys of this type were made by Steiff, who included a splendid white felt swan and a grey and white spotted velvet goose in their 1913 range. Their pull-alongs were described as 'High Class Riding animals' and were sold in sizes ranging from nine to twenty-four inches or more. The lion was highly impressive and ornamented with an abundant silky mane that contrasted with the light brown plush of his body. The lambs in 'curly white lambskin' were appealing, as were the Irish terriers in light brown plush. Steiff did not provide children simply with 'a dog' but made a number of specific breeds such as dachshunds and pekinese which were convincingly accurate models. The circus horses, with arched necks and very delicate legs, were quite beautiful and were provided with both a steering apparatus and a coloured saddle with stirrups. Another particularly delicate wheeled model was a young deer in brown imitation sealskin. All these toys were made with wood or metal frames and fixed to metal bases with spoked iron wheels. They originally carried the characteristic Steiff trademark of a hexagonal metal button in the ear and models over seventeen inches were provided with

A child's turned wooden pushalong horse with a paper saddle and harness, similar to those made by the London firm of Patterson Edwards. *Circa* **1900. Bethnal Green Museum of Childhood, London.**

Facing page : **This fur fabric polar bear with a wheel attached to each foot is similar to those made by the German firm of Steiff, but is unmarked. The muzzle is made of leather. Height 8½ inches. Ipswich Museums.**

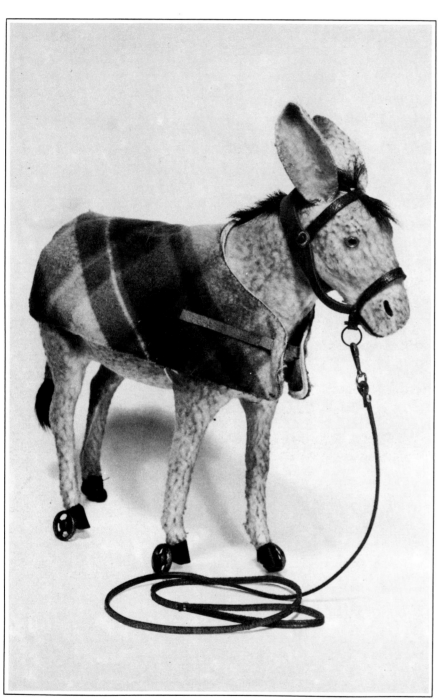

This pushalong donkey in a plaid blanket dates from around 1905. Similar toys were made by several manufacturers and this example is unmarked. Height 8½ inches. Ipswich Museums.

To generations of American boys a coaster wagon was as essential in childhood as a doll was to a girl. These wagons were usually painted red and were pulled by a shaft with a swivel axle. With some dexterity the child could, after attaining a good speed, stand on the vehicle and coast along, steering by the shaft. These sturdy toys were often passed from father to son and though not decorative in appearance have a sentimental appeal for many American adults to whom they were once cherished possessions.

Toy making practically ceased in Europe during the First World War and the really fine quality toys did not reappear. Instead, the manufacturers turned their attention to eye-catching novelties that were frequently made of shoddy materials, and these have deteriorated so quickly that some examples are dated to a much earlier period simply because of their decrepit state. The Chad Valley company remained very traditional in its output and continued to produce fluffy animals worked either by clockwork or simply pulled along. Their basic range included the usual cats, lions, bears and elephants. The products of Dean's Rag Book Company were much more whimsical and their 'Wheeled on Series' mounted on strong iron frames was introduced in 1920. 'True to Life Animals' including a pug dog and a tabby cat could be mounted on wheels for an extra 1/6d as could their 'Kuddlemee' range that included a fat Jumbo. When scooters enjoyed a surge of popularity in 1923, the firm mounted many of their basic soft toys on these simple vehicles and sold them as pull-alongs, though a few, known as 'Scooterkids' and 'Scootazoo' were especially made. Many of the toymakers in the 1920s seemed to share the heavily humorous turn of phrase used for the 'Toota the Skoota' which was included in this series. Plush as well as fur-fabric wheeled toys were made by this firm, and their 'Bulldog Drummond' with a brass spiked collar was very striking. 'Quack Quack', 'Woof-Woof' and 'Puss-Puss' were joined in 1923 by Beatrix Potter's 'Peter Rabbit', her 'Bobby Whitetail' having been introduced in 1920. 'Dismal Desmond', one of the best known of Dean's products appeared in a wheeled version which was produced in 1928.

appropriate automatic animal voices. A similar steering device to that used on their circus horse is also encountered in their donkey, a model that could also be supplied with dismountable rockers. Steiff also sold a range of 'Natural Running Animals' which included a stuffed monkey, a felt rabbit and a waddling and quacking duck. These toys were linked by metal rods that moved the limbs as the animal was pushed along. They were very strong and not as likely to break as clockwork figures of this kind.

Many of the larger wheeled toys can still be purchased quite cheaply, as the majority of collectors do not have space for their display, but the miniature versions often fetch surprisingly high sums, as they look effective when displayed with antique dolls.

Horses and velocipedes

The possession of a splendid horse was a matter of pride to men of all classes from the beginning of civilization and model horses for children are among the earliest surviving toys. Few pre-16th century examples have survived but from 1516 there are both woodcuts and surviving models which illustrate the very high standard of construction achieved in this sphere at a time when dolls, for instance, were still being made with minimal realism. The knight wearing the Holzschurer arms at the Bayerisches Nationalmuseum in Munich is a case in point; although his horse is covered with a decorative blanket for a tournament and the body detail cannot be seen, both the legs and the neck of the animal are realistically jointed. Early 17th century prints show children riding hobby horses and playing with well-made toy carriages, both of which could be purchased from market stalls. By this time, good toys were no longer solely for princes, but were produced on a commercial scale, particularly in the Berchtesgaden area of Germany. A visitor to this region in the 18th century described an effective horse and rider leading a foal and this type of naturalistic detail is quite common to the toys made by the skilled workers both of this region and Oberammergau. Composition substances were also experimented with in the mid 18th century, but proved unsuitable for larger horses. They crumbled if exposed to damp and were therefore mainly used for small toys.

Despite the number of hobby horses that appear in prints, very few have survived, as their construction was of necessity rather fragile. They varied in quality, some being exquisitely carved with manes, and their forelegs in realistic positions, while others were merely roughly cut outlines, decorated with paper or tinsel in the manner of fairground gifts. Skin-covered horses are mentioned from 1591, and these were always more expensive than the carved versions, though they called for less detailed workmanship. The standard of carving seen in the model horses in the Nuremberg cabinet houses is startlingly high, and in the Stromer house, dating from 1637, they are even provided with grooming brushes and other stable equipment. Some of the finest 18th and 19th century carved rocking horses also came from this region of Germany. The manufacturers were eager to expend their skills generously even on toys that were to be sold quite cheaply, and exhibited an ability to improve and adapt designs that is not seen for instance in the work of the British makers.

There are no references to rocking horses before the 17th century, when they appear as simple structures with board sides, rather like children's rocking boats. The shoulder and head were carved in some detail, but the legs and lower body were painted on the flat sides. This solved the problem of making necessarily slim legs with sufficient strength to support not only the weight of the horse's body but also that of the young rider – a problem that was later overcome by firms such as Lines Brothers in Britain, by making the legs of beech and the bodies of pine. One of the earliest surviving examples of the board type is believed to have been owned by Charles I of England, and there is another good example in the Museum of London at the Barbican. The Stromer cabinet house also contains a toy of this type, which is interesting as the condition is particularly good and the painting of the legs still very distinct. Ann

This fine 17th century rocking horse illustrates the plank-sided construction which continued to be used occasionally until the late 19th century. Note the remains of the foot rests and the dummy pistol in the wooden holster. Museum of London.

Children's horses of the rocker type took a variety of different forms. *Above:* A miniature example of the basic plank-sided rocker, complete with rider. Similar toys were exported in vast numbers from the Bavarian mountains throughout the 19th century. Bethnal Green Museum of Childhood, London. *Right:* The classic horse on curved rockers is illustrated by this example, which is made of carved wood and painted in grey. Mid 19th century; length 7 feet. Saffron Walden Museum, Essex. *Below:* A fur fabric covered 'Gee Swing' of the type sold by the London firm of Gamage's before the First World War. The horse is suspended on straps attached to strong metal lugs which run through the wooden body. The harness and stirrups are original. Length 34 inches. Author's Collection.

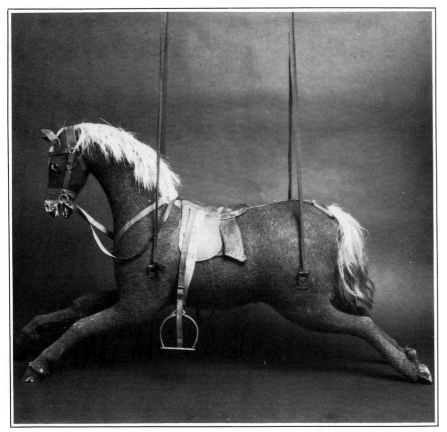

Sharp's house in England also contains a good example of an early rocking toy that dates from around 1700. Probably of German origin, it consists of two riders on simply but effectively carved horses fixed to a single solid rocking base. There were several methods of attaching the realistic horses which were popular in 18th century nurseries to their stands. They could be almost spreadeagled across the curved rockers, fixed to a central platform or supported by some projection from the base which gave added strength. These splendid figures were considered as a means of teaching the young to ride and providing them with wholesome exercise, and stirrups and saddles were also provided. Some of these curved rockers are very large, and mounting a real horse could have held little fear for a boy who was used to swinging precariously some five feet off the ground. It was the lack of safety inherent in this beautiful construction that led in the second half of the 19th century to a whole variety of improvements such as the chair-like rockers known as shoo-flys, which are particularly American in origin, and various low seated trotting devices that are often too ugly in design to appeal to collectors. Safety, or swing rockers, where the horse is slung on metal bars from a secure base,

The tricycle horses known as velocipedes make particularly attractive collector's items. *Left:* A solidly made tricycle horse with an unusual method of propulsion. English, probably home made; *circa* 1900. Bethnal Green Museum of Childhood, London. *Below:* An elegant example, probably of English origin, with pedals mounted on the front wheel. Late 19th century; length 35 inches. By courtesy of Christie's South Kensington, London.

are mentioned from the 1870s, but most examples date from after 1900 since when they have been the standard form of construction.

Velocipedes or tricycle horses appeared in the mid 19th century and early examples are characterised by their slim bodies and narrow heads. They appeared on the European and American market at almost the same time and an advertisement in the *Philadelphia Public Ledger* for 1850 offered 'Velocipedes – a few superior ones, suitable for using in the house'. Wheels of early examples were usually made of wood with metal treads, but during the 1860s these were superseded by metal spokes. The patent office records abound in improvements to the basic velocipedes and collectors possessing unusual mechnical examples are advised to consult these lists, though the majority found are those of the basic tricycle construction that were made until the First World War. Like so many horses, velocipedes are very rarely marked and the collector has to purchase purely from the quality and condition of the item. In comparison with doll's houses or tin toys, rocking horses and velocipedes do not attain particularly high prices, not because these toys are not appreciated but simply because the majority of collectors only have space for the display of a few examples.

MAIN PRODUCERS OF HORSES AND VELOCIPEDES

Askam & Son–Philadelphia, USA. Were manufacturing hobby horses in the 1860s.

Barnes & Co.–Covington, Kentucky, USA. Were producing velocipedes *circa* 1879.

Bliss, R.–Rhode Island, USA. Established in 1832. This firm produced a toy stables in their characteristic brightly lithographed style from 1895. Their 1911 catalogue states that the horses with which the toys were supplied were imported, in all probability from Germany.

Bushnell, E. W.–Philadelphia, USA, 1847 to 1857. Manufactured hobby horses and velocipedes.

Christian, A.–New York, 1856 to 1880s. Manufactured horses of various kinds including velocipedes, hobby horses and various carriages. Sometimes known as Christian & Son, after 1868 as Christian & Dare.

Cole, T. H.–Sparkbrook, Birmingham, England. Working before the First War. This company produced cycle horses, push horses and hobby horses.

Converse, Morton E.–Winchendon, Massachusetts. The firm was known as Mason and Converse from 1878 to 1883; there were then several changes of name until in 1905 it became Morton E. Converse & Son. Converse began to produce toys almost by accident after making a simple plaything for his daughter. The firm produced good quality horses including, in the 1880s, some with a skin finish and manes and tails of real horsehair. Cheaper horses were traditionally supplied with such additions made from cow hair. As in England the cheaper versions made by Converse were given the basic painted finish.

Crandall, Benjamin–Born in Rhode Island, USA. From around 1840 to the 1890s he and his four sons, Jesse A., William E., Benjamin junior and Charles, either worked for the family firm, Crandall & Co, or set up their own smaller concerns in Brooklyn and New York. Benjamin Crandall began to manufacture horses after looking at a German example and deciding that he could improve on the model. Originally his horses were of the skin-covered type, but eventually carved wood was used. The firm developed great skill in the construction of such toys and oscillating, leaping and spring-type versions were made. During the Spanish American war 'Teddy's Horse' was made to capitalise on the popularity of Theodore Roosevelt, the leader of the Rough Riders. In 1859 Jesse Crandall patented a design that consisted of two boards cut in the outline shape of a horse joined by a seat, a type of construction known as a shoo-fly and very typically American. This prolific company also made high quality velocipedes and won a gold medal at the Philadelphia Exhibition of 1876. They made a whole series of variations on this basic design including a 'Cantering Tricycle' that moved up and down.

Erste Schweizerische Spielwarenfabrik–Langenthal, Switzerland. A firm that was working in the late 19th and early 20th centuries in the production of papier-mâché stable animals, wild animals of all descriptions and carts of all kinds as well as special fur, imitation fur and varnished rocking horses. This company could also supply life-sized show horses that could be used by tailor's shops and toy-sellers. They also patented what an advertisement described as 'wood surrogate' horses.

Gabriel, William–Goswell Street, London. Recorded on his trade card as a rocking horse maker in 1784.

Gamage's Department Store–London. This store, whose fine annual catalogue was eagerly awaited by British colonial children, supplied a number of toys including rocking horses made to their own designs. In 1913 they produced 'Bronko, the Safety Hobby Horse', registered design No 467670. Though described as a hobby horse, it was in fact of the basic safety rocker type and was fitted with a sharply upswept 'cowboy saddle' to keep the child safely in position. The tail of this toy was particularly abundant. In the same year their 'Gee Swing', the 'latest novelty for nursery and gymnasium with adjustable hemp ropes' was patented. This was a fairly conventional horse which hung from ropes threaded through heavy metal lugs attached to the wooden body of the horse. Their tricycle horses all had glass eyes and padded saddles.

Graeffer, W.–Schleiz, Germany. This firm produced skin- and plush-covered rocking horses as

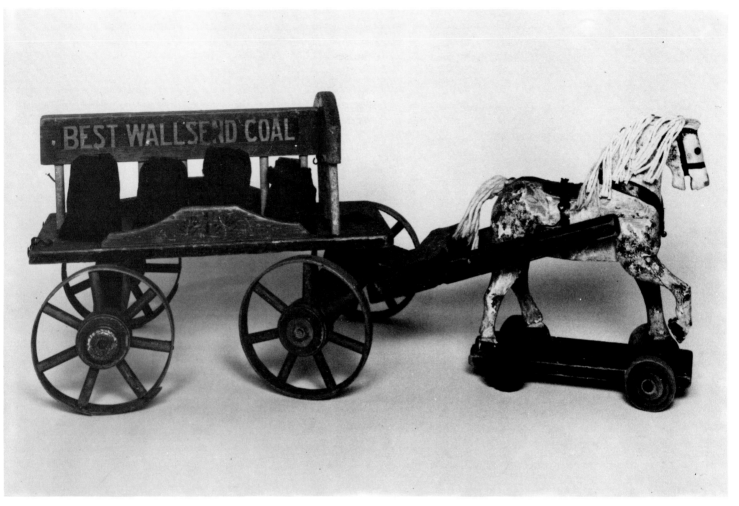

Gamage's "Bronk" Safety Hobby Horse.
Registered No. Ty. 467,670. This horse is specially constructed our own designs. Fitted with cowboy saddle and stirrups, **which** not only give it an elegant appearance, but render it a much **safer** horse for a child than the old style. Made in four sizes.
No. B .. **34/6** No. C, **42/6** No. D, **63/-** No. E, **75/-**
Hei. to saddle, 27½ in. 31½ in. 36½ in. 40½ in.
Len. of stand, 36½ in. 44 in. 52 in. 57½ in.

well as some in carved wood. Some paste-board horses, described as a novelty line in 1908, were said to be durable and unbreakable and made in elegant shapes.

Kendrick, R. F. & W.–Loughborough, England. Produced a strange but very functional horse in the early 20th century to develop the child's muscles while bouncing him up and down. The seat was attached to the bellows.

Keystone–Brand name used by the A. Mecky Co, Philadelphia, USA, who specialised in good quality velocipedes.

Lines, George and Joseph–London. (See also Child-sized Cars.) Some of their horses are found marked with a brass thistle plate. Horses marked 'G. & J. Lines' were made before 1919. The sign over the brothers' premises in the Caledonian Road read 'Velocipede horses, rocking horses, horses for fair and steam circuses and life-sized show horses'. In 1895 they were mainly producing

Above: **A late 19th century British made coal cart and horse. Almost identical horses were attached to a variety of vehicles. Bethnal Green Museum of Childhood, London. Gamage's 'Bronko'** (*left*), **registered in 1913, typifies the basic type of safety rocking horse.**

the old style rocking horses on curved rockers, some stretching to $7\frac{1}{2}$ feet long. Skin-covered versions were more costly. The best horses of the safety type were suspended from polished wooden bases, and the cheaper versions were brightly painted. In 1913, they produced a splendid Scots Grey on safety rockers with a detachable cavalry harness, shoe cases, valise, holsters, martingale, saddle cloth, military bridle, etc. In the same year they introduced the 'Wobbling Goblin' which had a trotting motion, and a 'Starter Tricycle Horse', Registered No 1905, with the horse's head in a more raised position than usual. At this time this very traditional company was still producing hobby horses with well carved heads but with quite large metal spoked wheels fixed to the end of the pole.

Long, William – Pennsylvania, USA. A cabinet maker and turner who in 1785 advertised himself as a maker of rocking horses 'in the neatest and the best manner to teach children to ride and to give them wholesome and pleasing exercise'.

Louis Lindner & Sons – Sonneberg, Germany. Made skin-covered horses in all sizes around 1900.

Luckett, Thomas & Sons – Petershore St, Birmingham, England. Made a variety of rocking horses in the early 20th century, also pole horses etc.

Marqua, W. A. – Cincinnati, USA. Made several types of horses including one patented in 1880 that stood on a stand instead of rockers and provided an up-and-down motion as well as the usual to and fro.

Midland Tent and Strong Toy Company – Birmingham. Made well equipped safety rocking horses on polished bases as well as velocipedes, hobby and pole horses before the First World War.

Patterson Edwards – Old Kent Road, London. A manufacturer of wooden toys who in 1908 advertised go-carts, pole and gig horses, beech and hobby horses, and galloping horse gigs. Their beech horses were of the barrel type. Their velocipedes were particularly good, being well carved and equipped with padded saddles.

Roithner & Co – Schweidnitz, Germany. This firm made well finished wooden toys including nursery seats with horse's heads fixed to the fronts of the chairs.

Star Manufacturing Co – Davis Street, London. In the early 20th century made a large number of velocipedes constructed from well seasoned timber and fitted with rubber-tyred wheels. They were supplied in all sizes to suit all ages. In 1909 the firm's swing horses were claimed to be rapidly ousting old fashioned rockers from popularity.

This advertisement from *The Toy Trader* of July 1909 shows some of the products of the Midland Tent & Strong Toy Company which was active in Britain in the years before the First World War. Though unmarked, the rocking horse shown below is markedly similar in detail and dates from the same period. It was used at Millbank School, Ely, Cardiff, in the early 20th century. Height 4 feet. Welsh Folk Museum, Cardiff.

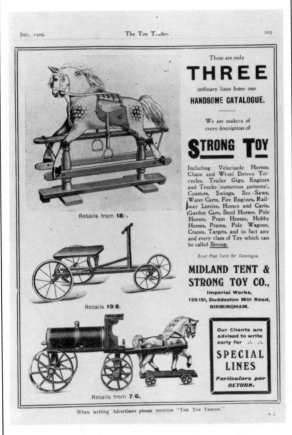

Child-size cars

Motor cars do not appear to have been imitated in child size until around 1905, after which they were advertised in increasing numbers. They were at first constructed mainly of wood, but the bodywork was mounted on a strong metal chassis. Many of the British cars were purely imaginative, but the French were manufacturing a few models, resembling Renaults in the first few years of the 20th century. The use of wooden bodywork on the early cars meant that a large variety of sizes and designs could be produced without the construction of special machinery and the range of cars advertised even in single catalogues is remarkable when compared to the very basic metal toys of today. Wheels on these early models were of the spoked or spider type and the tyres were solid; a few were supplied with hoods. As many as six children could be carried in the largest motors, but few have survived, and the majority that are still discovered are of the smaller and usually cheaper type of motor vehicle.

The manufacturers were very conscious of the criticism that their new models were merely a 'cross between a perambulator and a tricycle' and Joiboy Toys in 1909 claimed that their motor was most carefully designed to imitate the adult vehicle. Some of the French-made models, attractive to the collector because of their wild improbability, are indeed very reminiscent of doll's prams; the backs of the seats are similar to those used for mail carts and constructed of artistically patterned cane. In 1908, E. Hubner of Birmingham claimed in the *Toy Trader* that they were the 'Original Manufacturers of Toy Cars in England', and though such claims are not always reliable it is improbable that an incorrect statement would be made to a readership who could so easily have corrected it.

Although the majority of model cars were made of painted wood, one unusual exception has survived, in the form of a metal reproduction of the Italian car that was driven from Peking to

This splendid child-sized car is made mainly of wood and dates from around 1910. It boasts a pedal and chain drive to the rear wheels and a rear wheel brake. The wheels are of the spoked type characteristic of early models, with solid tyres. Museum of Childhood, Rottingdean.

Paris in sixty days in 1907. This child-size car is an accurate scale model, made in 1910, with the words 'Parigi' and 'Pechino' stencilled on the bonnet and petrol tank and 'Itala' on the radiator grill.

Children's toy motor cars were given separate sections in the pages of the mail order catalogues of large stores by 1912, indicating that a considerable number must have sold despite their comparatively high price. They were, without exception at this time, moved by pedals and virtually all the models were fitted with speedometers, rubber tyres and 'motor clocks'. The more expensive versions were provided with adjustable upholstered seats, extra wide mudguards, windscreens and two headlamps. Single seater cars were sold in sizes suitable for children from 3 to 6, 4 to 8, 6 to 10 and 6 to 12 years old, a list that gives some indication of manufacturers' eagerness to satisfy exactly a customer's requirements. The 'Last Word in Children's Automobiles', advertised in Gamage's catalogue for 1912–13, was mounted on tangent-spoked wheels with pneumatic tyres for which a special pump was provided.

There was at first little development from the tricycle type of model, though from around 1918 the chain drive was sometimes omitted and two levers, one for each pedal, were used instead. One of the finest Italian pedal cars, which carried a Fiat trademark on the cowling, was produced in

wood in 1925, indicating that good quality toys often continued to be made for some time in somewhat outdated techniques. This car was supplied with electric headlights and wheels with tubed tyres – refinements that were used only on better models.

A milestone in the development of the model motor was passed in 1927, when an almost perfect scale model of the Type 52 Bugatti was made, which was created especially by the firm to be used as a display piece at the Milan show. The standard of model cars was further advanced by André Citroën in 1928 with his Citroën C6. This was battery driven and could move forwards or in reverse, while variations of speed could be effected by the movement of the accelerator pedal; there was even a voltmeter on the dashboard for checking the batteries.

Prestige model cars have continued to be occasionally produced by the large automobile companies, but they have always been too expensive for general sale. On cheaper cars the outdated pedal propulsion has continued to be used up to the present and simply disguised by up-to-date bodywork. Since 1935, the whole construction has usually been of metal and any that fairly accurately imitate a particular adult model are worth buying if the collector has plenty of room for display.

As luxurious and sophisticated as its full-sized counterpart is this child's model racing car in the form of a 4 litre Bentley with an electric motor housed in the boot. Its features include rack and pinion steering and pneumatic tyres, and it is finished in British racing green with applied transfers. *Circa* **1930; length 6 feet 6 inches. By courtesy of Sotheby's Belgravia, London.**

This child's pedal car with painted decoration dates from around 1912. It has the wood and metal construction typical of the period and the original horn and lamps. Tolson Memorial Museum, Huddersfield. *Below, left:* 'The Last Word in Children's Automobiles', from Gamage's catalogue of 1912-13. *Below, right:* An electric two-seater made by the London firms of Lines Brothers under the Tri-Ang trademark around 1928. The triangular trade mark is incorporated into the radiator cap. By this time, most model cars, like this one, were made of metal. Sold at Christie's, London, on 12th July 1973.

For Children 6 to 10 years old.

Order

Style

H.

THE LAST WORD IN CHILDREN'S AUTOMOBILES

It is mounted on tangent spoke wheels with pneumatic tyres, and includes all fittings shown as well as a pump for tyres. Finished in suede grey, French grey, dark green, or dark blue.

Price   .. **£7 10 0**

MANUFACTURERS OF CHILD-SIZE CARS

Auto Speciality Manufacturing Company Inc – Indianapolis, USA. This firm advertised model cars of wooden construction in 1912.

Brassington and Cooke – Cable Street, Manchester, England. 'The British Strong Toy Manufacturers', established in 1875. Very fine two-seater cars were advertised in 1909 with nicely upholstered seats with braided edgings. The horn was mounted on the steering wheel and the car had two headlamps and strong running boards.

Bugatti – Italy. A Type 52 car was made to specific order of firm and shown at the Milan Motor Show in 1927. It carried two children and was driven by a 12 volt electric motor with a battery located behind the seat. It was made of steel but had aluminium wheelrims with correctly made tyres. The radiator was imitation and the opening bonnet was secured by leather straps. Forward and reverse gears were provided.

Citroën – France. Model cars were made with the aim of encouraging a child to buy a Citroën when an adult. The firm produced a child-size car based on their 5 hp model, but their most successful was that created by André Citroën for his son Miky, and the advertisement illustrating the car showed the boy riding in it. It was not a lavishly produced car and offered the driver minimum comfort. It was made completely of sheet metal and represented the 1928 Citroën C6. It was driven by two 12 volt batteries and supplied with working lights and a glass windscreen.

Cole, T. H. – Sparkbrooke, Birmingham, England. Made high class wooden cars from around 1908.

Eureka – France. Made good model cars and racing cars as well as an original box truck. Many had lighting fitted or available. In 1933 one model was based on a 35 Bugatti. Cars made in 1938 to 1940 have bonnets similar to those on Peugeots or Renaults. Styling of the models was good. The name 'Eureka' is on the dashboard of some.

Perhaps the most famous of all children's cars was the Type 52 'Baby' Bugatti, made to the order of the car firm and first shown at the Milan Motor Show in 1927. Here, Ernest Friderich, Bugatti agent in Nice at that period, is seen with two of the 'Babies' at Barcelonettes.

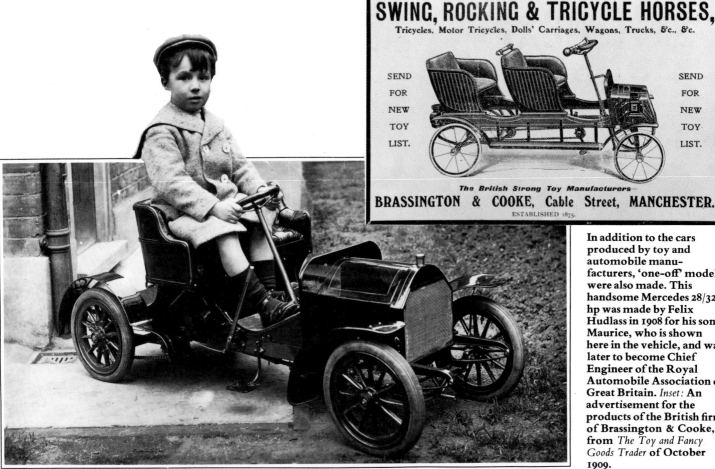

In addition to the cars produced by toy and automobile manufacturers, 'one-off' models were also made. This handsome Mercedes 28/32 hp was made by Felix Hudlass in 1908 for his son Maurice, who is shown here in the vehicle, and was later to become Chief Engineer of the Royal Automobile Association of Great Britain. *Inset*: An advertisement for the products of the British firm of Brassington & Cooke, from *The Toy and Fancy Goods Trader* of October 1909.

Gendron Wheel Co – Superior Street, Toledo, Ohio. Established 1872. In 1925 this firm advertised 'Juvenile automobiles with windshields, airflex extenders, clocks, motometers, Facsimile play reproductions of real autos'.

Hubner, E. – Ladywell Walk and 124 Petershore Street, Birmingham, England. 'The original manufacturer of toy cars in England'. Also made doll's prams of cane and pressed cardboard.

Joiboy Toys – Kettering, England. In 1909 Joiboy were advertising realistically modelled cars with pneumatic tyres and wide mudguards. No headlamps were supplied but they had the usual side handbrake.

Lines Brothers – London. Established by the second generation of the Lines family, the firm was registered as Lines Brothers in 1919. In the same year the Tri-Ang works were purchased. The firm was one of the largest manufacturers of model cars and even made one in basketwork. Early cars were of wood and included a model Vauxhall with working steering, springs, Lucas headlamps and pneumatic-tyred spoked wheels. From around 1930 the majority of cars were made of metal like their full-size counterparts.

Lines, G. & J. – London. (See also Horses and Velocipedes.) Originally established *circa* 1848, the firm occupied the Thistle Works in 1913 and some of the toys from this period bear a thistle trade mark. Some cars made around 1913 had lithographed tinplate radiators and headlamps. It was the sons of Joseph Lines who set up the firm of Lines Brothers.

Loffler, M. – Hamburg, Germany. In 1910 Loffler were producing seven different model sports cars suitable for children aged between three and fourteen. They were heavily made of wood and had rubber tyres.

Luckett, Thomas, & Son – Mark Lane, Petershore Street, Birmingham. Advertised a range of toy motors in 1908.

Manufacture Française d'Ameublement – Saint Etienne, France. In 1921, this firm made a car that was propelled by the child with levers and had large pressed metal wheels.

Patterson Edwards – Old Kent Road, London. This wood toy manufacturer advertised model motors from 1908.

Star Manufacturing Company – Davis Street, Manchester Road, London. Made two-seater cars in the first ten years of the 20th century.

Toledo Metal Wheel Company – Ohio, USA. Claimed to be the 'largest manufactory in the world devoted to the production of children's vehicles. In 1907 this company issued fifty-three new models. They are also known as the American Metal Wheel Co. In 1908 they were making wheeled sledges and similar toys as well as cars.

4

METAL TOYS

Model soldiers

The model soldier enthusiast views the development of this toy as a progression towards an almost completely realistic figure which can be used effectively in war games. The collector of antique toys on the other hand will almost certainly prefer the flat figures produced by makers such as Hilpert because of their rather primitive charm. The finest completely realistic soldiers are those produced by 20th century specialist makers, who are creating figures almost exclusively for an ever growing army of collectors. Though few of their names are recorded in this book, which deals only with antique toys, their achievements should nevertheless be recognised.

Miniature figures of warriors are found in the remains of several civilisations, but their use as toys is debatable and it is not until the medieval woodcuts of boys playing with model jousting knights that we are upon safe ground. The earliest tin figures of German origin were found in Magdeburg and date from the 13th century. Though closely resembling soldiers they were made in all probability for purely ornamental use. In 1578, the Council of Nuremberg authorised pewterers and jewellers to make tin figures as toys for children and from this time it is the town of Nuremberg that is primarily associated with the development of their manufacture. The well documented purchases of the French kings give some indication of the magnificence of the German toys, an example being the army with moving figures which was ordered by Louis XIV for his son. Louis XIII had even owned a silver army, which was later increased with figures of lead and earthenware, while other French princes did not despise the paper armies which were to become so cheap by the end of the 19th century.

German engravers of flats at first based their designs upon the soldiers represented in woodcuts but, from the end of the 17th century, there were sheets that showed the uniforms of soldiers fighting in various campaigns in precise detail

Often preferred by collectors of antique toys to the completely realistic model soldiers are the lead flats of the type made in Nuremberg. These examples date from the mid 19th century and have articulated arms. Bethnal Green Museum of Childhood, London.

and these were copied by craftsmen who had probably never left their native regions. The work of individual early engravers is almost impossible to identify, as they often moved between firms. Their soldiers were made in a variety of sizes which made it difficult for a child to collect several sets and assemble a battle scene. There was no great advance until Johann Gottfried Hilpert, known as the 'father of the tin soldier', regularised his production of soldiers at between five and six centimetres high. The Hilpert family also issued their own catalogue so that very specific items could be ordered, and sold their toys in characteristically labelled chipwood boxes. Their early flats were made purely of tin but lead alloys were eventually substituted for this material.

The toy soldier industry gained quickly in strength and by 1792 there were eight foundries in Fürth, near Nuremberg, and factories in Switzerland, Strasbourg and Denmark, as well as a large number of very small concerns employing only

A contrast to the Nuremberg type flats is provided by these fine examples of modern model soldiers. *Above:* Henry, Duke of Lancaster in full armour, made by F. Ping. *Left:* Joan of Arc, made by Richard Courtenay as one of his Poitiers series. Height 4 inches. Both English. By courtesy of Phillips, New Bond Street, London.

The Napoleonic Wars gave a new impetus to the making of model soldiers in Europe. This effectively costumed Napoleonic soldier is made of wood with a composition head. *Circa* 1800; height 5 inches. Luton Museum and Art Gallery, Bedfordshire.

Facing page, top: **Some idea of the wide range of Nuremberg flats which were made is given by this group which includes the three knights shown on page 134, a set of infantrymen, a military band, cavalrymen with guns and an unusual elephant with an assortment of armed soldiers in its howdah. 19th century. Bethnal Green Museum of Childhood, London.** *Bottom:* **A Berlin-made military parade of flats by G. Sohlke dating from the first quarter of the 19th century. Germanisches Nationalmuseum, Nuremberg.**

a few people. Ammon, Allgeyer and Gottschalk were among the great firms which were established by the beginning of the 19th century and whose work was given a wealth of inspiration by the Napoleonic wars. Soldiers made by these various manufacturers still varied considerably in size and were not standardised until the introduction of the Nuremberg or Heinrichsen scale in the 1840s. Ernst Heinrichsen saw how sales could be vastly increased by encouraging boys to build up large armies, and he even produced a book on the subject for his customers. Realising the difficulty of staging a battle with flats of different sizes, he cooperated with several other makers to establish the 30 mm scale that has remained the basic standard to the present time. These flats became essential toys for boys all over Europe and they were exported in quantity both to Britain and America, so that examples are not difficult to find. Some of the firms used a surprisingly large number of different moulds – J. C. Haselbach of Berlin used between five and six thousand. Other firms, such as J. E. du Bois, were far more concerned with the accuracy of their models, and it was upon this aspect of the soldier that attention was concentrated around 1900, leading eventually to a completely three-dimensional figure.

A few solid lead figures were made in France in the 16th century and though they were too expensive for any large scale production, it is thought that solids continued to be manufactured in very small numbers in Paris. These early solids were a mixture of lead and antimony and are characterised by their very accurate painting. The greatest French manufacturer was the firm of Mignot, which produced well designed figures and made the famous series of historical characters such as Joan of Arc. Despite the superiority of these figures over the flats because of their greater durability, they provided no serious rival on a world scale as they were necessarily more expensive than the latter.

In their effort to introduce more realism to their work, several German firms produced semi-flats with the bodies of the horses and their riders slightly rounded, but the legs still fixed in a straight line on the base. A few German makers in the 19th century also began to market solids, amongst them Johann Carl Fraas and Georg Heyde of Dresden, whose work was widely exported and who sold spectacular boxed scenes of historical battles. Surprisingly, the great break-through in the rendering of realistic figures occurred at the end of the 19th century in Great Britain, where

Above: **This painted wooden army barracks is particularly well equipped and contains lead soldiers of British manufacture marked 'Johillco' and 'John Hill & Co.'. By courtesy of Christie's South Kensington, London.** *Right:* **Carved wooden soldiers of this type were made in many regions of Germany in the 19th century. Welsh Folk Museum, Cardiff.** *Bottom:* **An unusual variation on the model soldier theme is this 'Centennial Soldier' – a jointed flat wooden figure patented and manufactured by Charles M. Crandall of Montrose, Pennsylvania.** *Circa* **1877. Margaret Woodbury Strong Museum, Rochester, New York.**

production of model soldiers had so far been minimal. William Britain created hollow cast figures that were light to handle and fairly cheap to produce. Right from the start, the firm concentrated upon absolutely accurate uniforms painted in the correct colours. So great was the company's success that before the First World War they were even exporting soldiers to Germany.

In America, as in Britain and most other European countries, there was little manufacture of soldiers except in wood and paper until the 20th century, as the German and to a lesser extent the French products were so widely exported. American soldiers did not assume any real importance until the collectors encouraged specialist manufacturers to create prestige pieces specifically for this discerning market, though it should be remembered that a few makers such as J. E. du Bois were creating showcase figures in the latter part of the 19th century.

MAKERS OF METAL SOLDIERS

Allgeyer, Johann Christian – Fürth, Germany. Originally a maker of tin children's clocks, J. C. Allgeyer was established as a manufacturer of flats before 1800. He was followed by his son Johann Friedrich (1821 to 1876). Semi-solids and solids were also made but in small quantities. Both his son and grandson were fine engravers. The family name was signed on the bases of the figures. It is thought that until 1890 this firm was the only one whose products were imported into France. After Konrad Allgeyer's death in 1896, the firm was put into liquidation and the moulds dispersed.

American Soldier Company – Glendale, New York. Made some hollow cast figures *circa* 1904 that are virtually copies of the work of William Britain of London.

Ammon, Johann Wolfgang – Nuremberg. Ammon became a master pewterer in 1794 and made a number of flats based on soldiers of the Napoleonic wars. He was followed by his son Christoph, who became a master in 1836. Christoph was followed by his son Christian, who continued the business until 1921. The firm used several marks on their fine quality soldiers including 'C. A.', 'C. Ammon' and 'C. Ammon in Nürnberg'.

Bergmann, A. J., C. T. and Charles – Strasbourg, 1800 to 1904. Made a number of flats and was the most important firm to work in this town.

Blondel et Fils – Paris, 1839 to 1851. Made solids.

Britain's Ltd, William – London, 1893 to present. Founded by William Britain, whose eldest son, Alfred, was the general manager of the factory. His other son, William, superintended the modelling department and designed and cut the costly brass models for the casting of the figures. The use of a hollow casting of alloy instead of solid lead made the models light and easy to handle. The figures were first displayed in large numbers by Gamage's. The Life Guards

This group of knights by C. Ammon of Nuremberg is part of a tournament setting. The figures are decorated in gold and red, and their visors and both their arms move. *Circa* 1840. Germanisches Nationalmuseum, Nuremberg.

Above, left: **An example of the soldiers made by William Britain is this rare American military band. These sets were made mainly for export to America in the years preceding the Second World War.** *Above right:* **One of William Britain's rarest groups is the Salvation Army, made around 1914. By courtesy of Phillips, New Bond Street, London.**

were the first to be made, then Grenadier Guards and kilted Highlanders. The early models can be distinguished by a separate sword or rifle plugged into the cuff of the right hand and are known as 'plughanded Highlanders' by collectors. Other lines were soon introduced, so that by 1902 one hundred and four different regiments were being made, including the West India Regiment and the South Australian Lancers.

The City Imperial Volunteers were the first to carry the label 'Copyright Wm. Britain Jun. 1 1900' and from 1900 the firm's mark was embossed on the horses. The firm placed great emphasis upon completely accurate rendering of colours and uniforms and their products were almost invariably sold in shiny red boxes. Their main concentration was upon the regiments of the British Army and these became popular with enthusiasts in other countries, so that before the First World War Britain's were even exporting to Germany. The labels initially used on foot-soldiers were replaced by embossing in 1905. After 1906 oblong bases were used for the foot-soldiers, which had previously stood on round or oval bases. Their mounted soldiers are fixed in place and cannot be removed. Britain's made vast numbers of soldiers and military type processions. Individual figures can be found easily but complete boxed sets are now sought after. They are priced purely according to rarity.

An early set of Britains 9th Royal Lancers with their original box. Early 20th century. By courtesy of Phillips, New Bond Street, London.

Bois, J. E. du – Hannover, established in 1830. J. E. du Bois was originally an engraver to Wegmann (see below). Main production was of flats but a few rare solids were also made. He was followed by his son Ernst, and the firm was in operation until the end of the 19th century. The firm made troops modelled on the Hannoverian army, Napoleonic troops, and both foot and mounted Roman soldiers. Some work was marked 'J. E. du Bois', but it was generally unsigned, though of excellent quality.

Comet Metal Products – New York. The first figures were made in 1938 and sold under the name Brigadier, and can be distinguished by the thickness of their stands. Comet made flats, semi-flats and solids. During the last war, specialist models were made and afterwards the name was changed to Authenticast and a regimental uniform series was made. The designer Eriksson's initials, 'H. E.', are found on some models.

Crescent Toy Company – London and Cwmcarn, Wales. (See also British Metal Toys). Founded in July 1922 in a small North London workshop, the firm made model soldiers and cowboys which retailed at a penny each. They were cast hollow in lead alloy and were painted mainly by women. In 1922 a man earning £2.15 per week would cast 300 soldiers an hour. The women painted 600 to 800 models in a nine-hour day with six colours to each figure. A large number of British regiments were made and detachable riders with moveable arms were introduced in 1948. The quality of the painting was generally mediocre and the hollow-cast figures were marked only 'made in England'.

Denecke – Brunswick, Germany. The founder made flats in the early 19th century and part of the firm was sold by his widow to Wegmann in 1820. The remainder of the firm was taken over by Wollrath Denecke in 1842 and was later sold in 1870 to L. Link. The firm's products included Napoleonic troops and Brunswick militia and they also made figures to the Nuremberg scale. The firm's workshop eventually passed to Bernhard Borning and it can now be seen in the Stadtisches Museum. Brunswick. The figures made by Wollrath are signed 'W.D.'.

Dorfler, Hans – Fürth, *circa* 1890 to 1945. Made semi-flats and solids. Models included the armies of the Great War and some large German pre First World War figures with riders that could be detached from their horses.

Fraas, Johann Carl (1828 to 1912) – Breslau. Fraas was a master founder and between 1854 and 1912 made both flats and solids, including a few civilian models.

Gottschalk, J. W. (1768 to 1843) – Nuremberg. Made the usual variety of flats in various sizes, some of which were signed 'F. E.' for F. Eggimann, his most important engraver.

Left: **A rare officer of the 11th Hussars, made by Britains around 1900. The figure is one from a set of five; the horse has a throat plume, a feature that is highly regarded by collectors. By courtesy of Phillips, New Bond Street, London.**

A page from the 1915 catalogue of the Grey Iron Casting Company, Mount Joy, Pennsylvania. Margaret Woodbury Strong Museum, Rochester, New York.

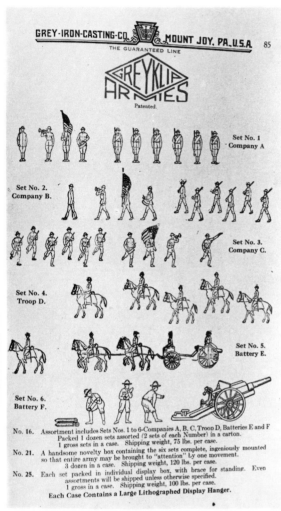

Grey Iron Casting Company – Mount Joy, Pennsylvania, USA. Founded *circa* 1904 and unusual in that cast iron figures of decidely crude construction were made.

Haffner, Johann – Fürth. J. Haffner founded the business in 1838 and it was continued by his son. Later known as the United Toy Factories, it made the usual range of Franco–German War figures, and some French dragoons. Won a prize at the Paris Exposition of 1867 for pewter toys. Made flats, semi-flats and solids. The firm was eventually taken over by Albrecht Stadtler, an engraver to Heinrichsen (see below).

Haselbach, J. C. – Berlin, *circa* 1848 to 1900. A very large production which used between five and six thousand different moulds. Haselbach made figures from the Thirty Years' War, the Crusades and an unusual series of sailors. He worked in the 40 mm or Berlin scale. The figures came in boxes bearing a large 'H' on the lid.

Heinrichsen – Founded in Nuremberg in 1839 by Ernst Heinrichsen, who had worked as an engraver in the workshop of Christoph Ammon and in 1842 won a gold medal for engraving. He was also an effective businessman and employed the most skilled designers. The firm produced flats of the Prussian Guards, Bavarian Infantry and French lancers, as well as tournament figures and scenes. Among its special commissions was a complete set of the mounted regiments of the Russian Guards for Czar Nicholas I. At first the figures were made in different sizes but around 1848 he began to use the 30 mm Heinrichsen or Nuremberg scale which was also adopted by other manufacturers and which in 1924 gained international acceptance as the standard size for tin flats. Heinrichsen provided his young customers with a book on war games written by himself. The firm was taken over by his son Wilhelm from 1869 to 1908, and by another member of the family, Ernst Wilhelm in 1908, production ceasing in 1945. Wilhelm Heinrichsen was also a highly skilled engraver and increased the firm's range by thousands of figures from all periods. His son modernised the type of figures the firm produced and also added a large number of new subjects. After his death in 1938, his widow continued the firm for a short period and is still thought to occasionally cast a few soldiers to special order, as the moulds still survive.

Heyde, Georg – Dresden. Maker of semi-solids and solids. The precise date of foundation is unknown, but the firm was certainly in production by 1870. Heyde exported huge quantities of soldiers and worked to a standard size of 6 cm for dismounted figures, though he did make figures in other sizes also. Boxed sets of spectacularly large size were made and settings included trees, farmhouses and fences. The heads of figures were plugged to the bodies and the mounted men were detachable. A few hollow cast figures were also made. Among the subjects produced were Romans and Greeks, Hannibal's march on Rome, North American Indians back from a scalping raid and scenes from the American War of Independence. Many of the figures were later pirated, so it is not always easy to identify the firm's work. The factory was bombed during the Second World War and production ceased. Box lids show facsimile medals won at exhibitions.

Hill, John & Co – Founded in London *circa* 1900 by a Mr Wood, who had previously worked for

/orange bastards

William Britain and in the new company attempted to produce figures that were cheaper, but still of the hollow-cast type. The firm achieved its peak just after the First World War and set up a particularly good export to America. It was known variously as John Hill, J. Hill, J. Hill & Co and Johillco, all marks that sometimes appear on the figures.

Hilpert – Coburg and Nuremberg. Several generations of the same family producing flats from 1720 to 1822. Johann Georg Hilpert was the son of a tinsmith who left Coburg to set up business in Nuremberg and after working as a journeyman for seven years, was made a freeman of the City of Nuremberg in 1760. The early models were made of pure tin and are arrestingly modelled, but despite the vast numbers produced, there are relatively few of them still available to collectors, as most are now in museums. They are marked on the bases with an 'H', 'Hilpert' or 'J. G. Hilpert'. The firm mass-produced toy soldiers but also made some prestige figures such as Frederick the Great and the Prince de Ligne. Their sets of toy soldiers were exported to Britain, Holland and Russia. J. G. Hilpert's son, Johann Wolfgang, became a master pewterer in 1787 but worked with his father until 1795. The range of scenes and animals are possibly more lively than the soldiers. The firm was the first to make use of mass production methods and also produced a catalogue. The production of model soldiers was considerably encouraged by the interest children took in the Seven Years' War. This firm is thought to have been the first to create large scale model armies. The agent Johann Ludwig Stahl probably took over the Hilpert stock since figures from the

Hilpert moulds were included in his 1805 catalogue. These later, recast figures are not considered to be as finely detailed as those produced by the Hilperts themselves.

Lucotte – Paris, *circa* 1795. Makers of solid figures. Little is known either of the founder or the origins of the firm. It was taken over by Mignot at an unknown date.

McLoughlin Brothers – New York. Made copies of Britains' hollow casts from 1900 to 1912.

Mignot – Paris. Founded in 1825, this firm is the most famous by far of French makers, producing solids, flats and some hollow cast figures. The mark 'C.B.G.', composed of the initials of the three founders of the firm – Cuperly, Blondel and Gerbeau, was not used until 1838, the year in which the production of model soldiers began. There were several amalgamations and reorganisations of the firm; at some stage Lucotte was incorporated

Above: **An interesting group of flats of battle scenes made by the Nuremberg firms of Heinrichsen and Hilpert. Mid 19th century. Germanisches National-museum Nuremberg.**
Top: **Part of the splendid collection of soldiers by Lucotte which can be seen at Blenheim Palace, Oxfordshire.**

A display box of Roman soldiers with two tents in the corners made by Heyde of Dresden. *Circa* 1890. By courtesy of Phillips, New Bond Street, London.

and his mark of 'L.C.' with the Imperial bee is found on some work. The mark 'C.B.G. Made in France' has been used since 1945. As Lucotte was in existence from 1789, the firm of Mignot itself claims to originate in the 18th century. They are generally thought to have amalgamated around 1825. The solids produced were five to six centimetres high and the firm's main concentration was obviously on figures from the French armies. One of the finest groups can be seen at Blenheim Palace. As solids were more expensive to produce, they never became as widely popular as flats but the work of this firm is characterised by its detailed decoration. John G. Garratt comments on the basic differences between models made by Mignot and Lucotte and observes that the tails of Mignot horses are short whereas those of Lucotte horses are long. While both makers created figures with detachable riders, the Lucotte models also have removable saddles and saddle cloths. Mignot produced a very wide range of subjects including historical as well as military figures. Among the historical figures are Joan of Arc, Lincoln, and George V and Queen Mary. Among their great prestige pieces was the large army made for the Prince Imperial and commissioned by Napoleon III, which was designed by the sculptor Fremiet.

Renvoize, J. – London. Made hollow cast soldiers between 1900 and 1914. The horses are marked 'J. Renvoize' on the base.

Reka Ltd – London, *circa* 1908 to 1930. Owned by C. W. Baker, this firm produced a very large number of soldiers which were obviously based on the hollow casts made by William Britain. These included most of the British regiments and the Cowboys and Indians of around 1922 were among the last to be produced. It is thought that some of the models were sold to Crescent in 1933. Pieces are marked either 'Reka' or alternatively 'Reka/C. W. Baker'.

Rieche, Gebrüder – Hannover. Founded in 1806. Made flats based on various subjects including the Indian Mutiny, Waterloo and the Conquest of Mexico. Also produced some portrait figures, such as the Duke of Wellington, which were engraved by Franz Rieche and designed by Richard Knotel. The firm ceased operation in the year 1938.

Schweizer, Adam – Diessen-Amersee, Germany. A tin founder who made flats which were sold by the pound in 1821 and were probably unpainted. Produced a series of infantrymen, Bavarian dragoons etc, all very much in the manner of fairly cheap toys.

United Toy Factories – Nuremberg. 20th century, but took over the firm owned by Christian Schweigger of Nuremberg (1763 to 1829).

Wegmann, Carl – Brunswick, before 1820 to 1895. Maker of flats, Carl Wegmann worked from 1820 to 1825 and was succeeded by his son Theodor. The firm used Denecke moulds and marked the bases 'C.W.' It was later purchased by B. Borning. Products included Napoleonic troops, Prussian infantry and figures from the Franco–Prussian War.

Wehrli, Rudolf (1801 to 1876) – Went to Gottschalk as an apprentice and set up his own concern in Aarau making 'tin composition figures'. His son continued until 1887, both making flats.

Weygang, Carl – Göttingen, Germany. A maker of flats who worked from around 1820 to his death in 1872, and was followed by his son Victor who worked until 1919. The models were of Hannoverian infantry and civil characters, signed 'C.W.G.', 'C.W.', or 'W'. Very occasionally the full surname was used. The moulds are now in the Göttingen Museum.

Wright, J. L., Inc – Chicago, 1910 to 1943. This firm traded under the name of Lincoln Logs USA and made a number of log forts as well as metal alloy figures of various types.

Toy and model trains

The distinction between model and toy becomes as blurred in the collecting of trains as in miniature furniture, though the majority of enthusiasts include both within their sphere of interest. The earliest miniature trains were made by the associates of the men who were later to develop the full sized railway and there was even one model peopled with dolls, which was made to encourage a ruler to build a railway system in his land. The first working miniature locomotive was that created by William Murdoch, who was James Watt's assistant, and this model attained an apparently terrifying speed for the time of some six to eight miles an hour. Another famous early model was that made by Trevithick in 1797, which he later followed with several others. All these early models were really in the nature of experimental prototypes and the production of toy trains did not begin until the opening of the Hetton railway in 1822. Stephenson had built his first engine in 1814 and there was some home workshop material available for enthusiasts shortly after this date. Despite their somewhat crude appearance, the majority of early models discovered were however made professionally, as few amateurs could afford the workshop equipment.

The early trains obviously commanded great general interest and models of many of them were produced by instrument makers. With their shining brass and fine workmanship these models make superb display pieces. The manufacture of trains by instrument makers continued for some time, and as late as 1875 firms such as Newton & Co of London were still manufacturing breathtaking models. The earliest toy trains were probably commissioned from instrument makers for the amusement of rich children, but the world of the toy train really began with the opening of the Nuremberg–Fürth railway in 1835. This event was almost instantly recorded by the makers of metal flats, who produced simple models to add to their range. The first recorded exhibition of a model railway was that held at the Leeds Mechanics Institution in 1838, where a steam train ran around a model island.

Very few pre-1850 trains are now discovered though those made much later are often so retrospective in design that they suggest a date much earlier than that of their actual manufacture. The good quality brass locomotives were made to run on the floor and are known as floor- or carpet-runners, though they were sometimes bought complete with rails. A number of the great American toy businesses were established in America by the late 1830s but the first self-propelled tinplate train known to have been produced in that country was that made by W. Brown & Co in 1856. The commercially produced model steam train seems to have first appeared in Europe in the 1860s, though their manufacture did not become widespread until the 1880s. The French were at this time producing some charming but rather thinly painted carpet-runners modelled in a completely retrospective style. One of the earliest methods of moving a toy train by clockwork was to connect the locomotive to the motor by a bar which would then draw the train round in a circle.

This primitive early train set is made of painted wood and was sold with a wooden track. Also shown is its original chip wood box. German, *circa* 1845; height $3\frac{1}{4}$ inches. Museum of London.

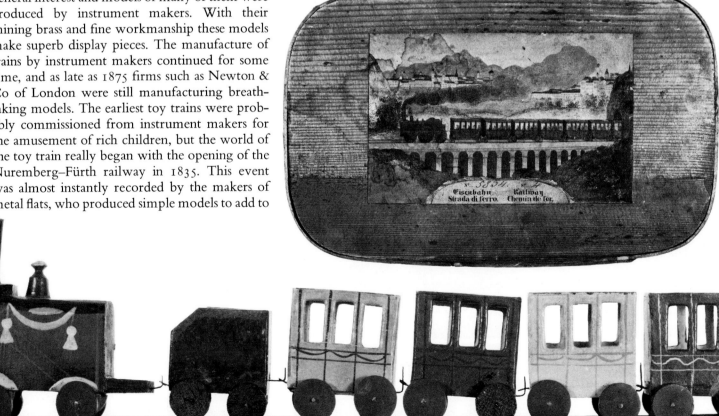

The rotary models, the French carpet-runners and the steam trains were all made very much in the idiom of toys and frequently with little effort at realism. As a result, the division between toys and specially commissioned models remained wide until the late 1880s, when the great tin-toy makers began to realise that much more accurate models of up-to-date trains were required by children, and they began to compete with each other to produce not only the most authentic but also the most complete systems.

The golden age of the model train, which for purists ended with the First World War, abounds with such famous names as Carette, Märklin, Bing, Plank and Bub. The efforts of these companies, in combination with the improved litho-

graphic processes of the 1890s, produced much more realistic contemporary models at a relatively low price, so that good trains came within the range of most middle class boys.

Märklin's introduction of their sectional tin-plate track enabled a lay-out to be extended into several rooms. Their figure eight formation, introduced in 1892, was also something of a sensation and it was this firm which first used a numerical system of gauges – 0, 1, 2, 3 and 4. One of Märklin's more diverting models was a silver-plated train propelled by an electric motor which was made to the special order of the Maharajah of Gwalior to carry decanters around his dining table. The early steam models would have been most unsuitable for this purpose, as they left

Above: **A lead flat, made in four sections, representing the first train to run between Nuremberg and Fürth in 1835. Note the guard sitting on the roof of the last carriage, as in horse-drawn coaches of the period. Germanisches Nationalmuseum, Nuremberg.** *Right:* **William Trevithick's second loco model of 1796. Screw jacks are fitted to the underside of the main driving wheel which could be used to convert it into a stationary engine. Science Museum, London.**

Top: **An effective model train given to the original owner in 1903. It has an indistinct mark reading 'G ... & Co.'. Length 7 inches. Luton Museum and Art Gallery, Bedfordshire.** *Centre*: **'The Jewel in the Crown', a clockwork floor runner made by the French firm of Dessin. The train has been restored by C. Littledale.** *Circa* 1880; **track width $2\frac{5}{8}$ inches. Reproduced by courtesy of New Cavendish Books.** *Bottom*: **One of the earliest electric trains, a Bing steeple cab locomotive and carriage in gauge 3 ($2\frac{1}{2}$ inches). The small turnstile building is a contemporary Märklin railway accessory. David Pressland Collection.**

Above: **A gauge 0 clock-work streamlined train set in Union Pacific livery made by Louis Marx.** *Below:* **A Bing gauge 1 clockwork 0–6–4 tank locomotive finished in its original maroon livery, with trackside equipment also made by Bing for the London firm of Gamage's. *Circa* 1920; length of engine 17 inches. Both by courtesy of Sotheby's Belgravia, London.**

untidy pools of water behind them as they moved along and were consequently termed 'Birmingham dribblers' or 'piddlers'.

European trains were often adapted for the American market by the simple expedient of adding a cow catcher to the front, but the Americans were not dependent on the German producers. American manufacturers produced a steady flow of trains, many of them distinctively modelled in cast iron. Among the cast-iron engines made by Ives was one that emitted smoke from a lighted cigarette and another that fired caps. A great American landmark in the development of model railways was the electric train patented in 1884 by Murray Beacon. The first electric train sets in Europe, made by Märklin, were not issued until the year 1898.

Another important landmark in the development of the model railway was the meeting of Stefan Bing and W. J. Bassett-Lowke at the Paris Exhibition of 1900, at which Bing agreed to manufacture particularly realistic models to be

marketed by the Northampton firm. Bassett-Lowke were soon to achieve considerable success and promoted the whole concept of playing with trains by skilful advertising and marketing.

The years before the First World War were the high point in the creation of quality models, and the range and variety of equipment that can be seen in old catalogues is breathtaking. Buildings, figures, station lights, working signals and level crossings and even uniforms and ticket collector's equipment were all available, fathers were obviously willing to spend quite large sums on a pastime which they could share with their sons. During the war the trainmakers' factories were diverted into activities such as the making of munitions. Many never recovered from the effects of the war and the depression that followed, and in the 1920s only Märklin and Bing remained as giants in Europe.

In Britain, the scene was a little brighter. Bassett-Lowke were still very successful, and were joined immediately after the war by Hornby trains, produced by Meccano. A system which could be continually added to was adopted. The clockwork trains were economical to produce and there were few families unable to afford at least a small Hornby layout for their children.

As such a large quantity of equipment was produced it is still possible to acquire quite extensive clockwork layouts fairly cheaply. The earlier steam trains on the other hand, are now so sought-after that they are expensive. The collecting of trains is highly specialised and demands a knowledge of engineering as well as an appreciation of antiques. The novice collector is therefore advised to buy only from the most reputable sources, as there are so many pitfalls for the unwary and the uninformed.

MANUFACTURERS OF TRAINS

American Flyer (trade name) – Chicago. Manufacture commenced in 1907 and their early carriages were almost copies of those made by Ives. The firm was successful, and in 1910 a new partnership, the American Flyer Manufacturing Company, was formed. Between 1915 and 1916 electric models were also included. Their trains until 1936 were made in $2\frac{1}{8}$ inch gauge. It was this firm that acquired most of Ives' stock in 1928 (see below). In 1938, it was taken over by A. C. Gilbert, who was to become the first president of the American Manufacturers' Association. Under Gilbert's direction, the company became one of the most important manufacturers of model trains in America. It was taken over by Lionel in 1967.

Bassett-Lowke & Co – Founded by Wennman J. Bassett-Lowke in 1899 at Northampton, England. His family had manufactured steam boilers etc in the area for some years. Aware of the interest in

the home construction of model engines, Bassett-Lowke decided to supply rough castings for this purpose. After his meeting with Stefan Bing at the 1900 Paris Exhibition, the decision was made to manufacture realistic model trains. In 1901 Henry Greenly was employed as consulting engineer. Already a popular and respected contributor to the magazine *Model Engineer*, he was responsible for the design of the Bing/Bassett-Lowke models, which were actually made in Germany. From 1904, large-scale passenger railways such as those seen at fetes and fairs were also produced. Bassett-Lowke's London showroom, known as the 'Mecca of Model Railways', was opened in 1908 and interest in their products was also fostered by the *Model Railway Handbook* which was first published in 1906. Greenly improved the model of the 'Black Prince', which was the first train to be made by Bing and Bassett-Lowke, and the perfected version appeared in 1910. The company also sold hand-made model locomotives for larger gauges. Carette was also

Above: **The only American manufacturer to produce a European type of model train, American Flyer made this clockwork 'GNR' tank loco in gauge 0 with a tender and two lithographed coaches. The set was marketed as the 'British Flyer'.** *Circa* **1920. Reproduced by Courtesy of New Cavendish Books.** *Below:* **One of the most famous English producers of model trains was the firm of Bassett-Lowke, which was founded in 1899. A typical product is the upper model, a gauge 1, 4-4-2 'Precursor' tank locomotive, finished in its original black livery with red and white lining. Originally steam-powered but converted to centre-rail electric; length $16\frac{1}{2}$ inches. The lower model is a specimen of miniature engineering rather than a toy – a $2\frac{1}{2}$ inch gauge live steam coal-fired locomotive, the 'Lady Iris'. Length 2 feet 8 inches. Both by courtesy of Sotheby's Belgravia, London.**

to produce locomotives especially for the North-ampton company and these sometimes appear in Carette's German catalogue, whereas Bing made trains specifically for Bassett-Lowke and did not sell the models in Germany. The First World War halted the supply of German-made trains and the factory found it necessary to increase their own production, though this was soon augmented by Bing again after the war. Between the two wars, the name of the firm was associated with all that was fine in British-made trains, and overseas agencies were set up. W. J. Bassett-Lowke died in 1953 and the manufacture of trains ended then, despite an attempt to rekindle interest in them in the 1960s. Since then, the firm has concentrated on industrial and museum models.

Bateman, J. & Co – London. Established in 1774 and also known as the Original Model Dockyard. This firm made parts both for model steam engines and ships, and from 1879 was manufacturing model steam locomotives. In the 1880s the firm ran its own museum of models in High Holborn in central London.

Beeson, James S. – London. Began manufacturing trains under his own name in 1924. They are the finest models of this period known to enthusiasts and are perfect in every detail. Since 1924 some 1,500 locomotives, mainly in 0 gauge, have been produced. Some of Beeson's trains were sold by firms such as Bassett-Lowke.

Beggs, Eugene – New Jersey, USA. Beggs had worked in the locomotive works of Danforth and Cooke and also worked as a foreman on the Mariette and Cincinnati Railroad in Ohio. He later returned to his native town of Paterson and in 1871 was producing miniature steam powered locomotives of patented design, some of which were relatively expensive. His toys were marketed through Ives and James McNair and by the National Toy Company. The production of steam trains ended in 1906.

Bergmann, Althof & Co – New York. Founded in 1856 and one of the first American firms to make floor-runners with or without clockwork and made of either tinplate or cast iron.

Bing, Gebrüder – Founded in Nuremberg (see German Tin Toys for detailed history). The Bing brothers had the largest toymaker's stand at the Bavarian Trades Exhibition of 1882, and they

Facing page: **A Bing spirit fired gauge 1, 4-4-0 loco and tender. It has its original filler plug, whistle and spirit burner. Early 20th century: length 22½ inches. By courtesy of Sotheby's Belgravia, London.** *Below:* **The classic toy train: a Bing gauge 3 (2½ inches) live steam 4-4-0 LNWR locomotive, tender and carriage in pristine condition. 1904. David Pressland Collection.**

were manufacturing trains from this date. An advertisement of 1886 shows that their trains were made entirely of sheet metal with wheels of cast brass, and ran on zinc rails. Similar floor-runners were also produced. In 1898 the firm was selling a variety of railway accessories including remote-controlled points, and were soon claiming that it did not matter if a boy paid one shilling or one pound for their steam engines, all would have been individually tested under steam. Their display at the Paris Exposition of 1900 included a 4-2-2 miniature Midland Railway engine. The firm also made prestige trains for window display in gauge 2 ($2\frac{1}{8}$ inch). In 1912 a steam pilot loco with reversing gear, reduction gearing to increase the power and brass fittings was advertised, as was 'The New Model Express Steam Loco. Entirely reconstructed and brought up to date'. The advertisement claimed of the latter: 'This is the first really good model of an eight wheeled steam locomotive in this small gauge 0'. Much of the rolling stock produced was very detailed and there were cattle trucks, motor traffic trucks and mail vans in abundance. The firm encouraged model railway enthusiasts by selling copies of a publication called *The Little Railway Engineer*, which showed how to assemble effective layouts. Some of their finest and most accurate trains were supplied to Bassett-Lowke and these were not sold in any way by Bing themselves. In 1934 the firm was finally wound up. Not only had it suffered from the Depression of the 1920s, but the family which had been the driving force no longer owned it and a lack of centralised policy caused financial difficulties.

British Modelling and Electrical Company – Established in 1884. Made a wide variety of locomotives, usually with pierced footplate railings.

Brown, George W. & Co – Forestville, Connecticut, USA. This firm produced the first American self-propelled tinplate trains that ran by clockwork, in 1856. The early locomotives were unusual in that they ran on three wheels. They were simply decorated with stencilled patterns executed in bright colours.

Bub, Karl – Founded in 1851 in Nuremberg, the Bub company manufactured a variety of tinplate models. Around 1905 they produced clockwork trains that ran on rails, and these were to become one of their main products. They were also producing electric trains before 1914. They were eventually to take over some of Bing's equipment and after the war an English branch factory was opened in Aylesbury to avoid import duties. This was run in conjunction with Tipp (see German Tin Toys). The firm closed in 1967.

Carette, Georges – Founded in Nuremberg in 1886 (see also German Tin Toys). This firm used particularly fine wheel castings for their trains and were one of the first makers in Europe to introduce electric models between 1897 and 1898. The quality of lithography used on their trains after 1905 was particularly good. The firm went into collaboration with Bassett-Lowke before the First World War, in order to gain a foothold in the lucrative English market. The locomotives made for Bassett-Lowke were not available from Carette's catalogue but the Bassett-Lowke/Carette coaches in non-standard livery were available from both firms. The years 1905 to 1914 were the most prosperous, as the war resulted in the return of Carette to his native France and the firm closed in 1917, though Carette locomotives continued to be produced by Bassett-Lowke after the war.

One of the live steam models produced by Georges Carette: a gauge 1, 2-2-0 locomotive with twin outside oscillating cylinders and matching tender in its original dark green livery with red, yellow and slate grey lining. *Circa* **1910; length 1 foot 3 inches. By Courtesy of Sotheby's Belgravia, London.**

Carlisle & Finch – Founded by Morton Carlisle and Robert S. Finch in 1894 at Cincinnati, the firm was manufacturing two-inch gauge electric tramways from 1897. It was the first to produce a model railway builder's instruction book, entitled *Miniature Electric Railway Construction*. The firm closed in 1916.

Clyde Model Dockyard – Glasgow. Founded in 1789 originally to manufacture model ships for Admiralty use. They also produced parts for the home assembly of steam engines. In 1902 they produced a representation of a Webb four-cylinder compound locomotive. They claimed that all their advertised products were British, but in fact some were made by the French firm of Radiguet & Massiot (see below).

Doll & Cie – Nuremberg. Founded in 1898 as a partnership between Peter Doll and J. Sandheim, initially in order to produce simple steam engines. The first factory was set up in 1913 and by 1930 there were 150 employees. The firm was taken over by Fleischmann in the 1930s and no trains were made after 1938.

Dorfan Co – Newark, New Jersey, USA. Founded by Milton and Julius Forchheimer, this firm had strong links with the Nuremberg factories such as Bing. It was the first to investigate the possibilities of pressure- and die-casting from zinc alloys and produced trains of this material with the help of the New Jersey Zinc Company. In 1926 they were making gauge 0 and $2\frac{1}{8}$-inch gauge electric trains. After 1929 it became necessary to try to produce cheaper trains and this resulted in a rapid loss of quality; the factory's output had ended by the Second World War.

Fleischmann, Gebrüder – Nuremberg. Founded in 1887. No early production of trains, but after taking over Doll they produced trains after the Second World War.

Fournereau, J. E. – Seine-et-Oise, France. Were producing models of locomotives from 1928. They took over other quality firms and produced particularly fine models and kits. In 1937 Fournereau published *Loco Revue*, the first French model railway magazine.

Gilbert, A. C. – (See also American Flyer and Constructional Toys – Erector.) A prominent figure in the American toy trade, Gilbert helped set up the American Toy Manufacturers' Association, and formed a lobby for high duties on imported German toys after the First World War. He took over the Meccano Company of America in 1930, but his involvement with model trains did not really begin until he took over American Flyer in 1938. He died in 1961 and was succeeded by his son, but the company was soon split up.

Hafner, W. F., Manufacturing Company – Chicago, around 1914. The company at first imported German trains, but were forced to increase their own production greatly because of the First World War. The company went through several mergers and eventually became part of the Louis Marx toy empire.

Above: **A Hafner 'Overland Flyer' clockwork train set of the cheaper type. Made in Germany,** *circa* **1914. By courtesy of Sotheby's Belgravia, London.**
Below: **A small train of the Penny Toy type, with its original box bearing the 'H' trademark of the Hess company. The engine is red and the carriages are brown and yellow. Note how the realism of the box illustration contrasts with the simple execution of the model.** *Circa* **1895; length 6 inches. Author's Collection.**

Above: **A setting of 0 gauge Hornby including an engine shed, trackside equipment and rolling stock. All late 1930s.** *Right:* **A Hornby Dublo engine and carriage. The engine, an 0–6–2 LNER, utilises the three-rail electrical system.** *Circa* **1954. Both Author's Collection.**

Hess, Math. – Founded in Nuremberg in 1826. This was one of the first companies to make toy railways from pressed steel. The early versions were simple pull-alongs, but they were later provided with clockwork. In 1866 the firm was inherited by the founder's son, John L. Hess, and his initials were used in the sign.

Hornby, Frank (1863 to 1936) – Liverpool, England. The idea of making model trains was investigated before the First World War by the makers of Meccano, but the 'Hornby Train' was not marketed until 1920. The early trains were built from standard units so that they could be taken to pieces and rebuilt. The standard gauge 0 was used and there were two standard curves for the rails. A continually growing system like that used in the construction sets was envisaged but it was soon found too limiting, and after 1925 specially made components of the traditional type were used. The first Hornby trains were in the livery of the Great Northern, Caledonian, London and North Western, and the London, Brighton and South Coast railway systems. In 1925 an electric train was introduced based on the trains of the London Metropolitan railway. In 1926 the Hornby Control System was introduced, enabling the whole layout to be controlled from a single cabin. A variety of accessories including figures and luggage were available, as well as name- and destination-boards and miniature posters. The development of these trains was aided by the *Meccano Magazine*. The firm is important as it was one of the last manufacturers of 0 gauge model railways. In 1964 it was taken over by Lines Brothers. Its largest and probably most popular engine was the Princess Elizabeth Pacific, introduced in 1937. In 1938 00 gauge trains known as Hornby-Dublo were introduced. The firm is still in operation.

Issmayer, Johann Andreas – Established a factory in Nuremberg in 1861. In the 1870s, the firm produced some of its first trains, which ran on rails and were clockwork driven. By 1894 some 150 hands were employed. There is no record of the firm after 1932.

Ives – Established in 1868 by Edward R. Ives in Plymouth, Connecticut. In 1870 the firm moved to Bridgeport and was to become famous with its well-known slogan 'Ives Toys make Happy Boys'. The business included a succession of firms, and the Ives name was retained after Edward Ives

Two examples of
American model train
production. *Above:* An Ives
gauge 0 electric locomotive
shown with Ives and
Lionel carriages, *circa* 1932.
On the right of the picture
is an earlier '3200' series
Ives electric locomotive
with a cast iron body,
circa 1916. *Below:* Two
gauge 0 electric loco-
motives made by Lionel, a
Union Pacific 'City of
Portland' three-car diesel
unit, *circa* 1934, next to a
Mini Scale NYC 'Hudson',
circa 1937. They are shown
beneath another Lionel
product, the 'Hell Gate
Bridge'. The Mini Scale
loco could be obtained in
kit form and was made
from castings. NYC
'Hudson' from the Torry
Collection. All reproduced
by courtesy of New
Cavendish Books.

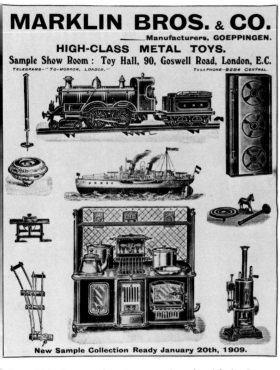

himself had ceased to be associated with it. It was unusual in showing an apparently genuine interest in the children for whom its products were made. The first toys made by the company were floor-running tin locomotives of brightly painted metal, some of which were clockwork powered. In the 1880s and 1890s, however, their toys were mainly of cast iron, and the trains were again mainly floor-runners, with some additional clockwork trams and locomotives. They also marketed steam trains, but these were made for them by Beggs. In 1900, a fire destroyed the old factory and, as it was decided that floor-runners were outdated, they introduced clockwork trains in US gauge 0 which ran on tracks. These were followed in 1912 by trains in gauge 1. The company put great emphasis upon quality and offered an excellent replacement service. There was a great interest within the firm in its own history and in the 1920s a collection of Ives trains was arranged in the New York showrooms. It is thought that this display did much to encourage collectors' interest in the subject of old toys. In 1928 the company went bankrupt and were taken into joint partnership by American Flyer, Hafner and Lionel. In 1931 the firm was completely absorbed by Lionel of Irvington, New Jersey, together with the exhibition of old trains in the New York showroom.

Lionel – The firm's founder, Joshua Lionel Cowen (1881 to 1965), was born in New York. In 1901 he set up business in a small electrical shop in New York. At first he traded under the name of The Lionel Manufacturing Company and produced good quality miniature trams. In 1906 he also began to produce smaller, more economical, models. He patented his own gauge for trains, which he described as 'standard gauge'. Complete train sets were manufactured by 1908 and a move to bigger premises was necessary. In partnership with others, he was to buy out Ives and by 1937 his staff exceeded a thousand and the output was huge. After this there was a very gradual decline and the firm became part of the Roy M. Cohn group, though the brand name was still used. In 1968 the railway production department was acquired by Gilbert.

Märklin – The firm's founder, Theodore Märklin, was born in Göppingen, Germany in 1817 and died in 1866. The firm traded as Gebrüder Märklin from 1888, when his two sons took command of the business, which had been run by his wife after his death. From 1892 to 1907 it traded as Gebrüder Märklin & Co and from 1907 to the present as Gebrüder Märklin & Cie. In 1891, the firm produced the first tinplate sectional track, to be followed in 1892 by their figure-eight layout, which caused a sensation. They were producing good quality model trains propelled by both steam and electricity before 1900, and were the first to use a numerical system of gauges. Their

Above, left: **An advertisement from** *The Toy Trader* **of January 1909, showing the variety of metal toys produced by Märklin, including an English 'GNR' locomotive.**
Right: **An LNWR model train made by Märklin and bearing the firm's initials 'GM' on the front of the engine. It also carries a label which reads 'Gamage's, Holborn. Made in Germany'. Ipswich Museums.**

Above: **The 'Black Prince',
a gauge 2 live steam locomotive made by Ernst
Plank.** *Circa* **1903. E.
Hoffmann Collection.
Reproduced by courtesy of
New Cavendish Books.**
Right: **Scarcely qualifying
for the title of 'model train'
is this Penny Toy in fine
original condition bearing
the trade mark of C.
Rossignol on its box.** *Circa*
**1895; length 7 inches.
Author's Collection.**

1891 catalogue included floor-runners on high wheels with some figures in the carriages. Some of their scenic settings, with a train running in a circle around a pond or under a castle are extremely effective, but they are now almost impossible to find. They were offering at this time a very good selection of floor-runners including some with wood-carrying wagons. In 1895, their railway stations were of an excellent standard and there were also line-keeper's houses, tipper trucks and some quite complex landscape settings that were sold complete with the trains. The products of this period are particularly interesting, as the carriages and locomotives were still hand painted. In the early 1900s, it was felt necessary to produce more accurate models, but flights of fancy were still occasionally indulged, such as the superb model of Stephenson's Rocket made for live steam in 1903, which is thought to be the only model of this famous train made by the early manufacturers. Another interesting model was that made in 1935 to commemorate the centenary of the Nurem-

berg–Fürth railway, an accurate reproduction which included seated figures. By 1959 the firm employed some 2,000 staff.

Merriam Manufacturing Co – Durham, Connecticut, USA. Produced tin trackless push-alongs in the late 1830s.

Newton & Co – London. This firm of instrument makers produced some of the best models of the 1870s. The models are of brass and made in very accurate detail.

Plank, Ernst – Nuremberg. Another instrument-making company, founded in 1866. In 1882 Plank showed an electric railway at the Bavarian Trades exhibition. The firm produced a large number of steam locomotives in the 1890s and by 1899 was producing some 80,000 steam engines, locomotives and ships each year. The brass locomotives were mainly of the 0-2-2 oscillating cylinder type, and the wheels had very large flanges. After the First World War there was a very limited production of trains.

Radiguet, M. – Paris. Produced steam engines from 1872 as well as parts for home workshop manufacture. It is thought that they first made steam trains in the 1880s. In 1889 Radiguet formed a partnership with a man named Massiot. This firm supplied parts and even some complete trains to British companies.

Rossignol, C. – Paris. This firm was in existence by 1890 and producing carpet-runners before the First World War. Around 1914, gauge 0 trains with rails were produced and by 1919 electric trains had appeared.

Stephens' Model Dockyard – Founded in 1843 in London, until 1912 this firm was producing brass locomotives in at least eighteen designs that became larger and increasingly complex. A few of their trains made in the 1880s had mahogany tracks, and the construction of some of their early models is both heavy and somewhat primitive.

Trix – Nuremberg. Stefan Bing established this firm around 1927 with two partners. At first producing constructional toys, they showed the Trix Express at the Leipzig Fair in 1935. After the Second World War Trix operated from Northampton, England, but eventually passed out of the control of the Bing family.

German tin toys

The life of the German tin toy industry, which reached its peak between 1890 and 1910, was of fairly short duration in comparison with, for instance, the production of wooden toys. As Nuremberg was a traditional centre of the toy industry with trading channels already established, the new techniques also became centred on this town, and its skilled workers of both sexes were quickly harnessed to the production of colourfully decorated boats, horse-drawn transport and fairground scenes. Metal toys were made in the area by firms such as Hilpert from 1775, but it was the improvements made in punching and pressing machines together with cheaper methods of applying colour that led to the great general interest in toy making of this type at the end of the 19th century.

Toy kitchenware was made in the middle years of the century by firms such as Bing and Märklin, who began by manufacturing simple pressed toys of this type but gradually moved into the creation of the most extravagant of models. The success of the German makers lay both in the strength and durability of their toys and in their willingness to manufacture items specifically for sale in particular countries. They would not only print different names on boats and fire stations but also make vehicles in imitation of full-sized models just introduced into various countries. One third of the entire German tin toy production after 1900 was exported to America and that country's new models were quickly copied. It was also possible, despite the cost of shipping, for the Germans to undercut other toys in price because of their skill in manufacturing and the low wages demanded by their workers.

The range of toys produced was vast and though the largest factories often marked their work, there were many small firms employing only a few members of one family whose products are completely unidentifiable. The tin toy industry differed from the traditional German pattern in that very few outworkers were used and in general the toys were made in factories, between which there was considerable competition. New models were carefully guarded and admission to the premises refused until the new car or boat was revealed at the next trade fair.

Before 1900 the majority of toys were hand enamelled and even after the introduction of photolithography in 1895, it was some time before the technique was in general factory use. A journalist visiting one of the larger factories in 1907 does not mention the process, and this suggests that the tinmen were slower to adopt new ideas than we now think. Despite the availability of pressing machines in the 1890s, many toys continued to be hand made, though sometimes with machine-pressed additions. They were decorated either by the use of stencils, spray or painting, while the men who lined the toys were considered among the most skilled workers. Many collectors prefer the earlier methods of construction and decoration

Fairground amusements made apt subjects for tin toys in the period before the appearance of the motor car. *Right:* **A set of swing-boats from a German-made fairground setting for which pieces could be purchased separately.** *Far right:* **An unmarked German tin toy representing a roundabout.** *Facing page:* **A highly decorative German tin toy representing a ferris wheel. All late 19th century. Bethnal Green Museum of Childhood, London.**

and enjoy, in their acquisitions, tracing the development of the industry from simple hand-made pieces to the sophistication of the mass produced toys of the early 1920s. Any examples marked by the great firms, such as Bing or Märklin, are obviously popular, but fortunately much of a toy's worth still depends upon the workmanship, quality and general decoration of a piece. It was once felt that as the better tin became more expensive collectors would diversify into the more recent examples, but while this has happened to some extent in named pieces the general trend is not in this direction and it is obvious that even the very new collectors wish to acquire those pieces made when the German toymakers were at the peak of their success and popularity.

Top: **A baker's cart driven by a flywheel mechanism. Welsh Folk Museum, Cardiff.** *Centre:* **A pair of cars dating from 1925–1930. One is painted red, the other purple. Luton Museum and Art Gallery, Bedfordshire.** *Bottom:* **A pair of German-made tricars dating from the early 20th century. One is marked 'Ruck-Ruck' and has a clockwork mechanism and reversing action. The other is named 'Beatrix' and has a barrel spring. Both are lithographed tinplate and were made by the firm of Walter Stock of Solingen, which operated from about 1906 to the 1930s. Tolson Memorial Museum, Huddersfield.**

This open car with a driver
and two officers was made
by Gebrüder Bing around
1900. The general construction is much lighter than is
usually associated with
early Bing products.
Germanisches National-
museum, Nuremberg.

GERMAN TIN TOY MAKERS

Adam, Richard and Carl–Königsberg, East
Prussia. The trademark of a girl standing on a
globe was used from 1894. The firm made light,
colourfully printed toys such as beetles, thought
similar to those made by Lehmann (see below).

Arnold, Karl – Nuremberg, founded 1906. At
first made mainly boats and light novelty toys.
Ceased production during last war but later became one of the most successful producers.

Bing, Gebrüder – Founded by Ignaz and Adolf
Bing in 1863 or 1865 (the family claim 1865 to be
the actual date, though German sources give
1863). Ignaz had worked as a traveller in tinware
and, being aware of the market, set up a factory
with his brother in Karolinenstrasse, Nuremberg,
the firm at first being known as Nürnberger
Spielwarenfabrik, Gebrüder Bing. Within two
years one hundred workers were employed, as
well as 120 piece workers. Other finishing shops
were opened in the 1890s and a factory for the
manufacture of enamelled toys at Grünhain in
Saxony. Warehouses and administrative buildings
were firmly centralised in Nuremberg and it was
on this centralisation that the firm's success depended. In 1895, it was made into a limited company and known as Nürnberger Metall- und
Lackierwarenfabrik vorm Bing AG. Ignaz Bing
was now chairman, as differences had arisen
between Ignaz and Adolf in 1883 and their partnership had been modified. By 1908, some four
thousand men were employed on permanent
work. The firm won high honours at exhibitions
in Barcelona (1888), Chicago (1893) and Paris

(1900). Boats of all kinds including submarines,
key-wound figures and tableaux, fire stations, cars
and steamrollers were among the products of this
prolific firm. During the First World War, the
company helped in the war effort but a large
number of subsidiary companies continued to be
added. In 1917, a distribution company known as
Concentra was set up to market the whole range of
products under their various brand names. Tin
toys were still marked 'G.B.N.', standing for
Gebrüder Bing, Nürnberg, but after 1919 this
was changed to 'B.W.' for Bing Werke. Ignaz
Bing died in 1918 and in 1919 Stefan Bing became Director General. Because of differences
with the supervisory board, he severed all family
connexions in 1927. The firm encountered more
difficulties after this because of the downturn in
the world economy and less effective centralisation, and it was put into receivership in 1932. The
concern was split up, the ship department being
taken over by Fleischmann.

A brightly lithographed
car made under the brand
name of Bing Werke.
Circa **1925. Bethnal Green
Museum of Childhood,
London.**

Bub, Karl – Founded in Nuremberg in 1851. Made lacquered tinplate toys, some with clockwork mechanisms. In the 1880s the firm had offices at Tetzelgasse, Nuremberg. They made pieces in common with Carette and continued to sell them after the latter's collapse in 1917. A large number of cars and trains were made in the 1920s. The firm closed in the 1960s.

Carette, Georges – Nuremberg. Carette was the son of a Parisian photographer, who was a friend of a Nuremberg hop merchant. This family set him up in business in 1886 under the name of Georges Carette & Cie. Another backer was the firm of Bing, though there was some rivalry between the two. The early toys were mainly of brass and tin, with hand-enamelled finish. Little is known about these early products. Around 1897 to 1898 Paul Josephstal became a partner and worked with Bassett-Lowke until the First World War. Carette's 1911 catalogue shows a rather more solemn type of toy than those produced by the other firms, though the quality of surviving examples is usually good. Georges Carette retained his French citizenship and returned to Paris after 1914. The firm's production ceased in 1917.

Distler, Johann – Nuremberg. At the end of the 19th century this firm was making penny toys, some marked with a thistle, others with the monogram 'J.D.'. Later the firm used a globe trademark. Premises were originally at No 7. Leinhardstrasse. They were eventually taken over by the firm of Trix.

Doll & Cie – Nuremberg. Founded in 1898 by J. Sandheim and a tinman, Peter Doll, to make steam engines. Max Bein joined the firm in January 1911 and after this time clockwork toys were also made. Many steam engines were made in the 1920s and 1930s, and the company was taken over by Fleischmann in the late 1930s. The Doll name was, however, used until after the Second World War. The firm is remembered in particular for its gaily decorated toys with lavish use of cut and pierced decoration in the early years of the century. Some 250 people were employed by the firm in the year 1938.

Eberl, Hans – Nuremberg. Made some well finished toys in the early 20th century.

Einfalt, Gebrüder – Nuremberg. The firm was founded in 1922 and after 1935 used 'Technofix' as its trade-mark.

Above: **An interesting boat probably made by Fleischmann in the mid 1920s, which features a water circulating engine heated by a methylated spirit burner. Length approximately $11\frac{3}{4}$ inches. David Pressland Collection.** *Left:* **Four of the eleven different 'Bremen' type liners sold by Fleischmann in 1936. The examples shown have a length of $7\frac{1}{2}$, $8\frac{1}{2}$, $11\frac{3}{4}$ and 13 inches respectively. They were made again in the 1950s. Alan Whitehead Collection. Reproduced by courtesy of New Cavendish Books.** *Below:* **A clockwork tinplate car made by Hans Eberl of Nuremberg around 1910. Note the original bevelled glass in the windows. Length 11 inches. David Pressland Collection.**

Fischer, H. & Co – Nuremberg. Began production in 1908 when a fish trademark was used. It is thought that a figure in armour might also be a trademark of this firm. One of their best known products especially in America is the 'Toonerville Trolley' copyrighted in 1922. Marked pieces made by Fischer are not common and items are sometimes attributed to this firm because of similarities to marked pieces.

Fleischmann, Gebrüder – Nuremberg, founded in 1887. Little is known of the firm's early products, but they later specialised in magnetic floating toys and tinplate ships. In 1928 the firm of Staudt was taken over and after this time other types of mechanical toys were made. Fleischmann made a wide range of boats in the 1930s, many of which are similar in details to the work of Carette. Later they took over the firm of Doll. They are still in existence today.

Right: **An attractive floor toy made for the American market by Mathias Hess of Nuremberg.** *Circa* **1908; length 10¼ inches. David Pressland Collection.**
Below: **An advertisement for the Bavarian firm of J. J. Landmann, from** *The Toy and Fancy Goods Trader* **of February 1910.**

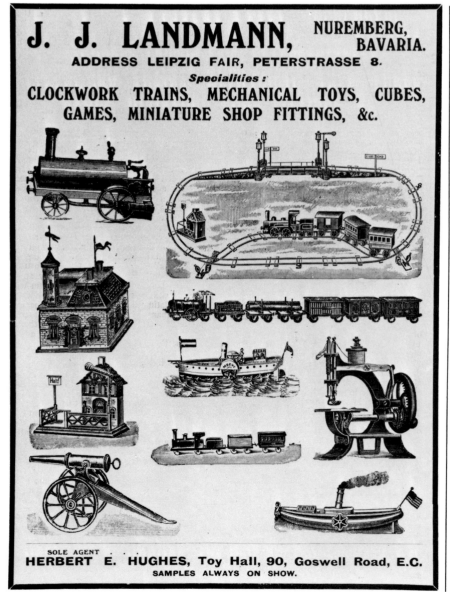

Greppert & Kelch – Brandenberg, Germany. Made toys, particularly in the 1920s, that are similar in mood to those made by Lehmann (see below), though the finish was not as good and the decoration not as skilled.

Gunthermann – Nuremberg. Founded by S. Gunthermann, the firm was mentioned in directories in 1880, when it was established at 32 Tetzelgasse. By 1901 some 250 people were employed. S. Gunthermann is sometimes considered as the pioneer of the Nuremberg tinplate clockwork toy manufacturers. He died in 1890 and his widow then married the firm's manager, Adolf Weigel, whose initials were included in the firm's trademark until 1919 when he died. After this the mark 'S.G.' was used again. The firm made the typical Nuremberg range of toys including horse-drawn vehicles, fire engines, a well known series of Gordon Bennett racing cars and aeroplanes. Production of good tinplate models has continued to the present. The company was taken over by Siemens in 1965.

Hausser – Neustadt, Germany. The firm was founded in 1904 and is perhaps best known for the composition figures sold under the trade name of Elastolin. Figures of this substance were sold to other tin-toy makers for inclusion in their models. Being a native company, they flourished during the 1930s when the Jewish owned companies were unpopular. A large number of accurate tinplate military vehicles were made in this period. Work ceased in 1942 but their toys were again on the market by 1946. Tin-toy production had almost ceased by 1957 but the company continued to produce a wide range of wooden toys.

Hess, Mathias – Nuremberg. This firm was one of the oldest of the Nuremberg toy makers, founded around 1825. Mathias's son, John Leonard Hess, took over the company in 1886. Early toys are rare, though they are known to have made trackless floor trains in the middle years of the century. The decoration of their toys remained consistently good, though different techniques were obviously used. Perhaps their best known products were the 'Hessmobiles' which were propelled through reduction gears by a flywheel. Before the First World War they made Dreadnoughts worked by clockwork that rolled along on wheels. Production ceased in the early 1930s.

Issmayer, Johann Emanuel – Nuremberg. Made pressed metal toys in the 1830s.

Issmayer, Johann Andreas – Nuremberg. The son of Johann Emanuel Issmayer, Johann Andreas had worked in his father's business as a traveller and at the factory itself. In 1861 he founded his own business at 20 Peterstrasse in Nuremberg to make toy kitchenware and magnetic floating toys. He is thought to have been the first Nuremberg toymaker to produce working tinplate figures. Comparatively few of this firm's clockwork toys are known, as their main production was of trains, but they made amusing tins in the form of toys in the early 20th century and charmingly decorated clockwork pieces in the late 19th century. Issmayer died in 1922 and the firm was then taken over by his son-in-law. The last entry for the firm is in the 1932 Nuremberg Commercial Directory.

Lehmann, Ernst Paul – Brandenburg, founded in 1881. This firm originally made tins and containers, but are particularly known to collectors for their bright and whimsical toys which were originally supplied with flywheel mechanisms. Later, identical models were sometimes sold fitted with clockwork motors. The colourful effect of their toys depended heavily on the lithographed decoration, though a few toys made before the First World War were hand-coloured. Their toys are very fully marked with even the patent specifications in many cases. In 1921 Johann Richter, a cousin of the founder, became a partner as he had studied production methods in other countries, and was prolific in new ideas. He remained in charge of the firm after the death of the founder in 1934. In the year when he had become a partner, the firm had some 800 workers.

The toys of Ernst Paul Lehmann relied heavily for their effect on the lithographed decoration, and this is illustrated in the models shown here. *Above:* A flywheel-driven Lehmann delivery man with his cart. *Circa* 1912. Ipswich Museums. *Left:* A clockwork tinplate car by the same manufacturer. *Circa* 1910. *Below:* An unmarked tinplate hansom cab. *Circa* 1910. Both Bethnal Green Museum of Childhood, London.

A pair of Lehmann tin toys with their original boxes. The box on the right bears the legend 'Baker and Sweep, or Good fighting Darkness', and the Lehmann trademark is clearly visible on the body of the tricycle illustrated on the box. The 'New Century Cycle' is 5 inches long. By courtesy of Christie's South Kensington, London. *Below:* A typical German-made tinplate car of the 1920s, made by Georg Levy. *Circa* 1928; length 6½ inches. From The Collector, Lavender Hill, London.

In 1949 the factory was sequestered by the Russians. Johann Richter fled to West Germany and by May 1951 he had begun to re-establish the firm near Nuremberg. He died in 1956 but by this time had managed to set the firm again on a successful road. It is now run by the third generation and still makes good metal toys.

Levy, Georg–Nuremberg, *circa* 1920 to 1934. Levy had been a partner in the Nuremberg firm of H. Kienberger and sold a number of the latter's products when he set up on his own.

Lineol–Brandenberg. Founded around 1906 by Oskar Wiederholz, the company flourished in the 1930s, when many military vehicles with com-

position figures were made which are highly effective because of their accuracy. Earlier, they had made horse-drawn military toys. The war caused a halt in production around 1942 but work was recommenced in East Germany afterwards.

Lutz, Ludwig–Established *circa* 1846 in Ellwangen an der Jagst. Specialised at first in decorative tin such as grave decorations but later went over entirely to the manufacture of toys, concentrating mainly on transport vehicles and doll's house furniture. Some soldiers were also made. In 1883 his son, August, took over the firm and expanded it, employing twenty-five full-time workers. August had learned improved techniques for printing on metal in Paris, and ships and trains that ran on rails were now made with either clockwork or steam power. The firm exported most of its wares and towards this end exhibited each year at the Leipzig fair. Lutz products were marketed by Bing under their own name. In 1891 Märklin also marketed Lutz toys, which although dated were highly popular because of their fine enamelling. Märklin purchased the firm in the same year and took over all the Lutz equipment, stock and registered designs. Dr Christian Vaeterlein suggests that the clockwork trains on rails that Märklin showed for the first time at the 1891 Leipzig Fair were actually the work of Lutz. He also comments that he has never discovered a marked example of the firm's work.

Märklin – Goppingen, Germany. Founded by Theodor Friedrich Wilhelm and Caroline Märklin in 1859. Märklin, a tinmaker, had gone to Göppingen in 1840 and the firm at first made tin kitchenware. Initially there were difficulties, despite Caroline Märklin's skill as a travelling sales representative, and despite her struggles to keep the firm together after the death of her husband in 1866. It was not until her two sons took over the company that rapid improvements were made. It became known as Märklin Brothers in 1888.

E. Fritz joined the firm as a joint proprietor in 1892, when the name was changed to Gebrüder Märklin and Co, which was retained until 1907. From that date to the present time the firm's name has been Gebrüder Märklin & Cie, a change of name that seems to have taken place while the 1907 catalogue was in preparation, as it appears in this in the two forms. Just before the First World War there were some 600 employees. Their reprinted catalogues indicate the wide range of toys made from 1895, including working fountains

Among the most impressive and elaborate tin toys are those made by the firm of Märklin. Here a large Märklin steam electricity generating plant dating from 1909 is being used to drive the 'Aeropal', a Märklin fairground toy from the same period. Base of generator 15 inches square; height of 'Aeropal' 18 inches. *Below left:* 'Chicago', a live steam Märklin battleship of 1904 destined for the American market. Note the wealth of detail which went into the more expensive toy boats at this period. Length 28¼ inches. All David Pressland Collection.

Above: **A Märklin closed coupe of around 1900 featuring beautiful quality paintwork, a detailed horse, plaster coachman and elegant carriage lamps. Overall length 18½ inches.** *Facing page, centre:* **Probably also by Märklin is this hansom cab which was bought new in 1875. The tin pressings used to make the horse are of particularly high quality. Overall length 17 inches. Both David Pressland Collection.**

and windmills. Their toys are associated with high quality and are always good acquisitions. During the First World War the firm was awarded the German rights of the British Hornby Meccano sets. Fritz Märklin, who had watched mass-production methods in the United States, went into the firm in 1923. The number of workers had risen to 900 by 1929. During the Second World War, munitions were made but toy production was afterwards resumed and by 1959 there were over 2,000 workers. The last of the Märklin family died in 1961, but the firm is still very active. The work produced by Märklin was always of the highest quality, and any marked pieces are of great interest to collectors.

Meier, J. Ph. – Nuremberg. Known for penny toys, sometimes with the dog cart trademark that was registered in 1894.

Moko – Trade mark used by Moses Kohnstam, who was established in Fürth in 1875 as a distributor of toys. By 1894 Kohnstam had offices in Milan, Brussels and London. In 1914, the London end was appropriated by the government, but after the war it was re-established as J. Kohnstam Limited.

Muller & Kadeder – Nuremberg. A firm that was mainly active between 1900 and 1912. They made clockwork toys which are not marked.

Above and facing page: **Two clockwork driven Märklin liners. On the left is a model from the mid 1920s which was bought in Dresden in the 1920s for an American schoolboy. Note the hand-painted tinplate flags and the radio antennae between the masts. Length 26¾ inches. The second model is the 'Carmania', dating from 1906. Length 29½ inches.** *Bottom:* **A penny toy in the form of a car made between 1900 and 1914 by J. Ph. Meier of Nuremberg. Length approximately 3½ inches. All David Pressland Collection. The 'Oder' liner reproduced by courtesy of New Cavendish Books.**

Top and centre: **Other penny toys made by J. Ph. Meier include this battleship belching smoke and two gnomes sawing.** *Circa* **1900–1914; length approximately 3½ inches. Both David Pressland Collection.** *Bottom:* **A vertical steam engine made by Ernst Plank of Nuremberg with a plate giving its name, the 'Noris'. Made of antimony alloy and brass.** *Circa* **1895; height 5¾ inches. Tolson Memorial Museum, Huddersfield.**

Plank, Ernst – Nuremberg. Founded in 1866, Plank at first specialised in stationary engines and magic lanterns. Around 1900 trains, boats, etc began to be made in some numbers. In 1894 there were some 120 workers. Their first car is thought to have appeared in 1904 and was steam driven. The production of tin toys ceased in the 1930s.

Rock und Graner – Biberach an der Riss. Founded in 1813 and now considered to be the oldest Württemberg firm to manufacture enamelled sheet metal toys. Over a hundred people were being employed by 1837. In 1851 the firm won a Gold medal at the Great Exhibition in London.

Their entry included doll's house furniture, horse-drawn transport and Christmas cribs and castles – all of course made of tin. The boom years of the firm were between 1850 and 1870 and a decline then set in so that by 1900 there were only thirty-six employees. Clockwork trains and their accessories were added to their products between 1896 and 1900 and sold under the trade name of R & GN. The firm was liquidated in 1904. Dr Christian Vaeterlein thinks it probable that Märklin took over the tools and patents of this company, as there are distinct similarities between pages in the catalogues of the two companies.

Schoenner, Jean – Nuremberg, founded in 1875. Made steam engines and magic lanterns. From around 1900 steam boats and fire engines were also made. There are no known toys after 1906.

Schuco – Germany. This firm was founded in 1912 by a Herr Schreyer and Heinrich Muller. The first toys were clockwork animals and some of these were wound by turning an arm instead of a key. In the 1920s and 1930s, products included a Dancing Mouse, a Trotting Dog wearing a cape, a 'Pick Pick' bird of brilliant plumage, a comical clockwork mouse and a 'Turn Back' car which would never fall off a table. Schuco sports cars were cleverly constructed and their 'Steerable Driving School Car' had a starting crank, changeable tyres, differential gears and rack and pinion steering. Each car was supplied with a miniature tool kit. The firm is still in production.

individual until the 1930s, when some fine model cars were produced. Some of these were constructed on a very large scale and are usually marked on the bonnet. Tipp's Mercedes military cars are particularly effective, as they are often peopled with composition figures of recognisable characters such as the Führer himself. The military vehicles which were also produced in quantity at this time have similar composition figures. Ullmann himself had been forced to flee to England in 1933. The production of tin toys continued until the firm closed in 1971. The cars made in the 1950s were of particularly good quality.

Above: **The Schuco Studio 'Steerable Driving School Car', loosely based on a Mercedes racing car, with a couple of advertising leaflets. Author's Collection.** *Below:* **A single-engined monoplane by Tipp & Co.** *Circa* **1936; wingspan 12½ inches. Tony Gross Collection. Reproduced by courtesy of New Cavendish Books.**

Striebel – Biberach. Working *circa* 1840 to 1860. Manufactured tin toys and trinkets, including a model of the French Emperor's grave.

Tipp & Co – Nuremberg. Founded in 1912 by a Miss Tipp and a Mr Carstens. Miss Tipp was succeeded the next year by Phillip Ullmann and by 1919 he was the sole proprietor. The typical Nuremberg range of tin was at first made and the firm's work does not stand out as particularly

French metal toys

The French metal toy industry differed from the German, in that the makers were prepared to cater for both the richest and the poorest children. Whereas German toys exhibit a fairly even quality, the French products range from the most trumpery to other pieces as fine and expensive as the Rolls Royce and Hispano Suiza made in 1930 by JEP. These cars were made from the best quality sheet metal, provided with a clockwork motor with both forward and reverse movement, a working steering wheel and even 'Dunlop Cord' tyred wheels actually made of rubber. These two cars were extremely expensive and yet were made at a time when other manufacturers were searching for more economical models to put on the market.

Several of the French toy firms were established in the mid 19th century, but there are also scores of small single-roomed factories, whose names are unrecorded, which produced the cheapest of toys from waste material. One example is a French toy car of around 1905 that was found to have been made from the remains of a Tate & Lyle syrup tin, and this re-using of scrap metal was a characteristic of the work of the back-street firms. The toys they made were of the simple two- or three-section penny toy type and were usually sold to retailers by the assorted boxful. As they were so fragile, they are now very difficult to find in good condition.

Many French toys also exhibit considerable ingenuity of construction, such as those made by Fernand Martin to represent the figures and occupational characters he saw every day in the streets

A particularly finely constructed carriage and pair which was probably made in France around 1865. As the horses move along, their heads nod. Length 12 inches. Luton Museum and Art Gallery, Bedfordshire.

of Paris. These figures are amusing and almost ephemeral in character and probably represent the French toy scene in the eyes of collectors to a far greater extent than the often soberly accurate road vehicles made by firms such as Citroën, who supplied rack and pinion steering controlled by the steering wheel on all their cars. The German toymakers produced their wares in much greater number than the French and also put much more effort into exporting, so that whereas the bulk of German products were going to America and Britain by 1900 and can still be found in those countries in some quantity, the French seem to have concentrated more on the Continental home market and examples are much more difficult for the collector to locate.

Left: **This attractive and highly decorative tin toy representing Britannia is probably of French origin. Items such as this which use a bisque-headed figure fall very much on the borderline between tin toys and automata.** *Circa* **1875–85; height 6 inches. Betty Harvey-Jones Collection.** *Below:* **'Les Pompiers', a French fire-fighting set with a steam-operated fire pump, wheeled escape ladder and metal crew. The set has a painted finish.** *Circa* **1900; length of engine 7½ inches. Tolson Memorial Museum, Huddersfield.**

MAIN FRENCH PRODUCERS OF METAL TOYS

Bonnet et Cie – Paris. This firm took over Fernand Martin around 1919 and continued to produce some of his toys, though they were now also marked 'V.B. et Cie'.

CIJ (Compagnie Industrielle du Jouet) – Paris. A firm that manufactured good quality detailed cars, including an Alfa Romeo P2 that was introduced in 1925 with wheel-operated steering and a fine clockwork motor. Four different versions of this car were made by CIJ.

Citroën, André – Model cars were first made in 1923 as promotional aids. Some cars had lights, others opening doors and windows and every effort was made to create the models as accurately as possible. The early models have sheet metal wheels, but these were later substituted with rubber. Many of the cars are marked with a stencilled trade mark. After 1936, Jouets Citroën were not produced by Citroën itself but constructed by CIJ and later by JRD. An extremely large number of different models were made. The last models to carry the Jouets Citroën mark were 'Petit Rosalie' and 'Rosalie V', both made in 1935 to the design of cars first introduced in 1933.

JEP – Paris. This firm changed its name several times. The name Jouets de Paris or J de P was used from 1928. The early toys are not particularly interesting, but a new and better range was introduced when the name was changed, possibly in an attempt to compete with the much more accurate toys that Citroën were producing. These well made cars are popular with collectors, as their size is impressive and they have great realism. Unlike the Citroëns, they were made only with

A splendid example of a French miniature car – the P2 Alfa Romeo introduced by the Parisian firm of CIJ in 1925. The tyres with shaped tread identify this example as one of the second series. It has been repainted in silver. Length 21 inches. Owned by Michael Ellis. *Below:* 'La Sirène', an elegant late 19th century French clockwork paddle steamer, probably attributable to Maltête et Parent of Paris. Length 29½ inches. David Pressland Collection.

painted doors and they were not fitted with lights. There were often only very superficial differences between the various model cars. Some very large scale racing cars with steering were produced around 1930. This year also saw the production of two of their finest cars, the Rolls Royce and the Hispano Suiza, and though there was some economy in the fact that the two cars shared the same chassis, body and wheels, they are by any standard excellent models. Around 1932 the firm's name was again changed to Jouets en Paris (JEP) and two of the finest later products were a 40 hp Renault and a Talbot Lago 6 Coupé de Ville, with distinctive features, such as a bonnet that opened to show the engine, lights and opening side doors. Both of these models were introduced in 1936. The firm ceased production in 1965.

Maltête, C.H., & Parent, G. – 19 Rue Debelleyme, Paris. A firm that made a wide range of mechanical toys including sculling boats, submarines, paddle boats, railways and various amusing fish and lizards etc.

Martin, Fernand – Paris. One of the best known French producers, Martin was born in Amiens and experimented with mechanical toys from an early age. By 1876 he was selling his ideas to various manufacturers and beginning to make toys himself. His own factory in Paris was founded in 1878 and it is recorded that he made as many as 800,000 mechanical toys in a year. Medals were won at Barcelona (1886), Paris (1900), Milan (1906) and Brussels (1910). In 1880, some two hundred people were employed in the factory on the Boulevard Menilmont. Martin was a member of the Jury of the Antwerp Hors Concours in 1894 after serving on the Paris Concours for two years and he was also president of the French toy industry. A collection of the toys he had created over thirty years was given by him to the Conservatoire des Arts et Métiers in 1909. This collection is invaluable, as it gives a clear picture of the range of the toys produced, from simple elastic band driven mechanical fish in 1878 to his first clockwork toy, 'Le Moulin mécanique à tic tac', produced in 1883. As late as 1908, elastic bands were still used by the firm for driving simple models. Among Martin's toys was a red-nosed drunkard, and a Dutch servant girl trying to carry a precarious pile of crockery. The bodies of the figures were stamped from metal and supplied with wire limbs, though the feet were weighted for balance. In 1912 the firm was taken over by Bonnet et Cie.

'L'Intrépide Jockey', a tin
toy with a fabric costume
made by Fernand Martin
of Paris. *Circa* 1911. By
courtesy of Phillips, New
Bond Street, London.

Facing page, top: **'L'Auto-
patte'**, a fabric-costumed
tin toy made by Fernand
Martin with its original
box lid. *Circa* 1909. By
courtesy of Phillips, New
Bond Street, London.
Bottom: Also by Fernand
Martin is this very clearly
marked toy, the 'Maréchal
Ferrand' forge. Width 6
inches. By courtesy of
Christie's South Kensing-
ton, London.

Above: **This model of a long
distance van was made in
the 1930s by the firm of
Charles Rossignol, whose
initials appear on the side.
It is one of a number of
different van models which
were copied from contem-
porary Peugeots. Length
19½ inches. Reproduced by
courtesy of New Cavendish
Books.** *Right:* **Also by
Rossignol is this Paris bus,
dating from around 1938.
Length 8½ inches. From
The Collector, Lavender
Hill, London.**

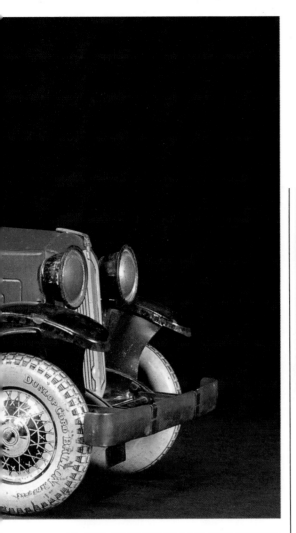

Radiguet, M. – Paris, established 1872. In 1889 Radiguet formed a partnership with Massiot. They made instruments and also good ship models with a great deal of detail in brass. The boats were precision made and steam powered with hulls of zinc and decks of polished wood. No toys are recorded after 1902.

Rossignol, Charles – Paris. Founded in 1868, the firm ceased production in 1962. The factory was at the Rue de Chemin Vert and the firm's name is often found, for instance, on the wheels of cars. Floor trains, motor cars, animals, singing birds, steam boats and even penny toys were produced. The firm is reputed to have made model cars before the Germans, and in 1880 an interesting experimental steam-driven tram was made. Their first known toy car, a model of the Renault taxi, the 'Taxi de la Marne', was made in 1905 and this was produced in both saloon and *voiture utilitaire* versions. Between 1923 and 1929 a series of Paris buses, with their routes painted on the sides, were made. Vans which were copies of Latil and Peugeot 201 motors were made in the 1930s, and these sometimes had opening roofs so that they could be used as cannisters. Large scale racing cars and other big models were produced between 1932 and 1938, many of which were supplied with battery-operated lights.

SIF (Societe Industrielle de Ferblanterie) – Founded in 1899. A forerunner of JEP.

Another Rossignol model, an attractive late 1930s racing car, loosely modelled on a Peugeot. Length 15 inches. Tony Gross Collection. Reproduced by courtesy of New Cavendish Books.

American metal toys

American children in the 18th and early 19th centuries relied for their toys upon imports from Europe, and it was only after the Civil War that they were produced on a really large scale in Connecticut, New York and Philadelphia in particular. There was, however, some manufacture of tinware and pewter even in the late 18th century and the industry is of great importance, as it is the oldest traceable sphere of the toy trade in that country. The early pieces were, in the main, produced by small tinsmiths for local use and the surviving examples are not always easy to identify, as the immigrant craftsmen often worked in the traditional methods of their original countries. The New England toys, in the form of simple pails, teapots and jugs with gaudily painted flower decoration are in themselves very reminiscent of the British barge ware made at about the same time in full size. Louis H. Hertz suggests that an extensive tin toy factory was operating in Philadelphia by 1838 and certainly a number of model kitchens with simple straight sides and very basic equipment are thought to date from this period.

The great development of the tin toy industry really began in the 1840s, and is thought possibly to have been a sideline of the great tinplate manufacturing concerns, though the traditional belief that scrap metal was used for toys is now largely discredited. Turner's of Meriden, Connecticut, were among the pioneer companies of this period. Cast iron was also used on a large scale in American toy production from the 1870s, though the peak of this particular manufacture was reached in the 1880s. These cast iron toys are very much a peculiarity of the American trade and were not made on any comparable scale in Europe. The indigenous tin toys are also somewhat unusual, in that their decoration differed considerably from that used in Europe. The toys were painted, often with a rather thin paint which age has caused to chip away, and then finished by stencilled lining and lettering. This charmingly primitive method of decoration gives toys made as late as the 1890s a curiously ancient appearance, which is most attractive.

The type of toy favoured by American children also differed and wheeled bell toys, often with a figure or animal that moved inside a hoop-like wheel as it ran along, were made in considerable number. Similar toys do appear in European catalogues of the time, but judging by the numbers that have survived, the main export of these was also to the States. River boats in a wide variety of sizes were also highly popular, and differed from

Tin toys invariably reflect contemporary means of transport, and these models were inspired by the vogue for trotting in mid 19th century America. Shown here is an example by the New York firm of Althof Bergmann; *circa* **1870–1890; length 15 inches. Bill Holland Collection. Reproduced by courtesy of New Cavendish Books.**

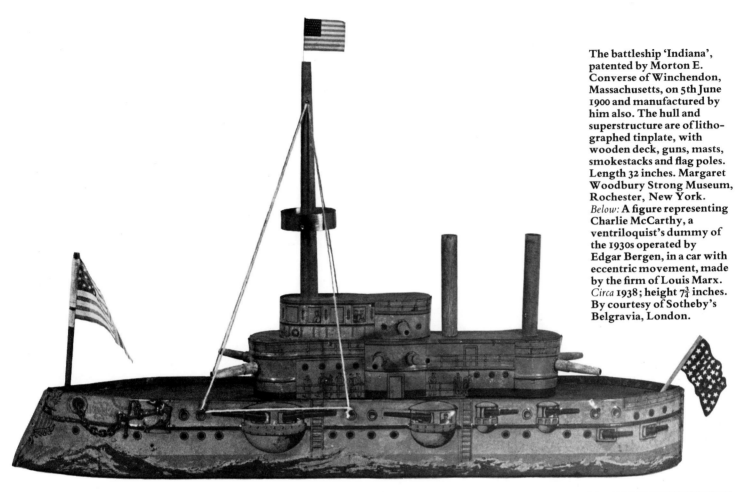

The battleship 'Indiana', patented by Morton E. Converse of Winchendon, Massachusetts, on 5th June 1900 and manufactured by him also. The hull and superstructure are of lithographed tinplate, with wooden deck, guns, masts, smokestacks and flag poles. Length 32 inches. Margaret Woodbury Strong Museum, Rochester, New York.
Below: A figure representing Charlie McCarthy, a ventriloquist's dummy of the 1930s operated by Edgar Bergen, in a car with eccentric movement, made by the firm of Louis Marx. *Circa* 1938; height 7¾ inches. By courtesy of Sotheby's Belgravia, London.

European boats, which were made to float, by being mounted on wheels so they could be pulled along the ground, often with a bell ringing. Toys such as these and simply constructed pull-along trains were the basic products of the firms such as Hull and Stafford, Bergman and Ives, all of which were established during the course of the second half of the 19th century.

Despite the success of firms such as these, it should be remembered that even in 1903 there were less than one hundred American toy manufacturers altogether and even in 1914 approximately one half of the toys played with were still imported from Europe. These figures are mentioned in the American toy trade magazine *Playmates*, which was first published in 1903, and provides a great deal of information regarding the early 20th century toy trade. The development of the industry was again accelerated as a result of the First World War, which seemed to stultify the inventiveness of the European designers, while those in America were more eager to experiment with new ideas. After the war, the German producers generally made good quality but rather conservative toys, while the American trade, aided by the skill of men such as Louis Marx, were

eager to represent in tin current screen idols and cartoon characters that held an immediate appeal for the buyers.

Attribution of unmarked American pieces to particular factories is not easy, as the construction and decorating methods were so similar. The problem is complicated by the fact that the larger firm often supplied parts to other makers. Edith Barenholtz, in her book *The George Brown Toy Sketchbook*, mentions, for instance, that shipments of both large and small horses, and men and women, were made to Stevens & Brown between 1851 and 1861 from a firm called the Union Manufacturing Company.

Because of the decorating methods used by the makers, surviving early American toys inevitably have a degree of scratching and surface damage. But this, combined with the fading and patination of the colours, is not unattractive, and collectors are usually happy to accept it. The iron toys are sometimes found to have lost almost all their original colour, and the collector then has to decide whether to repaint the item or leave it in its natural state. In general, the second solution would seem preferable, though it is advisable to remove any rust.

Right: **'Zip the climbing monkey', a tinplate string toy manufactured by the C. E. Carter Company. Height 8 inches. By courtesy of Christie's South Kensington, London.** *Below:* **One of the toys produced by Morton E. Converse between 1910 to 1920: a horse-drawn 'menagerie' wagon of colourful lithographed tinplate. Converse started business in 1878 and the firm continued in production until the early 1930s. Margaret Woodbury Strong Museum, Rochester, New York.**

MAIN PRODUCERS OF AMERICAN METAL TOYS

Automatic Toy Works – New York. This concern was run by Robert J. Clay. Between 1868 and 1873, he registered five patents for toys including a 'Woman's Rights Advocate', a crawling baby and fur-covered bears. These toys were supplied with moulded composition heads and resemble simple automata. They were eventually added to the Ives range.

Barnum, S. O., & Son – Founded in 1845 in Toledo, Ohio. Makers of metal wheeled toys.

Bergman, Althof – Founded in New York in 1856, this firm was a partnership of the brothers Charles, Louis and Frederick Bergman. The firm at first imported toys but soon manufactured their own. In the 1860s August Bergman and Gustav Cronemayer became partners. The company made floor trains, wheeled bell toys, boats and a variety of horse-drawn transport, especially the trotters that were so popular because of the great national interest in the sport. Their horse-drawn fire engines are particularly liked. These were often made with decoratively shaped wheels and provided with loud bells and highly stylised seated figures.

Boyle, Robert – New York. In 1781 was advertising pewter doll's dishes, plates and platters.

Brown, George W. & Co – Connecticut. In 1856, Brown formed a business with a clockmaker, Chauncery Goodrich, after himself working as a clockmaker's apprentice. It was the most important manufacturer before Ives. The company was one of the earliest in America to provide clockwork mechanisms for its toys. In 1869 Brown amalgamated with J. & E. Stephens to form the Stephens & Brown Manufacturing Company (see below). George W. Brown & Co produced a large number of key-wound items, such as a girl on a velocipede, hooped toys and paddle boats. Toys of a non-mechanical nature were also made, such as street-cars and baker's vans. They produced wagons, fire fighters, small tin toys, and a variety of cheap objects such as whistles. As a catalogue from the period between 1850 and 1870 survives, many pieces are identifiable. One of the more amusing toys is the 'Automatic Waltzer', with its three couples dancing on a platform. Brown apparently lost interest in toymaking after 1880.

Carpenter, Francis W. Harrison – Westchester, New York, 1844 to 1925. Registered patents for toys made of malleable iron. Many were for horse-drawn models and the parts were constructed by the Malleable Iron Works.

Fallows, James – Fallows had worked as a foreman for Francis, Field & Francis before founding his own firm in Philadelphia. He used the trademark IxL (I excel) and the main production was between 1870 and 1880. He made some horse-drawn models as well as Mississippi type river boats with bells and effective cut-out metal decoration of the bodywork.

Francis, Field and Francis – Also known as the Philadelphia Tin Toy Manufacturing Company. Established in 1838. Toys claimed to be 'superior to any imported' were among their japanned tin products. At first they made simple wheeled toys, but later a wide range including doll's-house furniture. They employed a young Englishman, James Fallows as their foreman.

Gong Bell Manufacturing Company – East Hampton, Connecticut. Established in 1866. This firm made a large number of bell toys, such as an 'Elephant Bell Ringer', horses with bells, a charming turtle with a bell mounted on its back and a clown leading a jumping dog.

Hafner, William F. – Made tinplate cars around 1901 with clockwork mechanisms.

Hill, N. N., Brass Company – East Hampton, Connecticut. Another maker of the popular iron bell toys. Included a 'Jonah and the Whale' among their products.

Among the most attractive and specifically American tin toys are hoop toys of the type shown here. This elaborate clockwork balancing figure was made by Althof Bergmann around 1870–80. Height 9¾ inches. Bill Holland Collection. Reproduced by courtesy of New Cavendish Books.

Hull & Stafford – Clinton, Connecticut. This firm may have derived from that of Hull & Wright, which operated from 1866 to the 1880s, though it is also thought possible that the Union Manufacturing Company of Clinton (1854 to 1869) was its predecessor. Made mechanical toys, horses, traps etc. Each toy was made in two halves and tabbed together. The name of the town of Clinton was itself to become mainly associated with the production of tin toys.

Ives, Edward R. – Plymouth, Connecticut. Ives was born in 1839 to parents who had both worked in a clock factory. His father, Riley Ives, ran metal stamping machines at his farm in the late 1850s, and with his son made tinplate thermal or hot air toys in the 1860s. There is a tradition that during the Civil War they stamped uniform buttons. In 1866 Edward Riley married Jennie Blakeslee, while his sister married her brother. In 1870 he moved to Bridgeport, where he established his own factory. In 1872 Joel Blakeslee, his father-in-law, joined the firm, which from this time was known as Ives & Blakeslee. Blakeslee was something of a character and was known as 'Deacon' Blakeslee, a man who himself worked in the factory's decorating room. The firm was highly successful because of Edward Ives' skill in finding new designers and in buying up potentially useful companies. Many of the Ives figures were more in the nature of automata than toys, and were suggested for use as window displays. The clockwork mechanisms were supplied by The New Haven Clock Company and ran long enough to be set up in a shop window. One of the designers Ives employed was Jerome Secor, who made singing birds in cages as well as moving figures such as a banjo player. Arthur Hotchkiss' walking man was also produced by Ives and Blakeslee, though again the figure is one that hovers in intention

between a conventional toy and an automaton, with the head made of composition and the body simply costumed. These men, representing characters such as Benjamin Franklin, Buller, Santa Claus and a 'Heathen Chinee' were worked by a clockwork mechanism and rolled along on wooden rollers under the heavily weighted feet. Among the firm's more conventional toys, produced in considerable number, were fire engines, boats and the usual range of horse-drawn vehicles as well as the trains discussed elsewhere. In the 1880s iron toys were added to the range. Ives and his father-in-law died in 1895 and 1896 respectively, and the firm was continued by Edward Ives and his son Harry despite a fire which burned down the factory in 1900. Ives are one of the most popular firms with collectors, as their work is both interesting and well constructed. Despite their long-standing reputation and success, however, they went bankrupt in the late 1920s like so many other firms and were taken over by Lionel.

Kingsbury, Harry Thayer – Kingsbury became involved in toy making when he bought a factory which made machinery, and in 1895 with the help of his father he purchased the Wilkins Toy Company. He continued to use this name until 1919, after which his own name was used on the toys. A sealed clockwork motor was patented by him in 1902 and this was used for many of the items. A 1930s catalogue shows some effective and elegant cars including a blue cabriolet with orange lining and wheels and a $13\frac{1}{2}$ inch '344 Coupe' with the latest rumble seat. A fire chief's truck and other fire-fighting vehicles were sturdily designed toys, and a breakdown lorry described as a 'Wrecking Car' of a type that appeared in most toy catalogues of the early 1930s was provided with a winding crank. Toys were not made after the Second World War.

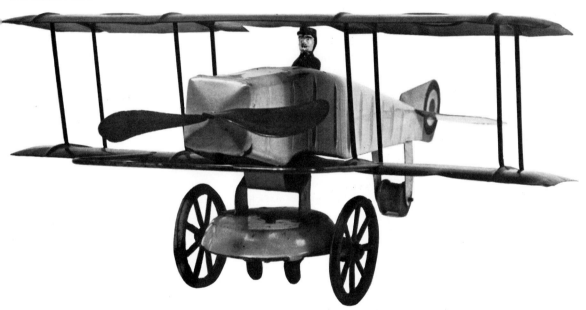

A group of toys manu-
factured by the Wilkins
Toy Co. of Keene, New
Hampshire. The barrel
truck and mail van were
originally horse-drawn
pieces. Around 1910 they
were converted to
automotive toys and a year
later they were fitted with
clockwork motors. The
aircraft was manufactured
in the 1920s. All were made
of stamped sheet metal and
brightly painted.
Established in 1888, the
Wilkins Toy Company
was taken over by Harry T.
Kingsbury in 1895. All
Margaret Woodbury
Strong Museum,
Rochester, New York.
Bottom: A particularly well
constructed tin toy made
by the Ives company and
listed in their 1876
catalogue as a 'Single
Galloper, Large Horse'
with a 'Dressed Boy
Driver'. Length 17 inches.
Holland Collection.

Cheap but lively tin toys were a speciality of the firm of Louis Marx, and a variety of their products is shown here. *Top:* A characterful painted clockwork goose with an articulated neck. 1930s; length 9¾ inches. *Right:* A clockwork milk waggon drawn by a single horse and decorated in very bright colours. 1930s; length 9 inches. *Bottom, left:* 'The Walking Porter', *circa* 1935; height 7¾ inches. *Centre:* The Walt Disney 'Donald Duck Duet'. Pluto dances on the larger drum while Donald Duck bangs the smaller one. *Circa* 1935. *Right:* 'Tidy Tim', *circa* 1935; height 7 inches. *Facing page:* The 'Merrymakers' clockwork mouse orchestra with functioning drummer, fiddler, pianist and conductor. *Circa* 1925; height 9 inches. All by courtesy of Sotheby's Belgravia, London.

Marx, Louis – Born in 1894, Marx ended as a director of the Strauss firm (see below), which he joined as an office boy. He formed a partnership with his brother and eventually took over the most successful lines made by Strauss. He bought several other factories and became a millionaire before he was thirty. He aimed at the lower price market and specialised in amusing but cheap toys, such as the charming 'Mouse Orchestra' and various stage and screen characters. These were sold in the chain stores and in the big mail order catalogues from which so many children ordered their toys in the United States.

Merriam Manufacturing Company – Durham, Connecticut. A firm which produced a range of tin toys between 1856 and 1880.

Patterson, Edward – Between 1730 and 1734, Patterson left Ireland to settle in Berlin, Connecticut, and later returned to his home country to fetch his brothers and sister. He then began with his family to manufacture tinware in Berlin, at first making use of imported tinplate. The firm grew steadily from the initial period when Edward peddled his toys from a basket. Eventually horses and wagons were used for distribution and from these other toys and books were sold. The toys were taken to Canada by Shubael Patterson, who traded with them for furs.

Rooney, T. – Made tin and sheet iron ware at Attleborough, Pennsylvania, and described themselves in the *Bucks County Intelligencer* of 1848 as making 'everything in the tinware line that has ever been thought of'.

Schwarz Toy Store – First opened by Henry Schwarz in 1849, at first chiefly for the sale of imported toys but eventually mainly selling American items. This shop was and is a major supplier of toys in the United States.

Shepard, Sidney – Buffalo. Began to manufacture tin toys in the 1860s.

Stevens & Brown Manufacturing Company – Cromwell, Connecticut. Founded in 1869 as an amalgamation of George Brown and J. E. Stephens, a firm making cast iron toys and money boxes. The company founded a distribution house in New York known as the American Toy Company. Their 1872 price list included a range of tin toys in the form of doll's house furniture.

Stiegel, Henry William – Established an iron foundry in 1758 as well as a glass works at Manheim, Pennsylvania. He produced iron toys during the peak of their popularity.

Strauss, Ferdinand – One of the major producers of clockwork toys in the early 20th century. His firm was eventually acquired by Louis Marx.

Warner, Nathan S. – One of the skilled designers whose work Ives used, Warner worked in a sewing machine factory in Bridgeport, Connecticut. In 1869 he patented a mechanical rowing boat with a man who rows in the water, which was one of the early toys made by Ives.

Weedon, William – Boston, Mass. In 1882 he founded the Weedon Manufacturing Company, which made steam engines, fire engines from which water squirted and steam boats. After 1939 the firm was run by his partner.

Wilkins Toy Company – This firm made tin toys in the 1890s and was taken over by Kingsbury in 1895, though the name was retained until 1919.

British tin toys

The British tin toy industry gained its main impetus as a result of the effects of the First World War on traditional imports. Previously, the toys of German or even French origin had been so cheap that there was little effort towards large scale production. German makers had applied English names and advertising to their models, and they were quick to copy contemporary vehicles of any country to which they were selling. As a result the native trade concentrated upon the so-called strong toys. The war cut off the flow of German toys and afterwards there was a move towards producing these at home. Great strides were made in improving the general quality of the work and it is from the 1920s and 1930s that the best known British toys, such as Chad Valley and Wells, mainly originate.

There was some small-scale production of metal toys in Britain from the mid 19th century, particularly in the Birmingham and Wolverhampton areas, though the main emphasis seems to have been upon toy kitchenware and similar, fairly simple items. There was also a small but high quality production of heavier toys, such as steam engines and model boats. Firms such as Sutcliffe have a long history in the manufacture of quality products, and their work is still available today. In the 1930s in particular, firms such as Wells and Chad Valley produced models of contemporary transport that were effectively decorated and quite sturdy, as many still work well. It seems highly probable that some of the less heavily decorated penny toys were made in Britain by such firms as the Reka company. In general, however, the British involvement in the mass production of tin toys came later than the period when the most decorative pieces were made on the Continent.

Many collectors now specialise in particular British products such as Hornby's Dinky Toys and though these are perhaps a little late for inclusion in a book on antique toys, the attention to detail, despite the small scale, and the decoration are of a quality equal to some of the better earlier products. Particularly memorable among recent products is the Matchbox series of vintage vehicles, which turned many children and their fathers into toy collectors.

Right: **A 20th century tinplate boxing ring, marked 'Made in G. Britain' on the box. By courtesy of Christie's South Kensington, London.** *Below:* **The British tin toy industry developed mainly after the First World War, and this lithographed tinplate locomotive is an unusually early example. It is operated by a wheel-wound spring inside the boiler. W. H. Hall patented a similar locomotive equipped with a whistle in 1882. Length 9 inches. Tolson Memorial Museum, Huddersfield.**

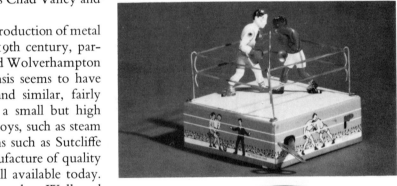

Lithographed tinplate toys by a variety of British manufacturers. *Top:* a group of tin-toys used as containers for confectionery. The motor bus was made by Burnett for the Cooperative Wholesale Society, for use as a biscuit container, while the tram is a toffee tin. Both *circa* 1910; length 7 inches and 6¼ inches respectively. The telephone box was sold full of biscuits by the Cooperative Wholesale Society. Height 6½ inches. All by courtesy of The Collector, Lavender Hill, London. *Centre:* A pair of early 20th century cars. The larger has a clockwork spring under the bonnet with transmission to the rear axle and rubber tyres. It was made by J. G. Brenner of Manchester. The smaller, which has a barrel spring, was made by Burnett Limited of Birmingham. Length 9½ and 7½ inches. Tolson Memorial Museum, Huddersfield. *Bottom:* A van made by Chad Valley in 1947. The Royal Mail livery is unusual, the van usually being lithographed with advertisements for a range of board games. Length 9¾ inches. Brian Garfield Jones Collection. Reproduced by courtesy of New Cavendish Books.

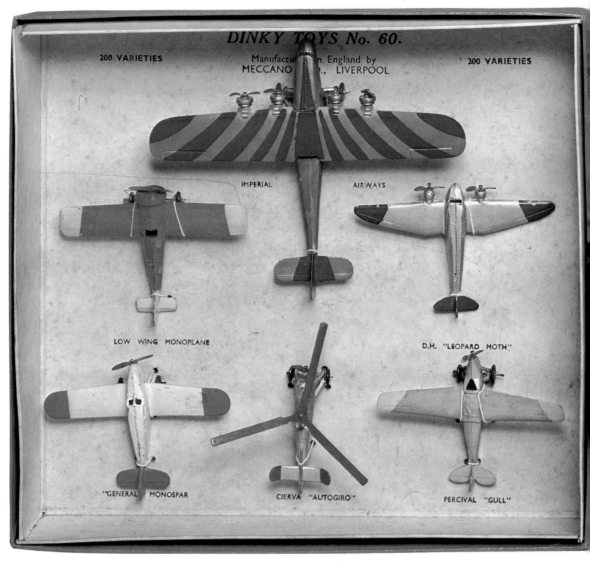

DINKY TOYS No. 60.

200 VARIETIES   Manufactu... n England by   200 VARIETIES
MECCANO ..., LIVERPOOL

IMPERIAL   AIRWAYS

LOW WING MONOPLANE   D.H. "LEOPARD MOTH"

"GENERAL... MONOSPAR   CIERVA "AUTOGIRO"   PERCIVAL "GULL"

Favourites with British youth and more recently with British collectors are the cast metal Dinky toys produced by Meccano Ltd. The style of the models in this boxed set of aeroplanes suggests that they date from around 1936–39. *Below:* A marked Brimtoy saloon of the 1920s which shows how the better made British toys were capable of rivalling the German. Length 11 inches. Luton Museum and Art Gallery, Bedfordshire.

BRITISH TIN TOY PRODUCERS

Bateman, John, & Co – Founded in 1774 and also known as 'The Original Model Dockyard', this firm had offices or premises in both Fleet Street and the Strand. It made components for model steam engines and ships. The 'Bateman & Co. Museum of Models' in High Holborn had the largest selection of working models in the world.

Bird, Alfred, & Sons – Birmingham, England. This firm used a weathervane trademark.

Brenner, J. G., & Co – Manchester, England. This firm used 'Brenco' as their trademark.

Brimtoy – London. From 1914 this firm used Nelson's Column as a trademark. They originally made tin road vehicles, possibly in cooperation with Bing, but were later amalgamated with Wells to form the firm known as Wells Brimtoy.

Britain, William – Britain came to London from Birmingham in the mid-19th century, when it seems he was already a toymaker who was able to create ingenious working models. Some of his early models are closer to automata than toys, and some were even costumed in fabrics, rather in the manner of Martin in France. William Britain's first recorded patent was for a Chinaman, in 1884, and he later made a 12 inch Mandarin who drank from a cup and a Scotsman who held a bottle and glass. Both of the latter were claimed to be suitable for window displays, as they had a clockwork mechanism which ran for a long time. In 1884, a patent was taken out for a metal dancing figure that spun in a socket. In 1886 a race game mechanism was invented and a type of flywheel that could be used in miniature toys. One toy still to be found is an equestrienne consisting of a circus girl who jumps over a bar as her horse circles. Heavy metal

Below, left: **An early metal toy representing the Mikado, made by William Britain around 1890. In the words of a contemporary catalogue: 'The Mikado-sian ornament for the mantelshelf is always amusing. When the umbrella is spun the figure will vigorously fan himself with the fan that he holds in his left hand.' Height 4 inches. Author's Collection.** *Right:* **Another early toy made by William Britain, operated by a top mechanism.** *Circa* **1910. By courtesy of Christie's South Kensington, London.**

toys with a flywheel movement were made at this time also, such as a figure carrying an umbrella on an elephant, and a Mikado who fanned himself while his umbrella twirled. Some of these figures were intended as ornamental items as well as toys. In 1893 patents for galloping animals were also recorded. The general manager of the firm was the founder's son, Alfred Britain. The firm also made a clockwork 'Blondin' cyclist and a steam-roller, railway signals and model cranes.

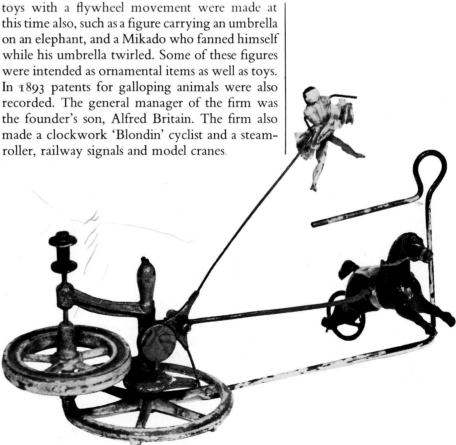

A selection of lithographed tin toys by Chad Valley, one of the famous names of British toy-making. The steam-roller, animal cage and gypsy caravan could all be used as biscuit containers. *Circa* 1946; total length 21½ inches. The London bus was sold by Carr's, the biscuit-makers, for the same purpose. *Circa* 1950; length 9¾ inches. All from The Collector, Lavender Hill, London.

Bull, Thomas Henry – Newington Causeway, Surrey. Made pewter toys around 1888.

Burnett Limited – Originally based in Birmingham. After October 1914 the firm's trademark carries the name of London. Later taken over by Chad Valley.

Cartwright, Sidney – Wolverhampton. Claiming to be established from 1850 this firm made toys in the 1880s. In 1909 they moved to Dudley, between Birmingham and Wolverhampton.

Chad Valley – Harborne, Birmingham. (See Constructional Toys for early history.) This name was used as a trademark from 1897 and the firm is still in existence. Some tin toys were sold from the late 1890s, including the 'Climbing Nigger' and the 'Miller and his Mill' both of which climbed a pole, received a coconut or a sack of flour on their heads and climbed down again. This toy is marked Chad Valley but an identical toy is also found marked Lehmann. The firm made a number of cars and other road vehicles, including some large-scale versions which could be pulled along.

Crescent Toys – Cwmcarn, Gwent. Established in 1922 and still in operation. The firm was started by Henry G. Eagles and Arthur A. Schneider in a 30 foot square workshop in North London. They originally made model soldiers and cowboys which were hollow cast in lead alloy and hand painted. In 1924 the firm became a limited company. Rapid expansion caused a move to Tottenham in 1937 and throughout this period a wide range of metal toys was produced. During the Second World War production almost ceased as the firm was involved in the war effort, but a few pieces continued to be produced at a much lower standard. At the end of the war Harry and Ernest Eagles helped to re-establish the firm and the move to Cwmcarn, Monmouthshire, began in 1949. The whole of the company was working at Cwmcarn by 1953 when it moved into the production of plastic models.

Fancy Tin Toy Company – Deritend, Birmingham. Made a variety of printed tin toys and were particularly known for their seaside buckets and spades. Sold sand moulding tools and printed buckets for moulding turrets and battlements.

Hornby, Frank – Maker of Meccano who introduced Dinky toys to his range of products in 1933. A huge variety of miniature road vehicles were made under this brand name and the various models of cars are particularly collected. Hornby boats, made first in the 1930s, showed a sensible use of parts, with an apparently wide range based on only a few basic hulls. The models show the same attention to detail as the Meccano sets. In 1964 the firm was taken over by Lines Brothers.

Lines Brothers – This family owned toy-making factories from 1858. The Tri-Ang trademark was registered in 1927 and the Minic mark was used on clockwork and tin cars made in the 1930s. The firm's interest in metal presswork and stove enamelling developed rapidly in the 1930s and a new factory on 47 acres was begun at Merton in South London.

Mettoy Company Ltd – Founded by Henry Ullman, who was a proprietor of Tipp & Co before the war. Made tinplate toys marked Mettoy in the 1930s and 1940s and Corgi toys in the 1960s.

Norris, Messrs James – Sherbourne Road, Birmingham. Around 1908 made a number of stamped tin toys including utensils, scales etc.

Reka Company – Wimbourne Street, New North Road, London. A wide range of penny toys were advertised by this firm in 1908 including a delivery van, a donkey and a barrow. Rainbow spinning tops were another of their lines. They specialised in light, hollow and solid castings in metal that were plain cast or finished in colours, gilt, etc. This firm also made pieces to special order as advertising material, as did some German firms such as Bing.

Stevens' Model Dockyard – Founded in 1843 in Aldgate, London. Issued catalogues of components for the construction of model steam engines and ships. From 1880 they marketed some toys of German origin and their clockwork submarines in a 1906 catalogue are surely made by Bing. The company sold boat fittings and made any type of boat to order. Many were a mixture of wood and metal. They also sold cranes and model steam engine parts on cards ready for assembling. The firm seems to have closed in the 1920s.

Sutcliffe, J. W. – This manufacturer is mentioned in Leek, Staffordshire, in 1882, but appears to have established a firm in Horsforth, Leeds, in 1885. The company still makes tinplate toys and is run by J. K. Sutcliffe. Their first battleships, which were powered by a water circulator engine heated by methylated spirits, were made in 1920. Speedboats were also made in the 1920s. These water circulation engines were apparently not made after 1928 and the same boats were supplied with German clockwork motors. From 1938 the firm made its own clockwork mechanisms. Today 40,000 tinplate boats a year are made by this firm, mainly on old machines.

Wells – London. The firm was registered in 1923 and a very large range of road vehicles was made throughout the 1920s and 1930s. Wells was in fact the main producer of lithographed toys until the late 1950s. Some of their toys were very tawdry in appearance, an example being their decidedly poor quality Rolls Royce.

Top: **The possibilities of lithographed tinplate toys as an advertising medium are amusingly illustrated by this 'Mackintosh's Toffee' lorry, one of a number of similar vehicles made by Hudson Scott & Sons of Carlisle.** *Circa* **1925; length 7½ inches. Reproduced by courtesy of New Cavendish Books.** *Above:* **An English saloon car made by Wells in 1935. Length 7¾ inches. From The Collector, Lavender Hill, London.**

5

BOARD
AND
TABLE
GAMES

Board games

Printed board games have a much more immediate appeal to the average collector than the often rather clumsy table amusements; they are also liked because it is usually possible to make a precise attribution, since the publishers added their names and, frequently, a date or details of the reigning monarch. The main interest in such games dates from the mid 18th century; early versions were printed from copper or steel plates and skilfully coloured by hand. They contain fascinating details of places, events and people of the time, as well as moral strictures intended to improve the minds and behaviour of the players. Around 1839 lithography began to be used, though many children's games continued to be produced in the traditional way until the last quarter of the 19th century. At first many games were simply printed on paper, but these were obviously fragile and soon the prints were backed with linen to withstand frequent folding and further protected by end boards of cardboard, often with a leathercloth or marbled finish. Card was eventually used to back complete games and these heavier boards were often contained in a leathercloth-covered box, with the counters and totum.

During the 18th century American children appear to have played mainly with imported games and even in the 19th century many of the boards available were adaptations of those originally published in Britain. F. & R. Lockwood of Broadway, New York, offered in 1823 'A large assortment of Juvenile pastimes, all of which are calculated to improve as well as amuse the youthful mind', and among these were the Traveller's Tours already popular in Europe. Ives, in 1844, offered 'The Game of Pope or Pagan or the Siege of the stronghold of Satan by the Christian Army', and another very positive native game was 'The Game of American Story and Glory' published by William Chancey Langdon of New Orleans with a board and cards that represented eleven presidents and twenty-eight states. To most American collectors, however, it is the name Parker brothers that is immediately thought of in conjunction with board games as the firm's production was so varied and prolific.

The manufacture of board games was at first a general publisher's sideline, but by the late 19th century the majority were made by specialist toymakers and it is from this period that identification becomes more difficult, as these games were rarely marked or dated in any way. Until quite recently, established collectors tended to look down on these later brightly coloured lithographed toys, but they are now appreciated in their own right. When buying board games condition is all important and they have to be considered almost in the same light as antique maps, which depend entirely on their state of preservation for their appeal. As in all fields of toy collecting, very rare examples are always worth acquiring, even if slightly damaged.

One of the many games produced by the 'Tiffany of the games business', Parker Bros. of Salem, Mass., in which players had to deliver letters by air mail from city to city. Like Parker Bros.' best known game, Monopoly, this one clearly has an educational intention. Margaret Woodbury Strong Museum, Rochester, New York.

PRODUCERS OF BOARD GAMES

Bowles, Carrington and **Bowles & Carver** – St Paul's Churchyard, London. Several members of the Bowles family worked in London as print and map sellers. Their 'Journey Through Europe or the Play of Geography' was printed for Carrington Bowles in 1759 and described as 'Invented and sold by the proprietor John Jeffrys, at his house in Chapel Street'. This game is of great interest as it is one of the earliest known and consists of a map of Europe mounted on canvas and hand coloured. The rules suggested that it should be played like the Game of Goose, a board game of very ancient origin. The rules were separately printed and glued in place, a method frequently seen in these early editions. In 1793, on the death of Carrington, the name of the firm was changed to Bowles & Carver and games such as the 'European Geographical Amusement', the 'Geographical Game of England and Wales' and the 'Geographical Game of the World' were issued. In 'British Geographical Amusement or The Game of Geography on a most Compleat and Elegant Tour Thro' England and Wales and the adjoining parts of Scotland and Ireland', the game began at Dover and ended in London. This firm's games are always packed with interesting detail.

Betts, John – The Strand, London. In 1875 the firm's stock was taken over by A. N. Myers & Co. They produced a very large number of games but their editions were not dated in any way. Among their issues was 'Betts' Tour Through England and Wales, an amusing and instructive game for children', which was published in the mid 19th century and was lithographed and hand tinted. It contained much interesting information, including the populations of the various towns. A similar 'Tour Through Europe' was also issued and both were mounted on linen. Their 'Journey to Lindley Murray's' had a board showing a house and its grounds, and the game was a race from the entrance gates to the house, situated in the centre. Lindley Murray was an American who settled in York and wrote a grammar of the English language. The firm had an educational bias and several tours were published, also an 'English Grammar', 'Contemporary Sovereigns', 'Roman History' and 'Royal Tiger Hunt'.

Darton, William Holborn Hill, London. William Darton (1755 to 1819) was later joined by Joseph Harvey and subsequently they and their families worked and published from several addresses, and the firm's name was itself changed several times. They were interested in instructional games, and one of these entitled 'Birds and Beasts' was described as 'Containing Instruction and Amusement for the Youth of both sexes'. It was hand coloured and enclosed in a slip case. A 'Survey of London' was published in 1820. It was to be played by 'A Party of Tarry-at-Home Travellers' and was described as 'A new game to instruct a company of friends'. The board showed interesting engravings of London, and a booklet illustrated all the famous buildings. 'Elephant and Castle or Travelling in Asia' was published in 1822 and

dedicated to Lord Henry Russel, to whom the publisher offered 'This Juvenile Game of Amusement and Instruction in token of the respect he entertains for every branch of the House of Russel'. It took the form of a hand-coloured engraving. 'Virtue Rewarded and Vice Punished. For the Amusement of the Youth of Both Sexes. By T. Newton, Inventor of the New Game of The Mansion of Bliss' was invented to deter juveniles from 'Pursuing the dangerous paths of Vice'. It was played from 'The House of Correction' to 'Virtue'. The 'Delicious Game of Fruit Basket. Containing a literary feast for a party of Juveniles, for their Improvement and Diversion' was published in 1822 and was accompanied by a 72-page explanatory booklet. This firm also published the series of Walker's games including tours through Europe and Ireland as well as 'The Mansion of Bliss' and 'British and Foreign Birds'.

Harris, John (1756 to 1846) – St Paul's Churchyard, London. John Harris started by working for Newbery (see below) and eventually took over the firm in 1801; in 1843 it was sold to Grant & Griffith. In 1804 Harris published his 'New Game of Emulation . . . calculated to inspire the mind with an abhorrence of Vice and a love of Virtue'. It was packed in a slip case and played as a race with 'Virtue as its own reward'. In 1809 the 'Panorama of London or a Day's Journey around the Metropolis' was issued, enclosed in a slip case decorated with the arms of London. Among the places of interest shown was Harris's own shop 'Harrises Original Juvenie Library' in St Paul's Churchyard. In the same year 'Geographical Recreation', another hand-coloured game, was published. Several of the games produced by Harris were provided with rule books printed by H. Bryer of Bridge St, Blackfriars. The 'Road to the Temple of Honour and Fame' was published in 1811 in the form of an engraving mounted on linen, and 'The Swan of Elegance', *circa* 1815, showed pictures of good and bad children and was eventually won by a character named Zealous Peter; an instruction book contained verses for each character. 'Punchinellography of England', 'Historical Pastimes', 'Bulwark of Britannia' and 'Swan of Apollo' were among the other board games published by this energetic firm.

Ives, W. & S. B. – Salem, Massachusetts, USA. Issued 'The Mansion of Happiness' with a different board from the British version in 1843. 'The Game of Pope or Pagan or the siege of the strong-

hold of Satan by the Christian army' appeared in 1844. Salem was a suitable location for a publisher of games as many were bought by sailors, who also brought in new ideas from abroad. In 1861 'Authors', invented by August Smith was published, though this game was later issued by several other firms. Parker Brothers, by 1898, had obtained most of the rights to the games published by Ives and some of the early examples were later reissued by this firm.

Milton Bradley – Springfield, Massachusetts, USA, established 1860. Bradley went into the manufacture of games almost by accident as a means of using a lithographic press he had purchased. His first published board game appears to have been 'The Checkered Game of Life' issued in 1860. During the Civil War patriotic and war games were published. The firm was mainly interested in the manufacture of entertaining amusements rather than moralistic exercises. When certain issues were beginning to sell more slowly they were packaged together with other types and sold as interesting bargain packs. A variety of other toys were also made, but always of wood, card-board or paper.

Myers, A. N. & Co – Leadenhall St, London. This firm took over the stock of John Betts. One of their best known games is 'The European Tourist', which was published in 1861 and was unusual for a London firm in that it was lithographed in Germany. All the places were described in the rule book by a character named Roderick Roveabout. 'Columbus or the Discovery of America', 'The Knight', 'Calculation', 'Bird Labyrinth' and 'The Ascent of Mount Blanc' were all published by Myers.

Newbery, E. – St Paul's Churchyard, London. One of the leading 18th century children's publishers who in 1802 sold out to her manager, John Harris. Among the published board games were 'Human Life' and the 'Royal Genealogical Pastime of the Sovereigns of England', which was published in 1791. The latter provided the names and dates of the monarchs in panels and was played over fifty-two shields with a teetotum.

Ogilvy, David – Ogilvy ran his Repository for Rational Toys and Amusements around 1835 in Brunswick Square, London. He published 'The Royal Race Course, a Merry Round Game', designed by G. E. Madeley with six very

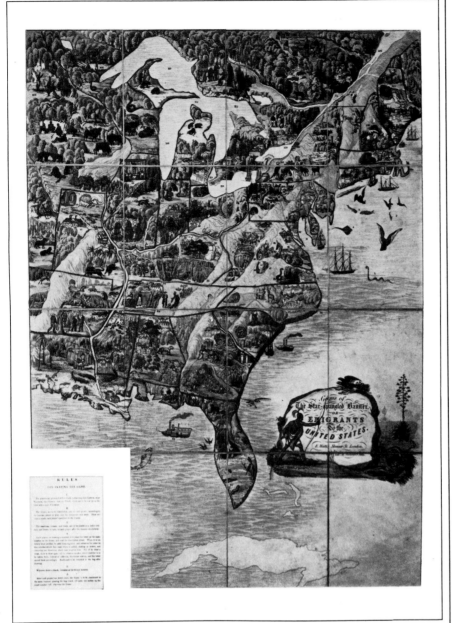

'The Game of the Star Spangled Banner or Emigrants to the United States', published by E. Wallis of Skinner Street, London. The game was provided with a book of descriptions of the places mentioned, and play involved the drawing of numbers which were to be placed 'in a lady's reticule'. Welsh Folk Museum, St Fagan's, Cardiff.

idiosyncratic differently coloured tracks for each player. 'Peter Puzzlewig's Game of Learning to spell' was also set out in this way, with stripes of different colour, and the design was copyrighted by Ogilvy. His 'Crowned Heads or Contemporary Sovereigns' was printed for him by L'Enfant Bros, Lithographic Printers, a firm which worked on occasion for several of the makers of board games. It showed a map of Europe with Victoria predictably occupying the central position and was mounted on linen folded in boards. The forty panels illustrated events from 1688 to 1844. 'L'Orient or The Indian Travellers' was a combined geographical and historical game which provided not only maps but also portraits of kings and queens and illustrations of historical Indian events between 1714 and 1846.

Parker Brothers–Salem, Massachusetts, USA, established 1883. Often known as the 'Tiffany of the games business', the firm began in Salem, where Ives had also worked. It was founded by George S. Parker, who was still at school when he invented 'The Game of Banking'; this was so successful that he decided to go into games pro-

duction. In 1886 he reissued 'The Mansion of Happiness', originally published by Ives, and in an attempt to make the game resemble the original, a group of children was used to paint the board in the traditional manner of one colour to each person. In 1887 'The Grocery Store', which had cards representing various commodities, was issued in an attractive box. 'The Doctors and the Quack', thought to date from the same period, was also accompanied by cards, printed with characters such as 'Clairvoyant Dr Humbug'. Not all Parker's inventions were equally successful. 'Chivalry', which was devised in 1887 and described as 'The greatest Modern Board Game of Skill' remained on the list for a very short time, though it was successfully revived in 1927 with the new title of 'Camelot'. The rapid expansion of the firm encouraged George's two brothers to join it in 1888 and a wide range of games then followed, all effectively packaged and well thought out. George Parker was different from the usual run of games producers, combining a keen interest in business with high moral principles, both of which were reflected in the types of games he marketed. Financial games included 'Speculation for Young Children' and 'The Game of Business or Going to Work', copyrighted in 1895. Instructive games such as Battlefields' and 'Famous Men' were also issued and others such as 'Christian Endeavour' in which the players aimed at 'Respect of Community', 'Justice' and 'Common Sense'. Of all Parker Brothers' games Monopoly is probably the most popular today. Picture blocks, puzzles, theatres and other novelties were also marketed by the firm, which, interestingly, copyrighted the name 'Ping Pong'. They are still one of the main producers of games in the United States and have a games museum at Salem.

Selchow & Righter–USA. Established by E. G. Selchow in 1864. He was joined by John H. Righter after their firm had absorbed A. B. Swift & Co. Their most famous game was Parcheesi, published in 1867.

Spooner, William–Recorded in Regent Street, London, from 1831, Spooner published various lithographic games. 'The Travellers or a Tour Through Europe' with views of each country was lithographed by W. Clerk and published in 1842. It was followed in 1852 by 'The Travellers through Europe with Improvements and additions' printed by L'Enfant and somewhat larger than the first version. 'Spooner's Pictorial Map of England

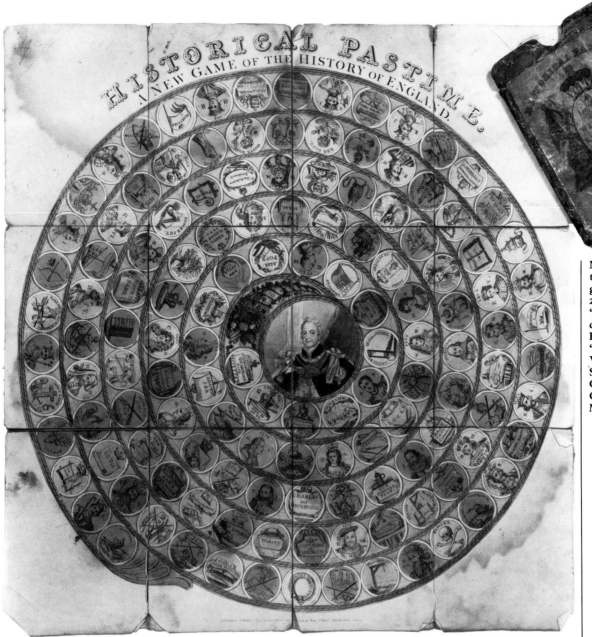

Notably similar in format to John Harris's 'Jubilee' game illustrated on page 200 is this educational game 'Historical Pastime', dating from around 1832. It bears the inscription 'Published by Edward Wallis, No. 42 Skinner Street & J. Harris & Son, Corner of St Paul's Churchyard'. Ipswich Museums.

and Wales arranged as an instructive game', published in 1844, was illustrated with 120 views. The game was also provided with a rule book in which were described the various counties and the assize towns. 'Wonders of the World. Chiefly in reference to the Architectural Works of the Ancients' was published *circa* 1843 and was provided with a separate key sheet and rules. Spooner's 'Game of English History', published in 1847, was a race from the invasion of Julius Caesar to 1845 and was later issued with a companion, 'Ancient History', published in 1850. More amusing games included the 'Funnyshire Fox Chase', which was played as an actual hunt. 'The Cottage of Content or The Right Roads and Wrong Ways', published in 1848, illustrated places such as 'Tittle Tattle Corner' and was later issued with a companion game, 'Country Fair or Rural Sports and Rural Rambles'.

Wallis – The firm was founded by John Wallis, who was followed by several other members of the family working mainly in London. In 1794 John Wallis, from his Map Warehouse, issued 'Wallis's Tour of Europe, A Tour Through England and another Round the World'. All his games cost six shillings each but this included counters and a totum. The 'Picturesque Round Game of the Produce and Manufacturers of the Counties of England and Wales' was published around 1830, and was interesting as the map was printed with an almost photographic three-dimensional effect; the game ended in the City of London. Wallis's 'New Railway Game' informed the child of the distances of all major towns from London and was published after the accession of Victoria. Their 'Wanderers in the Wilderness' was played on a map of South America and was a companion to 'The Star Spangled Banner or Emigrants to the U.S.A.'. A series of 'Historical Pastimes' was published that are dated purely by the last sovereign shown. A vast number of other titles was issued, including 'Wonders of Art', 'Scenes in London', 'The Destruction of Jerusalem', 'Pleasures of Astronomy' and 'Natural Philosophy', all illustrating the way in which purely moral games were giving way to those whose main aim was to impart useful knowledge on subjects such as the manufacturing industries of the nation.

Dissected puzzles, jigsaws & picture blocks

Few children of today would have the application necessary first to assemble and then to learn the facts contained in an 18th century dissection. However, the jigsaw puzzle was doubtless received as an entertaining diversion from the generally tedious educational methods of the 18th century. The date at which the first dissection was made is not recorded, though it is almost certain that John Spilsbury, a map maker and engraver, was the inventor. A London street directory of 1763 describes him as a 'Map Dissector in wood, in order to facilitate the teaching of Geography', the earliest known reference to a manufacturer of this kind. As Spilsbury worked in an area of London where the educated and the rich bought their books, his novel idea for the education of their children gained ground and the variety of specially engraved maps increased. The paper was glued to a mahogany backing and the cheaper early editions were contained in chipwood boxes, while the more expensive ones were boxed in mahogany. The pieces were generally cut along the border lines of counties or countries, so that the child would soon learn to identify the various shapes.

These map dissections remained popular to some degree until the 20th century, though their appeal was surely to the parent rather than the long-suffering child.

It was possible to print posters and bills very cheaply by the 18th century, and it was soon felt that a child would derive more pleasure from assembling a picture rather than a map such as Spilsbury's 'Europe Dissected'. The origin of picture puzzles is even less clear than that of dissected maps, but they were certainly on sale by the 1780s, and among the more amusing was 'Before and After Marriage', an upside down puzzle showing happy and miserable faces, published by John Wallis in 1789. Historical dissections, which used the new picture puzzle for an educational purpose, became popular in 1787, when William Darton published his 'Engravings for Teaching the Elements of English History and Chronology after the manner of Dissected Maps for Teaching Geography'. This publication was soon followed by John Wallis's 'Chronological Tables of English History for the Instruction of Youth', a much simpler construction that imparted less information and was therefore more popular with children. It was issued in a coloured edition in 1799. A flood of teaching dissections followed, variously intended to inculcate elements of the Bible, multiplication, arithmetic and letters of the alphabet. At this time morality was considered a subject to be taught in much the same way as arithmetic, and therefore appeared in puzzles such as 'The Pilgrim's Progress', published in 1794, which pointed a warning finger at the results of moral transgressions.

Attitudes both to children and educational methods changed steadily during the 19th century and this is clearly reflected in the much lighter subject matter of the puzzles produced at this time. In many cases they were intended for pure amusement and illustrated scenes from exciting stories, jungle beasts, contemporary happenings and children at play. These later examples are usually backed with softwood, as the mahogany formerly used was now too expensive. The colouring, even as late as the 1870s, was sometimes effected by hand and many collectors find little interest in the brightly lithographed versions of later years. The term jigsaw was not used until the 20th century and is believed to have originated in America. It refers of course, to the saw used for shaping the puzzle, which made possible the tightly interlocking pieces with which we are familiar today. Puzzles only became very cheap

Cheap colour lithography and the invention of a die which could cut a whole sheet of printed cardboard both contributed to the proliferation of jigsaw puzzles in the late 19th and early 20th centuries. The 'Yellow Kid Puzzle' shown here was published by McLoughlin Brothers of New York City. Yellow Kid was the subject of a colour comic strip published in the *New York Journal* Sunday newspaper. The character was copyrighted by its creator, R. F. Outcault, in 1896. Margaret Woodbury Strong Museum, Rochester, New York.

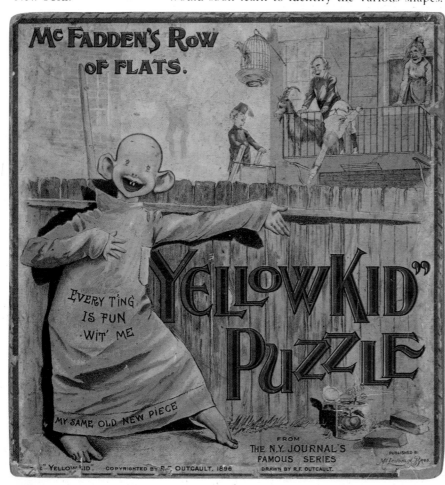

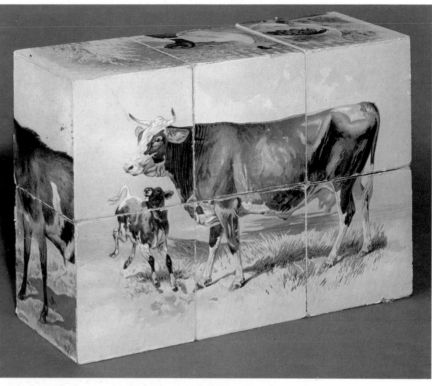

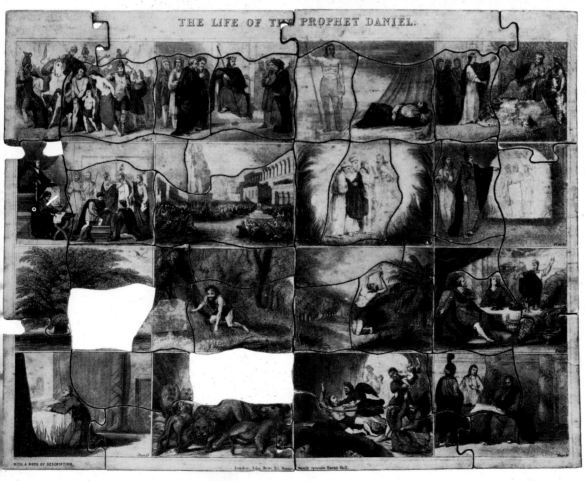

THE LIFE OF THE PROPHET DANIEL.

Hand-coloured dissected puzzles are of particular interest to the collector.
Above left: Hand-coloured lithography on 'The Young Volunteers', dating from around 1860. Unmarked; size 8½ x 12½ inches. Bedford Museum.
Left: 'The Life of the Prophet Daniel', published by John Betts of 115 Strand, London. Hand-coloured engraving; *circa* 1845. Ipswich Museums.
Above right: An unusual set of chromolithographic talking picture blocks of six different farm animals, each activated by pulling a string. Made in Germany in the late 19th century. Size of set 17 x 13 inches. By courtesy of Christie's South Kensington, London.

Alphabetical blocks in a variety of different formats. *Above:* **A set of pictorial blocks made in the United States around 1875. Bethnal Green Museum of Childhood, London.** *Far right:* **A colourful set of alphabet blocks which were probably printed in Germany, decorated with pictures of contemporary toys.** *Circa* **1900.** *Right:* **A set of bone alphabet letters contained in a mahogany box. Early 19th century; length of box 3½ inches. Both Ipswich Museums.**

after the introduction of a die which could cut out a whole sheet of printed cardboard – a development which accounts for the large numbers used as advertising material during the first half of the 20th century.

Picture blocks, with a separate scene glued to each of the six sides, are still among the most popular learning toys, but the exact date at which they first appeared is unknown. Several writers suggest that they only became available after the introduction of cheap colour lithography in the mid 19th century, but the author has handled sets illustrated with hand-coloured prints of late 18th or very early 19th century origin. These early examples were without their original key pictures and were almost impossible to assemble as all the scenes were similar and were coloured in soft blues and greens.

The main production of picture blocks occurred in the last quarter of the 19th century and in general those made after the First World War are of little interest to collectors. Children at play,

animals at the zoo, pets and domestic scenes all appear in brilliant gaudy colours and are contained in attractive boxes. The majority are completely without any maker's mark, though usually of German origin, and have to be valued purely on subject matter and condition. In the late 19th century a large number were based on scenes from the Bible and these are not as popular with collectors as others illustrating children with their toys or nursery rhymes. Sometimes the blocks have individual pictures accompanied by a letter of the alphabet. Such sets are often more collectable as there are specialists who buy items related to the learning of the alphabet.

Occasionally a very rare set of blocks such as those with a sound mechanism which are illustrated appear on the market, and these obviously create great interest. In general, however, few blocks are very valuable as they fall outside the interest range of collectors of dissections and jigsaws, and are often rather large for convenient display within a private house.

MAIN PRODUCERS OF PUZZLES

Anners, Thomas, S. – Philadelphia, Pennsylvania, USA, 1822 to 1829. Made bone alphabet blocks.

Barfoot, J. R. and J. W. – London. Made a very large number of puzzles in the mid 19th century. Their products varied in quality and some were backed with a green paper. Also made some double-sided puzzles. Marketed through retailers so the boxes are not marked with their name, though their initials are sometimes found. Subjects included 'Articulate Animals', *circa* 1845; 'England's Hope', with a map of England and Wales on the reverse, printed *circa* 1865; and 'Before the Flood or Noah's Ark', also *circa* 1865.

Betts, John – Another large publisher working in the mid 19th century, at Brunswick Square, London, from 1827 to 1845, and after this in the Strand. The firm's stock was taken over in 1875 by A. N. Myers and Co. Publications include 'Europe Delineated', *circa* 1830; 'Early Bible History', 1845; 'William Tell', 1850; and the 'History of a Load of Coals', *circa* 1880, a Betts dissected puzzle which was published by George Phillip and Son.

Darton & Harvey – Gracechurch St, London. Founded by William Darton, this firm traded as William Darton & Co from 1787. In 1791 Darton was joined by Joseph Harvey and the firm subsequently became known as Darton, Harvey & Darton to 1819, Darton & Clark from 1836 to

'My Grandmother, by Mr Upton', published on June 3rd 1813 by William Darton Jr., Holborn Hill, London. The Museum of London.

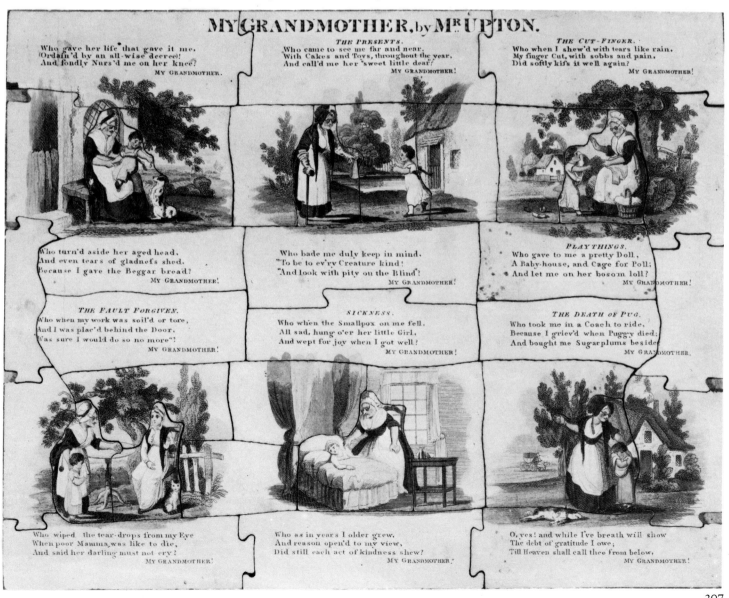

Right: **'My Uncle's Farm', a hand-coloured dissected puzzle published by John Betts at 115, Strand, London.** *Circa* **1845. Welsh Folk Museum, St Fagan's, Cardiff.**

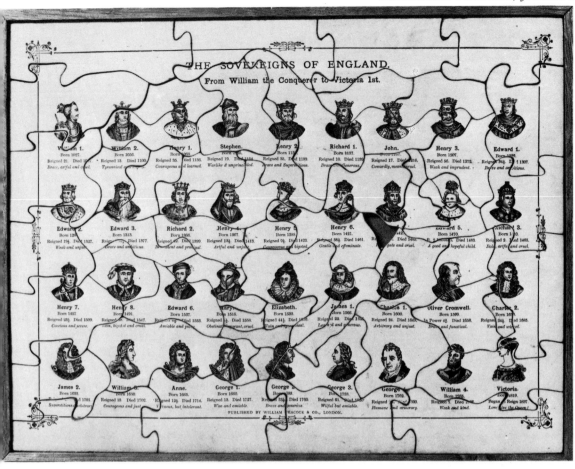

THE SOVEREIGNS OF ENGLAND.
From William the Conqueror to Victoria 1st.

PUBLISHED BY WILLIAM PEACOCK & CO., LONDON.

'The Sovereigns of England', published by William Peacock of London around 1860. Welsh Folk Museum, Cardiff.

1846 and finally Darton & Co in 1867. Products include 'Miscellanies for the Instruction of Infants', *circa* 1790; 'My Mother' in 1811, followed by 'My Son' in 1812 and 'My Grandmother' in 1813, as well as a very large number of maps.

Harris, John (1756 to 1846) – St Paul's Churchyard, London. Took over the firm of Newbury in 1801 but published only a few maps.

Hill, S. L. – Williamsburg, New York, USA. In 1858 Hill patented a spelling block and in 1863 a box-making machine. The blocks which he made had letters on some sides and numbers on the other. At least one side of each block was decorated with a colourfully printed, pasted-on picture. The sets of blocks were packed in wooden boxes.

Knickerbocker Company – Albany, New York, USA, *circa* 1850. Produced wooden alphabet blocks and some lithographed versions.

Milton Bradley – Springfield, Massachusetts, USA, established 1860. Producer of all sorts of lithographed games etc. Made both picture and alphabet blocks as well as dissected maps of the USA. Bradley's 'Kinder-Garten' alphabet and building blocks were issued in 1872. These consisted of a set of eighty-five blocks with the letters of the Roman and the script alphabets, numbers and effective pictures of various animals. They were contained in walnut boxes. Milton Bradley also absorbed the firm of McLoughlin Brothers, who produced a large number of puzzles during the 19th and early 20th centuries.

Newbury – St Paul's Churchyard, London. A leading firm of juvenile publishers in the 18th century which was sold to its manager John Harris in 1801. Published 'England Dissected', *circa* 1785; 'The New Game of Human Life', 1790.

Peacock, William – London. Working mainly around Islington, Peacock made a vast number of puzzles in the second half of the 19th century, including double-sided pictures and maps. He did not print his own maps. Publications included 'Sovereigns of England', *circa* 1860, with a map of Europe on the back; 'Map of England with the Railways', *circa* 1860.

Spilsbury, John (circa 1739 to 1769) – Worked from 1762 in Drury Lane, London. The firm was continued by his wife after his death. Published 'Europe Divided into its Kingdoms', 1766; and 'The World', 1772.

Tuck, Raphael & Sons – Founded in London in 1870 and still active. Made jigsaws in the 1890s and produced a vast number in the early 20th century which were largely printed in Bavaria.

Wallis – Founded by John Wallis in 1775. Both he and his sons worked from a variety of addresses in London and at the Marine Library, Sidmouth. Published 'Before and After Marriage', in 1789; 'Analytical Table of the Government of Great Britain' 1806; 'Dame Dumpling's Trip to Market', *circa* 1820; 'School in an Uproar', *circa* 1825; 'Whole Length Portraits of Kings and Queens', *circa* 1835; and 'The Farmer's Blunder', *circa* 1845.

Facing page: **The 'Locomotive Picture Puzzle', published by McLoughlin Brothers of New York City. It was copyrighted in 1901 and depicts the famous 999 New York Central locomotive which set a world speed record at the time. Margaret Woodbury Strong Museum, Rochester, New York. Started in the late 1820s by John McLoughlin, the firm which made this puzzle became known as McLoughlin Brothers in 1855 and was eventually absorbed by Milton Bradley of Springfield, Mass., in 1926.**

Table games

Games such as chess, knucklebones and draughts all have ancient origins and most of the games played by children up to the 18th century were based on these traditional pastimes. It was not until the late 19th century that competition amongst manufacturers resulted in a whole range of new and exciting games. These were packed in splendidly printed boxes which promised untold enjoyment for the recipient. Production of such parlour amusements reached its peak in the very early 20th century, before the First World War disrupted the supply of German printed material and before the advent of gramophones and the radio made it less necessary to provide evening amusements for both young and old. Many advertisements and box lids show adults as well as children enjoying the games and we are made very aware of how mass entertainment has changed family life. Today similar games would only be played on special occasions.

The finest of table games such as ivory chess sets or the splendid Victorian games compendiums, made to the highest specifications for adults, are obviously worthwhile acquisitions as antique objects. Versions intended for children are often simply made of boxwood and are not of any great interest unless still contained in the original box which sometimes gives the manufacturer or

A commercially made board for Nine Men's Morris, an ancient British game more usually played on chalked or carved lines. *Circa* **1870. Ipswich Museums.**

Facing page: **Two examples of the superior craftsmanship which went into many table games.** *Top:* **A set of bone spillikins with their original straw-work-decorated box. English; 19th century; length of box 6 inches. Saffron Walden Museum, Essex.** *Bottom:* **A particularly fine domino set dating from around 1800 and probably carved by French prisoners of war in Britain. The box has an interesting double lid, the top layer of which opens to reveal a painted figure of Napoleon. Welsh Folk Museum, St Fagan's, Cardiff.**

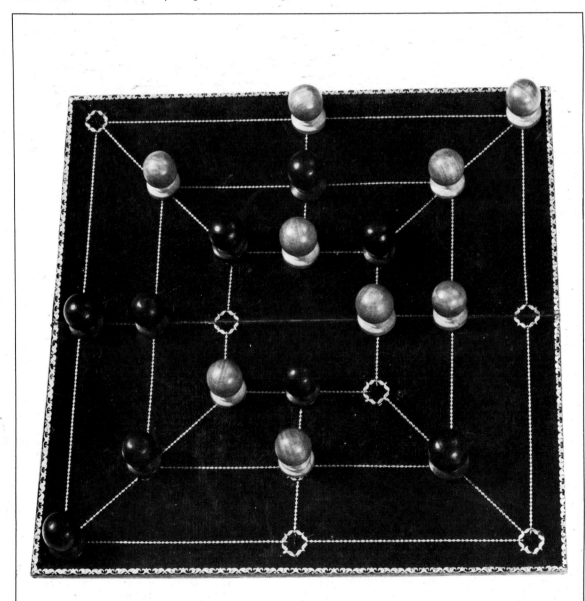

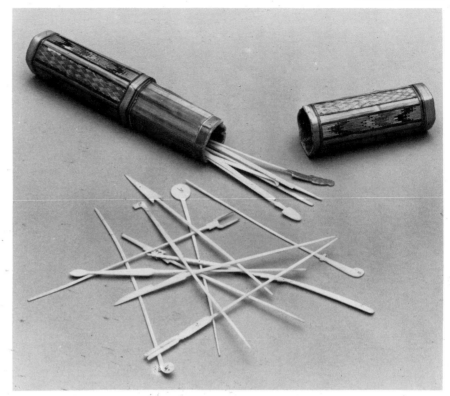

seller's name. Generally, the sets of draughts or chess men are found contained in simple unmarked boxes, with the exception of those produced by the London firm of Jacques & Sons, and this contributes to the low price they command. Some sets were specially made for younger children and have some form of painted or applied decoration and these do tend to interest collectors a little more, though prices are still low.

Colourfully painted Pope Joan boards have long been popular with collectors as they form effective decorative items. Like fine chess sets they were made for adult use, though they often eventually ended up in the nursery.

The 19th century is particularly associated with table games of the parlour type which could be played by all members of the family. Versions of charades, fortune-telling games such as Gypsy and a vast number of question-and-answer entertainments aimed at increasing word power, knowledge of geography and the Bible were common. In comparison with the vast number produced, there are few that have survived simply because they were such useful means of whiling away tedious hours that they soon wore out and were discarded. The major production of such games occurred in the late 19th century, when even the better off working-class families could purchase cheap toys and the noisy play of children was less frowned upon. The manufacturers in many cases actually encouraged noisy play as in 'The Naughty Piggiwigs', where the aim was to push marbles up a steep cardboard slope to a 'pen' at the top, with thin, easily bent wire pushers that made the marbles difficult to control. The 'Howitzer Game', in which small working cannons were used to fire pellets at the opposition must have also led to very noisy scenes. 'Storming the Citadel', produced by Chad Valley and consisting of a cardboard fort and a machine gun with ammunition must have also caused considerable disruption, and serves to indicate how the intention of parlour games was changing around 1900.

In advertisements for 'Fantails', adults were shown laughing and rushing about the parlour as they attempted to persuade paper birds into a large cardboard cage set on the table. 'The fun becomes fast and furious when birds caged by one player are fanned out again by another', commented one advertisement. An American game, 'Pillow Dex', manufactured by Parker Bros. of Salem, Massachusetts, involved batting a balloon around a table and was described as 'Fun for all Ages'. Once again, it was not intended primarily

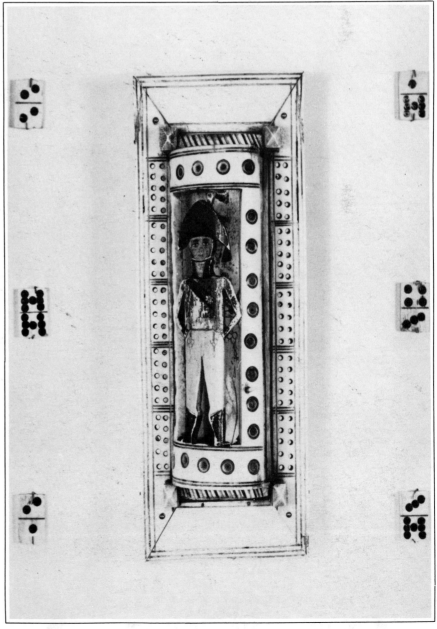

for children, and even in the book of rules it is adults who are shown at play. An English firm, Roberts Brothers, based in Gloucester, produced several novelty games of this type in the early 20th century including 'Howitzer', 'Pot in Egg' and 'Tipplee Web'. In the latter the apparatus consisted of a long strip of webbing not unlike a big razor strop and a ball about the size of those used in ping pong. The webbing was provided with a hole or pocket at one extremity and the balls were shot along the webbing to the goal. The appearance of this game when displayed is not particularly pleasing and illustrates the problems associated with toys that were highly successful in themselves but are not sufficiently decorative for the tastes of collectors.

Many of the skittle-type games are more attractive, as the targets are often brightly litho-

graphed. Examples are 'On the Tiles' and 'Cats and Catapults' in which children bowled at hinged cats sitting on the roofs of gingerbread-type houses. In 'Three Little Kittens', balls were aimed into the animals' widely laughing open mouths. Many variations on this basic game were produced, some featuring hunting scenes and nursery-rhyme characters. Others were made to represent well known personalities, such as the Kaiser or John Bull. Soft fabric skittles were made by several factories such as Dean's (see Soft Toys), who produced printed cotton versions aimed particularly at the very young.

The majority of Edwardian table games appear to be based on miniature versions of outdoor pursuits, such as the various attractive magnetic fishing sets in which old boots, fish and dead cats fitted with metal rings were picked up by a magnetic fishing hook. One more exciting version was 'Tarpon Fishing', where card fish were projected wildly about the room and caught in butterfly-type nets. Another improvement to basic magnetic fishing was 'Dangle' where the fish were 'weighed' in a scale according to the numbers printed on the tails and the first player with a bag of 14 lbs was the winner.

Cricket, though not ideally designed for table play, was made in many versions including Lamplough's 'Model Cricket' where the pitch was made by laying down a baize runner with a hinged wicket at the end. 'Oval cricket, a Capital game for boys' was claimed to work on scientific principles and runs could be scored. 'Parlour Cricket' was played on a board with numbered holes which represented runs; the player was 'in' until his ball hit the wicket or he was caught out. 'The Great Test Match and County Championship' included eleven men, a field, bat, ball and scoring board.

Fox hunting, midget croquet, table quoits, captive table tennis where the ball was suspended on string, and indoor model golf all provided family entertainment. Catalogues are also full of football games such as 'Wibbley Wob', produced by Gamage's and the new game of 'Kick' in which metal figures actually kicked the ball. In the 'Game of Socker or Associated Parlour Football' there was 'real passing, kicking and dribbling' and these noisy games indicate very clearly how children's play was no longer completely restrained. There were obviously still games for quiet Sundays such as 'The Missionary Journeys of Saint Paul' or 'Scripture Questions and Answers' both calling for the most detailed scriptural knowledge and great concentration. A much lighter game was 'Bargains' published by G. W. Faulkner in which 'Mr Clown the Auctioneer' knocked down various exciting lots.

In general, table games are not particularly attractive to established collectors, as the pieces of baize, net, sticks, balls and bats are most difficult to display effectively and very few are marked in any way, so identification has often to be obtained through tedious reference to old catalogues and advertisements. Frequently bagatelle boards, table croquet and variations on the football games sell at European auctions for a pittance and even good examples are cheap. Condition is obviously important and care should be taken to read the rules so that any missing pices of equipment can be noted. In particular the box should be almost perfect, as it is this feature that will catch the buyer's eye when it is eventually resold.

Card games

The origins of the playing card are surrounded by legend. One charming story suggests that they were devised by the favourite wife of a maharajah in the hope of diverting his attention from an irritating habit of continually pulling at his beard. Other stories link their invention to Persia, China and India, but there is no hard fact and all that can be concluded is that the beginning was almost certainly Eastern. The first European manuscript to mention playing cards dates from 1377, but as their use was prohibited in Regensburg in 1378, it would appear to have been established for some time. The unpleasantness and fighting often associated with the gaming tables was criticised as soon as cards began to attain widespread popularity, and sermons were preached on the dangers associated with card playing from the 15th century.

Very early cards are virtually works of art in miniature, as they were painted by professional artists and given as prestige gifts to princes and nobles. As card playing spread so quickly among the ordinary people, cheaper versions were created by the use of stencils, which meant that all the red on a card, for instance, could be filled in at a single stroke. The German printers, with their great skill in wood engraving, were highly successful in this specialised manufacture and by the 15th century they were exporting in quantity. The German lead was lost to France by the end of the century, as the French saw that economies could

be effected if the suits were simplified. These French cards are the basis of the designs still used today, as the dress of the figures has not changed to any great degree and still represents medieval kings and queens. This successful trade was also pursued in Belgium where the majority of the cards produced were exported to Russia and France with a lesser number being sold in England.

Playing cards first appeared in Britain somewhere around 1400 and by the end of the century, cards had become popular in all spheres of society. The earliest surviving card of indisputably English origin dates from 1675, though native production actually began much earlier than this. The Worshipful Company of Makers of Playing Cards was founded as early as 1628, with the intention of promoting the interests of members, who were continually hampered in their work by the high taxes that were demanded by the government. In 1710 an Act of Parliament was passed requiring that no set of cards should leave the manufacturers without a seal showing that duty had been paid. These seals have provided some help to collectors in dating early examples.

There was always a certain amount of opposition to card playing, though in general teachers of etiquette instructed the young to deal with the pastime in moderation and even children of just a few years old enjoyed games of this type. Louis XIII, who was born in 1601, was playing crambo

An early set of educational French playing cards, the 'Jeu des Rois de France', dating from 1638.

Left: **Some cards from the English card game 'Law and Security', published by S. Hooper and dated 2nd October 1775. Welsh Folk Museum, St Fagan's, Cardiff.** *Below:* **A page from the text accompanying an early instructional pack, 'Das Geistlich–Teutsche Karten-Spil', first published in 1603. The picture bears the legend: 'Joab under the oak tree runs Absalom through with three lances.'**

by the age of three and card games by the time he was five, and this was considered an achievement rather than the first steps on the road to ruin. The use of a card game as a means of instruction was soon devised by a monk, Dr Thomas Murner, who found it a convenient way of explaining the basis of philosophy to his students. The next instructional pack, 'Das Geistlich-Teutsche Karten-Spil', by Andreas Strobl, was issued in 1603 and included an astonishing three hundred pages of text to each suit.

One of the most famous early packs is that devised by Jean Desmarests, a French Academician in the first half of the 17th century, at the suggestion of Cardinal Mazarin. Four sets were produced with the intention of instructing the young king, and Della Bella, the Florentine artist, provided the illustrations. The first set illustrated the history of France from Pharamond to Louis XIV; 'Le jeu des Reines Renommées' contained portraits of queens and other famous women; the third set was based on fables, gods and goddesses, and the last on a geographical theme. Each illustration was accompanied by a few lines of explanatory text.

An English set based on mathematics, 'The Scolers Practicall Cards', was issued in 1656 and by 1665 there were a number of English cards instructing in heraldry and geography. A set issued in Nuremberg in 1693 illustrated the members and the history of the reigning families of Europe, and a M. Daumont, who had issued packs based on heraldry, also published an interesting series aimed at teaching boys the basis of military science, including the methods of dealing with corpses after the battle. Rather less aggressively military subjects included a Swiss pack that showed the uniforms of officers and these cards were particularly well painted.

In England, the main emphasis by the end of the 17th century appeared to be on cards of a geographical nature, but there were also a number that dealt with various threats to the stability of the

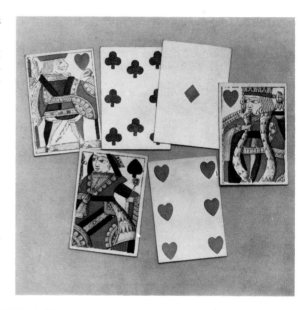

Top right: **A group of hand-coloured English playing cards dating from the late 18th century. Bedford Museum.** *Bottom right:* **'The Infant's Cabinet of Various Objects', a pack of 28 picture cards, each matched by a description in the accompanying book. Published by John Marshall, London, 1801. Size of box 3½ x 2½ inches. The Museum of London.**

A French instructional pack, the 'Boston de Flore' or 'Botanique Elément-aire', which relates the conventional suits to botanical subjects. 1820. *Below*: A hand-coloured mid 19th century English card game which explains character in relation to flowers. Ipswich Museums.

realm such as 'All the Popish Plots from the Armada in 1588 to the Popish Plot of 1678'. In Italy, Francesco Zaccarelli provided the drawings for a very desirable set that was published in 1748 and the same year saw the foundation of a notable French firm, B. P. Grimaud et Cie, who were associated with some fine costume packs.

The production of instructional cards was encouraged in the 18th century on the advice of educationalists who approved of learning through play, though much of the knowledge imparted by the cards was hardly entertaining in content. Educational packs appeared in America from the mid 18th century, though card playing by adults was first recorded in the country in 1633. The first American producer of cards was Jazaniah Ford of Milton, Mass., who was born in 1757, and he was soon succeeded by printers such as Amos Whitney and Thomas Crehore. At first there was considerable prejudice against home-produced cards in the United States; those made in England were preferred and a few makers stooped to such devices as printing the word 'London' on their packs to mislead the purchaser. Alphabetical, grammatical and geographical cards were all available in Boston from 1811 and though a large number were still imported, the native industry was becoming firmly established. One of the main 19th century advertisers of playing cards was G. & R. Waite who in 1808 offered 'Eagle Playing Cards from the best manufactory in the United States'. 'Conversation Cards' bearing topics on which each player had to talk were extremely popular, as were the 'Enigmatical Cards' sold from around 1817 in New York.

The greatest British manufacturer of playing cards, Thomas de la Rue, was born in Guernsey, and after working variously as a stationer and straw hat maker he issued his first pack in 1832. The decoration of the card backs produced by this company, which is still in existence today, was particularly effective. It was the work of Owen Jones, the architect and lithographer, who had decorated many of the buildings at the Great Exhibition of 1851. Almost simultaneously, the greatest of the American firms, that of Lewis I. Cohen, was established. Cohen was American-born but worked for a short while in England, and on returning to the States he set up as a card publisher, producing his first set in 1835. After his retirement in 1854 the firm was continued as Lawrence and Cohen until 1870, after which it became the New York Consolidated Card Company. Many experts comment on similarities

The late 19th and early 20th centuries produced a wide variety of card games. *Near right, top:* **Part of a set of satirical cards by Dante Gabriel Rossetti (1828–82). The king of clubs is a figure of Mr Punch carrying a club with the inscription 'Instituted for the suppression of humbug'. Victoria and Albert Museum, London.** *Near right, bottom:* **'Golly Misfitz' a colourful card game representing a series of dolls and toys with interchangeable parts. Printed in Germany by C. W. Faulkner, *circa* 1910. 72 cards made up into 24 pictures. Author's Collection.** *Main picture:* **An English card game entitled 'The Wedding', published around 1863. Unmarked, but 'Registered at Stationers' Hall' (London). Ipswich Museums.**

Facing page, bottom left: **Hand-coloured playing cards dating from 1815–20 and published by the English firm of Reynolds & Sons.** *Far right:* **'Welsh Counties', a card game published by Laird of Paisley, Scotland, on December 1st 1818. The cards list the county towns together with their major products and distances from London. Both Welsh Folk Museum, St Fagan's, Cardiff.**

between the cards produced by this company and those of de la Rue, but to date no definite connection has been established.

The publication of children's packs, which were mainly of an educational nature, reached its peak in the early 19th century and after 1850 there was a steady decline. Possibly parents remembered the boredom of using question-and-answer cards designed to inculcate unpalatable facts concerning the length of rivers and the population of obscure towns. The market for such cards was further depressed by the theories of the Swiss reformer Pestalozzi, who disapproved of their use and felt that learning should be based on experience. There was therefore a steady and gradual trend away from the rather grim presentation of facts to a much lighter tone. This was exemplified in the USA by Anne W. Abbot of Beverly, Mass., who invented a card game for the use of her own family which featured an amusing character known as Dr Busby. The game was such a success that she sold her idea to Currier & Ives,

who issued the first commercial pack in 1843. and sold a surprising 50,000 in the first year. In 1844 she invented a much less successful game, 'Master Rodbury and his Pupils'. Another tremendously popular American card game was 'Rook', devised and copyrighted by George Palmer with the aim of overcoming puritanical objections to the pursuit of card playing.

The publication of packs intended purely for amusement was much aided by improvements in colour printing in the late 19th century. These resulted in bright and entertainingly designed packs which must have had an immediate impact even on very young children. In England, some fairly substantial question-and-answer packs were still issued, including one by Smith's of Ipswich which included such items as 'Whom did the Princess Louise marry?' 'Who wrote Goblin Market?' and 'What country was the first to rebel after the Queen's (Victoria's) accession?'. Apart from these few exceptions, the general tone was much lighter after 1880 and subjects such as auctions

and games based on buying and selling became quite commonplace. The great production period for attractive card games was however in the early 20th century, when the manufacturers were able to appeal to a very wide market and even country workmen were occasionally able to purchase toys for their young. C. W. Faulkner & Sons, successors to Hildersheimer & Faulkner, produced some of the most colourful cards in the 1890s and early 1900s, most of their designs being printed in Germany. Among the best known of their products is the 'Misfitz' series, based on the assembling of characters from three separate cards and including 'Golly', 'Funny Folk', 'Wonderland' and 'National Misfitz', all contained in characteristic highly decorated boxes. One of de la Rue's most effective toy packs was 'Jumbo Jinks', with forty-eight pictorial cards illustrating the adventures and games of Dr Lion and his school and featuring Jumbo the Bull. A few cautiously educational packs such as 'The Language of Flowers', 'Flags', 'Authors' and 'Domestic Animals' were published just before the First World War, but care was taken that the visual appeal should be high. There were of course innumerable variations on Snip-snap-snorum, popularly known as Snap, and characters from stage, public life, fiction and nursery rhymes were all utilised in the creation of new versions.

When purchasing packs of Victorian and Edwardian cards, it is essential to see that all are in good general condition, as damage to a single card can mean that the set would be of limited interest to a specialist collector. Usually it is also necessary to obtain the original slip-case, as all too often in the case of the toy packs the manufacturer's name was only applied to this. Checking to be sure that a pack is complete can be an irritating task, especially in the saleroom, but the absence of a single card can radically affect the price, even if the pack is in otherwise superb condition. Early cards tend to be valued separately, as complete packs before the 18th century are almost impossible to find. Many late packs are lightly regarded by serious card collectors and could provide a promising collecting area for those wishing to spend only one or two pounds on acquisitions. Any cards including characters such as Teddy bears and golliwogs, Mickey Mouse or popular characters of stage and screen have a value of their own, as they are bought by the people who concentrate on these very narrow themes and therefore attain prices out of line with the majority of the sets from this later period.

6

EDUCATIONAL TOYS AND PASTIMES

The toy theatre

The toy theatre is thought to have developed from the crib sheets and sets of figures that were produced at Augsburg and Strasbourg and whose success probably inspired the publishers to print secular scenes as well. Prints of theatrical characters which were purchased as souvenirs from the late 18th century provide a much more direct link with the cut-out figures in melodramatic attitudes with which toy collectors are familiar. Both adults and children began to cut out these characters and they were eventually provided with simple scenes. J. F. Schreiber of Esslingen appears to be the first to have produced scenes specifically for children, around 1800, and some ten years later his first printed coloured sheets were sold, though in Britain such sets were hand coloured until the late 19th century. The theatre appealed greatly to continental children and the production of plays particularly in Germany was substantial. Walter Rohler, an authority on the subject, discovered that there were sixteen firms in German-speaking countries alone who produced sheets for the opera 'Der Freischutz'.

The English theatre developed independently from the Continental and was linked very completely to the current productions on the London stage. The sheets of actors with their names, the character they were playing and the title of the play were at first sold mainly for adults in sets of four, but from around 1810 they began to be supplied with a wing attached so that a very basic scene could be cut out and assembled. These were sold at a penny plain or twopence coloured. J. K. Green claimed that he was the first to have produced model theatres, but George Speaight in *History of the English Toy Theatre* considered it far more likely that William West was the first.

Although by 1820 there were several publishers it is often difficult to distinguish between their plays, as an almost rigid form of presentation quickly developed, aided by the fact that the artists worked for several different firms. Some publishers, such as William West, were a real trial to their young customers, as their plays were not provided with sufficient characters for all the scenes and it was sometimes years before specific missing sheets were printed. The artists who drew the figures went to actual performances with the actors already drawn in traditional attitudes, so that they simply had to sketch in the costumes and add a little character to the faces.

The model theatre was a type of activity that appealed mainly to the inventive and intelligent child and could not have held the mass appeal of a wheeled toy or a doll, so that by the 1830s it was already becoming less popular. In England, Martin Skelt began buying up the copper plates of firms that were closing down, and in a few years he was able to offer some sheets for as little as a halfpenny. He was the first producer to market his plays really energetically and they could be obtained from small shops all over Britain.

An unusual and fairly simple Spanish model theatre published by Seix y Barral in the late 19th century. Note the unusual realism of both stage front and scenery by comparison with the Pellerin theatres shown opposite. Pollock's Toy Museum, London.

The toy theatre was in almost complete decline by the 1880s, though fashionable interest in it was revived to some extent by an article which Robert Louis Stevenson wrote for *A Magazine of Art* in 1884. He described a shop in which all the year round 'there stood displayed a theatre in working order, with a forest set, a combat and a few robbers carousing in the slides; and below and about, dearer tenfold to me! the plays themselves, those budgets of romance, lay tumbled upon one another', adding nostalgically, 'Long and often have I lingered there with empty pockets . . . it was a giddy joy that shop, which was dark and smelt of bibles, was a lodestone rock for all that bore the name of boy'.

Toy theatres were not printed in any real quantity in America until the 1870s, when Scott & Co of New York published 'Seltz's American Boy's Theatre' which sold at 25 cents plain and 50 cents coloured. A new type of theatre was developing at this time that demanded less skill on the part of the child and was more in the nature of a simple constructional toy. This was produced in fairly cheap boxed sets by many toymakers and sold alongside such items as mosaic picture sets and basketwork outfits. The romance and imaginative qualities of the earlier toys have disappeared and these later sets are fairly obviously meant for very occasional amusement. J. W. Spear, for instance, issued a series of 'Pet's Plays' and shadow theatres that are entirely cheap and expendable. The shadow theatre originated in China and it is thought that the first European countries to hold shows were Germany and Italy. Toy shadow theatres were cheap to produce and these were also added to the inexpensive boxed ranges produced by firms such as Raphael Tuck. A few splendidly constructed theatres with good lighting and quite complicated sets were of course made especially for individual children, but well made commercial theatres did not appear after the First World War in any real quantity, and an effort made to rekindle interest in the subject after the Second World War was not a long-term success.

Many toy collectors like to own a small theatre of the commercially produced type, but home made models are not popular, despite the hours of work expended on their construction, and fine examples often fetch very small sums. The prints published in the early 19th century have been popular for many years, and good examples now only occasionally appear on the market, though there are many reprints from the original plates issued in particular by Pollock's in London.

Above: **The 'Opéra' Theatre, published by the firm of Pellerin at Epinal in France (see page 256). The stage is set with a shop interior in convincing perspective. Late 19th century.** *Left:* **Another Pellerin theatre, the 'Théâtre Français', with cut-out figures for a costume drama, including Pierrot and Harlequin. Late 19th century. Both Pollock's Toy Museum, London.**

PRODUCERS OF TOY THEATRES

Bestelmeier, Georg Hieronymus–Nuremberg. A toy merchant working from around 1793 to 1825. His catalogues, which are one of the most important sources of information on German toys made at this time, include theatres that were specially made for glove puppet shows. He also sold marionettes and a number of shadow theatres. His 'Chinese Shadow Play' included Chinese fireworks, which were in fact a purely optical effect created by two wheels. Their 1800 catalogue include marionettes, glove puppets and a number of shadow figures.

Green, J. K. (1790 to 1860)–London. In 1812 Green published a stage front and several characters which was sold through the firm of Burtenshaw. He then disappeared from records until 1834 when he laid claim to being 'The original inventor and publisher of Juvenile and Theatrical prints. Established 1808'. Green is thought to have worked for West, who was the most likely inventor of the toy in England, and in fact he published some plays from West's address. It is possible that he suggested the making of toy theatres to West, but this is very much conjecture. There are a few plays where it is not clear which man was copying the other, as there was obviously great rivalry and frequent pirating of plays. The plays published after 1834 are very well drawn and coloured and those to which he has sole claim are among the best produced. Before 1857 he had published some fifty halfpenny plays, some of which were copies. His subjects include 'The Wreck Ashore' (1837), 'The Forty Thieves' (1836), and 'Wapping Old Stairs (1838).

Hodgson & Co–London, 1822 to 1830. This group worked from several addresses and is thought to have included W. Cole, S. Maunder and Howes. Orlando Hodgson was probably connected with the company and he published plays until 1843. The plays published are very well printed and coloured and the firm was unusual for the period in that they invariably supplied sufficient characters for all the scenes. The plays are highly effective and are particular favourites among collectors. Orlando's plays are even more strongly drawn, with particularly amusing well decorated backgrounds. Their plays include 'The Vision of the Sun', 'Black Beard the Pirate' and 'Maid Marian', all dating from 1824. Altogether some sixty-eight different plays are recorded.

Jameson, J. H.–Theatrical Print Warehouse, Bow Road, London, 1811 to 1827. The sheets produced by this firm are now very scarce and it is thought that many of their characters were not actually intended for use in plays but were more in the nature of souvenirs. These sheets of characters, which were not very skilfully drawn but have considerable charm, were issued from 1811. In that year some six different sets were published. Some of the portraits are signed 'I. R. Cruikshank' or simply 'Cruikshank', while other sheets are signed by J. Findlay. A large number of plays were issued including 'The Americans' (1811), 'The Hag of the Lake' (1812), 'The Blood Red Knight' (1813), and 'The Vampire' (1820).

Pollock, Benjamin (1856 to 1937)–Hoxton St, London. Pollock was a furrier by trade and married the daughter of John Redington, a publisher of plays. When Redington died in 1876, Pollock, at the age of twenty, took over the shop and the stock. He was mainly a producer of reprints, and his only original publication was some scenes for Green's 'Sleeping Beauty'. His shop was given added fame by its mention in Stevenson's article in *A Magazine of Art*. In this it was suggested that he was the only remaining publisher and well known figures such as Chaplin, Edith Sitwell and Diaghilev visited him in consequence. In 1936 the British Puppet and Model Theatre Guild staged a

Right: **'Green's Characters and Scenes in the Red Rover', published by J. K. Green of London in the second quarter of the 19th century. The set included seven plates of characters, ten scenes and set pieces, and four plates of wings. Pollock's Toy Museum, London.**

This scene of an Egyptian palace was part of a large set issued by M. Trentsensky of Vienna around 1880. Bethnal Green Museum of Childhood, London. *Below:* The 'Theatre Royal', published by McLoughlin Brothers of New York in 1894. Though obviously a cheap toy set, the theatre is effective enough as shown here, set with a scene from 'Little Red Riding Hood'. The theatre front bears the name and address of the printer: 'Meyer, Merkel & Ottmann, Lith. 21–25 Warren St. N.Y.' Pollock's Toy Museum, London.

commemorative exhibition in honour of his 80th birthday. He did his own litho printing but sent out the letterpress work. Even at the end of his life, when he was well known, complete coloured plays could still be purchased for five shillings. His daughter continued the business until 1944. In 1946 the firm became Benjamin Pollock Ltd. Many plays are still reissued from the original plates and completely new plays have been published, including 'The Flying Saucerers' in 1956 and 'High Toby' in 1948.

Redington, John (1819 to 1876) – Hoxton St, London, 1850 to 1876. Redington was a printer, bookseller, stationer and tobacconist, who sold all kinds of printed booklets, paper games and toys. He originally sold the plays published by firms such as Webb and he was J. K. Green's retail agent. Around 1850 he issued some of his own rather crudely drawn scenes which were stone lithographed. His own plays included 'Charles II', Baron Munchausen' and 'The Mistletoe Bough', as well as a member of others.

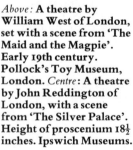

Above: **A theatre by William West of London, set with a scene from 'The Maid and the Magpie'. Early 19th century. Pollock's Toy Museum, London.** *Centre:* **A theatre by John Reddington of London, with a scene from 'The Silver Palace'. Height of proscenium 18½ inches. Ipswich Museums.**

Schreiber, J. F. – Esslingen, Germany. From around 1800 this firm began to publish children's theatrical scenes. Around 1810, the first printed coloured sheets were issued instead of the usual hand or stencil colouring. The 'Schreibersche Kindertheater' with notes, construction details, and sheets of figures was sold until the First World War in German, English and French versions.

Scott & Co – New York. This firm published 'Seltz's American Boy's Theatre' around 1870. The subjects issued included 'The Boy Sailor or the Pirate's Doom', 'The Red Skeleton or the Dead Avenger', and a pantomime – 'The Fiend of the Rocky Mountain'.

Singer, J. H. – New York. Around 1900, when the model theatre was really dying in Europe, this company published 'Blue Beard', 'The Young Soldier' and 'Robinson Crusoe'.

Skelt, Martin – Swan Street, London, 1835 to 1872. The firm was run by various members of the Skelt family, so that the initials M. & M., M. & B., B., and E. Skelt are found. Martin Skelt was an energetic snapper-up of other publishers' stock, which he reissued under his own name. He

did publish a few of his own plays at a penny a sheet and later some fifty halfpenny sheets were also sold. As a result of his policy of buying up other firms' stock, he issued several different versions of various plays. It is said that the plays were produced at the rate of one large sheet, that was cut by the retailer, a week. The Skelts could neither draw nor engrave themselves and different engravers were employed for the characters and the scenes. Other engravers were used for the lettering. The firm was over enthusiastic in its buying of plays and many were probably never issued by them. The running of the firm gradually became worse and Benjamin Skelt died in the workhouse. Their plays include 'The Wood Daemon', 'Der Freischutz' and 'Mazeppa'.

Trentsensky – Vienna. This firm issued over two hundred sets of sheets and 243 sets of figures for 41 titles. Their 'Big Theatre', issued *circa* 1825, used the technique of pen lithography and by 1860 was provided with 41 plays. The 'Mignon-Theater' or 'Complete Apparatus for the Presentation of the main features of popular plays from the repertoire of the Vienna theatres with faithful representation of decor and costumes' was published in 1830, though the characters are

rather more in the nature of fashion plates than conventional model theatre figures. In 1857 a series of plays was issued that were originally published by Joseph Myers.

Webb, W. (1820 to 1890) – Ripley, Surrey, and London, 1844 to 1890. Webb was apprenticed to an etcher and lithographer at the age of fifteen and learned the trade thoroughly from Archibald Park, who was himself a small publisher of plays. He then worked as a traveller before setting up his own firm. It is thought that his early sheets were engraved for other publishers. His own sheets can be marked W., W. G. or W. C. Webb and he was followed by his son H. J. Webb, who died in 1933. In 1847 Webb's first play, 'The Forest of Bondy' was published. Eventually some twenty-two plays were issued as well as the usual theatrical portraits. Webb was unusual in that he both drew, engraved and printed his products himself, a feat that no other publisher of the time performed. His plays are more Victorian in design than the melodramatic late 18th century style of the earlier designers, and his sheets are consequently less popular with collectors. His son simply reprinted his plays, the last of which was published in 1880. In 1926 H. J. Webb drew a special version of

'Robin Hood' for an exhibition, and the Webb shop in Old Street, London, was open until 1933. Plays include 'Union Jack' (1848), 'The Battle of Alma' (1854), and 'Jack in the Beanstalk' (1861).

West, William (1783 to 1854) – Theatrical Print Warehouse and Circulating Library, The Strand, London, 1811 to 1854. West was probably the first British producer of toy theatres, issuing some twelve plays in 1811. New plays were being published every month by 1812, and he sold a version of practically every play that was running in London. From 1812 scenes as well as characters were sold and 'Simon the Tartar' was probably his first complete set. His trade card claimed that he was a producer of 'Original tragic Fancy and Comic characters'. He also published and sold mildly pornographic books. Altogether some 140 plays were published, some of which were drawn in part by George Cruikshank. The colouring of the plays is particularly good. In 1812 the proscenium of the Theatre Royal was sold and West's other stage fronts include Covent Garden, Drury Lane and the Lyceum. Not a very good businessman, he had to sell most of his stock. Titles include 'Blue Beard' (1811), 'Pope Joan' (1819), and 'The Red Witch of Moravia' (1820).

A 'Globe' theatre, from a series published in the 1890s. It is set with the transformation scene from 'The Sleeping Beauty', and is of interest as the first English theatre to be printed in colour. Pollock's Toy Museum, London.

Children's books

The children's books that most interest the toy collector are generally those with an immediate eye-catching appeal, derived either from their lavish colouring or from a skilled three-dimensional effect, such as is provided by 'pop-up' illustrations. The often unpretentious early editions with few pictures are frequently ignored by the toy enthusiast and left to specialist collectors of antiquarian books. One of the first novelty books was published by Robert Sayer of Fetter Lane, London, in the 1760s. This had sections that could be opened in turn to show pictures accompanied by a short verse which ended with the words 'turn up' or 'turn down'. When this advice was followed another picture was revealed. As many of these 'turn-up' books described the adventures of harlequin, they were also known to children as 'harlequinades'. Other publishers quickly followed Sayer's example and by 1800 a number were in circulation, selling at sixpence plain or a shilling coloured. The pages were easily damaged, so that examples in very good condition are only occasionally found.

Among the most attractive of the early 19th century novelty books are those published by S. & J. Fuller at the Temple of Fancy, Rathbone Place, London, who sold some containing paper dolls as well as a variety of panoramas and peepshows. Their *History of Little Fanny* is well-known to collectors of dolls and takes the form of a narrative accompanied by figures in hand-coloured

costumes representing stages in the tale. Only one head was provided for each book, which meant that damage was easily sustained, and the buyer has to beware of replacements cut from prints of the period. Several other characters, such as 'Little Henry', were added to the series and all were contained in a sturdy card slipcases as they were comparatively expensive toys. Toy books such as these were imitated in America by William Charles of New York and Philadelphia between 1810 and 1825, but he issued the figures printed on separate sheets.

The 'illusion' books that were popular in the 1860s are also favourites with collectors. In these

The first book to be produced specifically for children was Jost Ammon's *Kunst und Lehrbüchlein*, published in Germany in 1578 and later issued in Britain as the *Book of Art and Instruction for Young People*. The wood engraving shown here (*near right*) represents Romulus and Remus. *Centre, top*: An interesting animated book with cutouts operated by a tab, *The Model Menagerie*, published by Ernest Nister of London and E. P. Dutton & Co. in New York. Late 19th century. Ipswich Museums. *Bottom: The Paignion*, a chart game in book form with sixty-five paper figures which could be placed in any of the views. Published by F. C. Westley, 162 Piccadilly, London. *Circa* 1838. Welsh Folk Museum, St Fagan's, Cardiff.

the child was instructed on how to see images on plain surfaces, through persistence of vision, after staring at the pictures in books such as *Spectropia or Surprising Spectral Illusions, showing Ghosts Everywhere and of every colour*. A whole variety of trick books appeared in the mid 19th century, though of course they were all relatively expensive. One of the main producers of novelty editions was Thomas Dean of Threadneedle Street, London, who was one of the first in Britain to use lithography and later chromo-lithography in the printing of children's books. Dean seems to have had some awareness of the needs of his customers, as even in 1859 he was offering a sixpenny series with

'coloured pictures and very little reading'. Some of Dean's books were printed on linen for durability and one contained a doll that was costumed in actual fabrics. This firm published some particularly ingenious books in which sections of the pictures moved when tabs were pulled. As the majority of children's books in the 1860s were still illustrated with woodcuts with very rudimentary hand colouring, these editions must have provided the recipients with real excitement.

Although firms such as Dean's were becoming aware of children's needs, it was the German companies that provided the bulk of colourful late 19th century literature, in particular the firm of Nister, which was based in Nuremberg but provided books to the specific needs of both American and British children. The Nister books are almost invariably colourful and enticingly produced, and those most often appearing in toy collections tend to be cut in the outline of, for example, a cat, Red Riding Hood or a small house, with the pages of text cut in an identical manner. Their 'stand-up' books are heavily collected by specialists, as examples in fine condition are quite rare. The figures lay flat on the pages but were pulled into an upright position by linen tabs. Later the firm also produced the much more common 'pop-up' books. Animated books such as those of Lothar Meggendorfer published by J. F. Schreiber at Esslingen, with sections that move when a tab is pulled, are highly collectable,

LINEN DRAPERS.

The earliest form of children's book, the horn book, consisted of an instructional text written or printed on parchment and covered with a thin sheet of horn to survive constant use. This interesting example includes the letters of the alphabet, combinations of vowels and consonants, and the Lord's Prayer and the Invocation. *Circa* 1660–1680. Saffron Walden Museum, Essex.

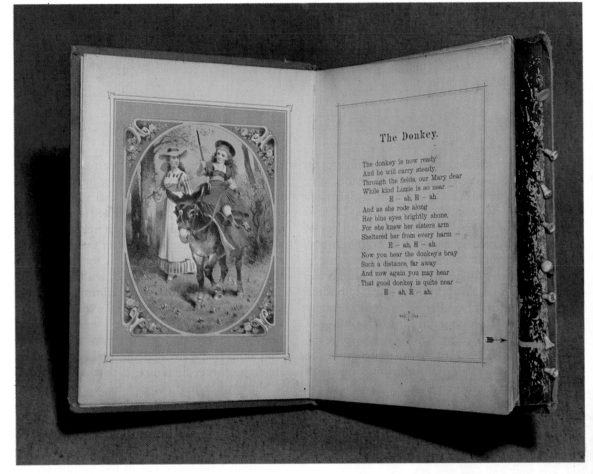

Right: The Speaking Picture Book, in which each picture is accompanied by a different animal noise, produced by pulling a cord at the side. Late 19th century; published by H. Grevel & Co., Covent Garden, London. Ipswich Museums. Below: Slovenly Peter, one of the 'Mechanical' series by Raphael Tuck (see page 239), designed in England and printed in Bavaria. It bears the 'Artistic Series' trademark no. 2523, and the inscription 'Publishers to the Queen' (i.e. Victoria). A pull on the cardboard tab activates the upper and lower pictures at the same time. Circa 1890. Author's Collection.

too, as they were so cleverly constructed. Among the most amusing of late 19th century publications was the 'Speaking Picture Book' in which different sounds were produced for each animal that was illustrated. The variety of novelty books seems to have declined rather than increased in the late 19th century, no doubt because wealthy children were already provided with a choice of colourful books aimed specifically at the imaginative needs of boys and girls.

The first artist to have worked with these basic needs of the child in mind was Jost Ammon, whose woodcuts were included in the first picture book that was designed specifically for children, *Kunst und Lehrbüchlein*, published in 1578 and later issued in Britain as the *Book of Art and Instruction for Young People*. Fairy tales were appearing from 1637 and, though not always intended for children, had an obvious appeal. The first known instructional picture book, *Orbis Sensualium*, was published in 1657 and by the end of the 17th century Locke was suggesting that children would learn with more ease if facts were accompanied by relevant pictures. In general, however, children were forced to make do with the few pictures in books such as *Foxe's Book of Martyrs*, or *The Pilgrim's Progress*, published in 1678. There was also a considerable supply of improving books teaching the elements of good behaviour, piety and etiquette, such as Robert Codrington's *Youth's Behaviour or Dancing in Conversation Amongst Women*, published in 1664. A moralistic book that was nevertheless of direct appeal to children of many generations was *Aesop's Fables*, published by John Ogilby

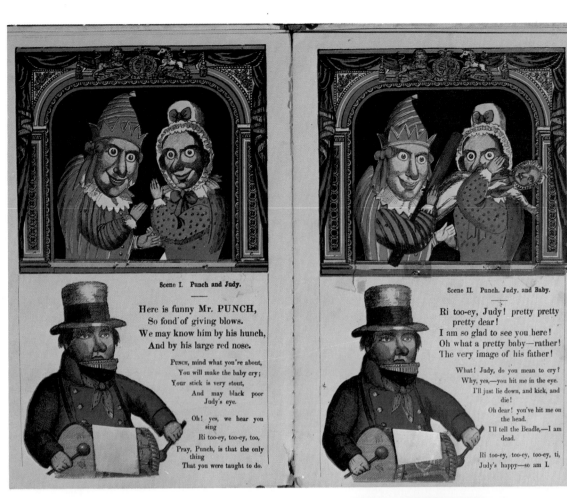

Scene I. Punch and Judy.

Here is funny Mr. PUNCH,
So fond of giving blows.
We may know him by his hunch,
And by his large red nose.

Punch, mind what you're about,
You will make the baby cry;
Your stick is very stout,
And may black poor
Judy's eye.

Oh! yes, we hear you
sing
Ri too-ey, too-ey, too,
Pray, Punch, is that the only
thing
That you were taught to do.

Scene II. Punch. Judy, and Baby.

Ri too-ey, Judy! pretty pretty
pretty dear!
I am so glad to see you here!
Oh what a pretty baby—rather!
The very image of his father!

What! Judy, do you mean to cry?
Why, yes,—you hit me in the eye.
I'll just lie down, and kick, and
die!
Oh dear! you've hit me on
the head.
I'll tell the Beadle,—I am
dead.

Ri too-ey, too-ey, too-ey, ti,
Judy's happy—so am I.

Left: **Two pages from** *The Royal Movable Punch and Judy,* **published by the British firm of Dean and Son in 1861. Bethnal Green Museum of Childhood, London.** *Below:* **High quality limited editions of children's books are always difficult to value. This plate from Charles Kingsley's** *Water Babies,* **with colour illustrations by Warwick Goble, was published in 1909 by Macmillan & Co., St. Martin's Street, London. Author's Collection.**

in 1651, illustrated with pictures for the adult reader but quickly appreciated by the young.

From the beginning of the 18th century, there was a much more substantial production of books intended purely for children, and it also became possible for relatively poor children to acquire literature, particularly from the baskets of pedlars and the packs of chapmen. The chap books, with simple but dramatic woodcuts, were often sold with the sheets still uncut and were printed mainly in the area of St Giles in the Fields, London. Children's songs and nursery rhymes also began to appear, and both Robinson Crusoe and Gulliver's Travels appeared in children's versions in the early 18th century.

A visitor to the Leipzig Fair in 1789 commented on the vast amount of children's literature that was available, and mentioned almanacs, newspapers, journals, stories, dramas, catechisms, history, grammars and other academic subjects. The general and amusing books appeared to sell mainly around Christmas, but the text books enjoyed steady sales throughout the year and must have been a necessity to the governesses, who were often relatively uneducated themselves. One of the earliest forms of text book was the so-called horn book, consisting of a sheet of parchment on which was written the alphabet, numbers and sometimes a prayer. The child followed and learned the letters by tracing them with a small pointer or his finger, and the sheet was protected by a thin layer of horn. These boards seem to have first appeared in the 16th century and were still used some two hundred years later.

WARWICK GOBLE

Leipzig and Frankfurt were becoming pre-eminent in the publishing of children's books from the late 18th century, while this period was characterised in Britain by the army of women writers, such as Hannah More, who wrote decidedly moral stories for the young, extolling the triumph of virtue over vice. A few lighter tales were gradually appearing, such as *The Diverting History of John Gilpin* by William Cowper, which appeared in 1782 and provided toymakers of several generations with promising subject matter.

The name of John Newbury (1713 to 1767) is pre-eminent in the history of children's publishing, as he was the first major publisher to realise

Jack the Giant Killer.

Pussy Jack the Giant Killer came skipping, sword in paw,
And the Giant, who was dining, dined never any more,

Above: **Pages from** *The Golliwog's Christmas* **by Florence Upton (see page 70), with verses by Bertha Upton. Published by Longman's Green & Co., London, 1907. Ipswich Museums.** *Right:* **An illustration from an untearable fabric-strengthened book,** *In Storyland with Louis Wain,* **which is notable for the rich colours used in the printing. It was published by Rapael Tuck (see page 239), and was designed at their studios in England and printed at their Fine Art Works in Bavaria. The book bears the legend 'Publishers to their Majesties The King and Queen & H.R.H. The Prince and Princess of Wales.'** *Circa* **1910. Author's Collection.**

Facing page, top: **Popular with American collectors are the books of Horatio Alger Jnr, which appeared in the late 19th century. The examples shown are** *Young Circus Rider or The Mystery of Robt. Rudd,* **published by Porter & Coates, Philadelphia, Penn., 1883;** *Way to Success or Luke Walton, the Chicago Newsboy,* **Porter & Coates, 1889;** *Tony the Hero A Brave Boy's Adventure,* **published by A. L. Burt, New York, 1890; and** *Tom Thatcher's Fortune,* **A. L. Burt, 1888. Margaret Woodbury Strong Museum, Rochester, New York.**

the vast possibilities of the new market. He designed his children's books himself and, as early as 1744, was promoting sales by offering 'gifts' such as a pincushion or a ball that actually cost an extra 2d with his volumes. The *Lilliputian Magazine,* the first periodical especially aimed at children, was sold by Newbury in 1751 and appeared monthly. After his death, the firm was continued by his son, whose main contribution to the development of juvenile publishing was to sell specially bound volumes so that even in childhood the beginnings of a library could be established.

Many of the favourites still enjoyed by modern children appeared in the early 19th century, including *Kinder- und Hausmärchen,* published in 1812 to 1815 and written by Jacob Ludwig Carl and Wilhelm Carl Grimm, and of course known popularly as *Grimm's Fairy Tales.* Hans Christian Andersen's *Wonderful Stories for Children* appeared in its first English translation in 1846, though it had appeared in Denmark in 1835, while *The Water Babies, a Fairy Tale for a Land Baby* by Charles Kingsley appeared in book form in 1863. This was closely followed in 1865 by *Alice's Adventures in Wonderland* written by the Rev C. L. Dodgson or Lewis Carroll, with its inimitable Tenniel illustrations.

In America *Peter Parley's Tales of America,* written by Samuel Griswold Goodrich (1793 to 1860), appeared first in 1827 and were immediately popular. The often found *Peter Parley's Annual* was published by Darton in 1848 with the addition of a coloured illustration and a coloured title page and continued until 1894. Because of the vast number of books he produced, Peter Parley was described as the most prodigious literary hack of his time, and similar criticisms are levelled at the work of Enid Blyton by intellectuals today. However, the fact that their books encouraged children to engage in the basic activity of reading should surely outweigh any criticism of their work as a whole.

As America is a comparatively young country almost any of their children's books that were actually published there in the early 19th century are of great interest even if not particularly decorative. One of the earliest children's books was

The History of a Great Many Little Boys and Girls— for the amusement of all good children of 4 and 5 years of age, published in 1815. Each page was provided with a picture. Chritmas annuals also appeared quite early and in 1831 the *Forget me Not* series was first issued, soon to be accompanied by a whole variety of annuals such as *The Hive,* which was published by W. & S. B. Ives. *The Youth's Companion* (1827) actually predated *The Forget me Not* and was published for over a hundred years. One of the more serious books was *McGuffey's Eclectic Reader,* which first appeared in 1836 and went through many editions. In 1833 *A Small Geography for Children on an Improved Plan, by Mrs. Beecher with Cuts* was announced by Benjamin Olds. Mrs Beecher was of course later to write the children's classic *Uncle Tom's Cabin.*

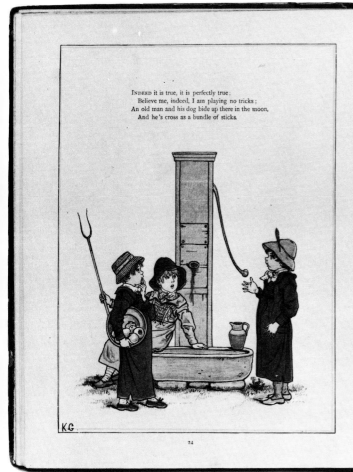

Indeed it is true, it is perfectly true;
Believe me, indeed, I am playing no tricks;
An old man and his dog bide up there in the moon,
And he's cross as a bundle of sticks.

K.G.

24

SCHOOL is over,
Oh, what fun!
Lessons finished,—
Play begun.
Who'll run fastest,
You or I?
Who'll laugh loudest?—
Let us try.

K.G.

25

Illustrators begin to assume greater importance than the authors of children's books to collectors after 1870, when artists such as Walter Crane and Kate Greenaway created their completely idiosyncratic designs. Walter Crane's 'Sixpenny and Shilling Picture Books', printed by Edmund Evans, appeared between 1865 and 1875. In 1873 Routledge began to publish the 'New Series of Walter Crane's Toy Books' at sixpence and in the following year a shilling series appeared. His illustrations are of interest because of the strength of their composition and their depiction of subjects such as fashionable contemporary interiors, which make the books an expression of the advanced taste of the period. Kate Greenaway's work is much less robust in character, but is also a charming expression of the aestheticism of the late 19th

century, when elegant mothers dressed their children in pseudo 18th century style. *Under the Window*, in which the characteristics of her work first appear strongly, was first published in 1878 in an edition of some 20,000 by George Routledge & Sons, those produced by Warne & Co being of a later date. Beatrix Potter (1866 to 1943) is another great children's illustrator and her *Tale of Peter Rabbit* appeared in privately printed editions from 1901, though it was later published by Warne & Co. All her books were produced in small sizes, so that they could be handled with ease by the smallest hands. Those most popular characters of childhood, Jemima Puddle Duck, Flopsy Bunnies, Timmy Tiptoes and Squirrel Nutkin had all appeared before 1912 and have remained popular to the present.

Two illustrated pages from Kate Greenaway's *Under the Window*, **a book of pictures and rhymes by one of the best known children's authors. It was published in 1878 by George Routledge & Sons at Ludgate Hill in London, and at 416 Broome Street in New York, and engraved and printed by Edmund Evans of London. Author's Collection.**

Scraps and scrapbooks

The colourful scrapbooks of the second half of the 19th century evolved from two quite distinct lines of development. The pasting of interesting verses, sketches, water colours and messages into books became popular in the late 18th century and was a very common pastime for women by the Regency period. These early books often show very clearly the personality of the compiler and though less immediately striking than later albums, reflect accurately the period and country in which they were assembled. The other distinct line of development was the use of decorative mottoes by confectioners and bakers. These were commercially printed in sheets and were cut out as required to be fixed to biscuits and icing sugar figures, a method of decoration that is still common in Germany and Holland. The improvements in colour printing and embossing meant that it was possible to produce these commercial scraps far more effectively, and from around 1860 the colourful embossed scraps that are so familiar began to be exported in vast quantities from Germany and to a smaller extent from France.

Sheets of plain or hand-coloured prints intended for adults were produced in Britain in the early 19th century by firms such as William Cole and J. Betts. Sheets with the title 'Tregears Scraps', usually with humorous subjects printed in a series of six or eight pictures, are still occasionally found in an uncut state. Unfortunately the publisher's name was usually printed deliberately on the section that would be cut away, so that when found in scrapbooks they are unidentifiable. There were no guide lines for cutting, so that some were trimmed quite literally around the outline of the figures while others appear as rectangles or squares. Fashion prints and figures intended for use in model theatres were often included and look effective when displayed on the variously coloured pages that became more common after 1820. After this time the German printers were gradually making more use of steel engraved plates instead of lithographic stones so that printing was also becoming steadily cheaper.

Fortunately, the compilers of early scrap books were pleased with their endeavours and added their names and the date on which the book was commenced. Even where this is not the case, an approximate dating is often possible from clues such as clothing fashions. The inclusion of cards also gives some help in dating, as the first Christmas cards did not appear until 1843 and it was several years before they were commercially produced in any quantity. The character of scrap books changes completely after 1860, when chromo-lithographed scraps began to appear in some quantity. Previously the involvement of children in the pastime was only occasional, but after this time it becomes much more common to find the books inscribed with a child's name and his age. The books themselves, which were often given as gifts, were attractively decorated and embossed and sometimes included protective sheets of tissue for the contents. They were produced in a variety of sizes and in qualities to suit all pockets, so that by the end of the century they were owned even by poor children.

A plain book with several sheets of gloriously coloured scraps made a useful Christmas present for children, providing them with a quiet and absorbing occupation. There is evidence of an adult hand in many surviving examples, for example in delicate water-colour backgrounds to some scenes which could never have been painted by a seven-year-old child. The technique of cutting and using scraps was variously known as decalomania, scrap work, decoupage and even Scrapiana, a term that was used on a scrap produced by Engelmann & Company in the 1840s. Scraps were produced mainly in Leipzig, Dresden, Frankfurt and Vienna and the manufacturers quickly saw the advisability of setting up distributors in the country of sale. The Mamelok Press was set up in England and the firm of Raphael

Tuck had branches in Paris, London, New York and Melbourne. It is not known when the first sheets were imported to England from Germany, but Gleeson White, writing in 1894, commented that 'Thiery of Fleet Street, known as the Father of the Christmas Card trade, was doubtless the first to introduce the elaborately embossed reliefs . . . then they cost eighty shillings per hundred but now their price has fallen to one shilling the hundred for large quantities.'

The greatest production of scraps was between 1875 and 1900. The subjects are usually typical of the sentimentalism popularly associated with the period and show chubby and beautifully dressed children, flower bedecked hearts and crosses and romantic country scenes. Special christening, marriage, Valentine and even mourning scraps were available, as were advertising sets, alphabets and educational groups teaching the correct names of various animals and shells etc. Though the sheets were usually purchased separately,

firms such as Raphael Tuck also sold boxed sets. As the maker's name when applied was usually on the white joining ties, the scraps that are cut are only occasionally identifiable. The swopping of scraps was a busy trade amongst children, and the insertions on a single page may have come from many different sources.

At the end of the 19th century, scrapbooks included much general printed matter, in particular the colourful advertisements that were appearing in large numbers. As a result, though perhaps less artistic in assembly, these later books are more lively as social documents.

Interest in this subject was until quite recently, very minimal, but is now steadily increasing, fostered perhaps by excellent exhibitions such as that held at the Bethnal Green Museum of Childhood in London in 1977. At this exhibition the collection of Alistair Allen was shown and the viewer was made aware of the astonishing range of both subjects and quality in scrapbooks.

MAIN PRODUCERS OF SCRAPS AND SCRAP SHEETS

Betts, J. – London, 1828 to 1874. This firm of stationers and booksellers sold scrap sheets entitled 'John Betts. The Juvenile Scrap Sheet'.

Benewitz, M. Appian – Leipzig. A firm of chromo printers selling reliefs.

Birn Brothers – London, 1882 to 1941. This firm published sheets which were printed in Germany, including Principal Buildings of the World, Fish and Crustacea, Children and Flowers, The Circus, Elephant and Rider, The Victoria Cross Gallery and The Hunter Caught Unawares.

Hagelberg, W. – Berlin. Founded in 1858. Ernest Falck & Co of London were their agents in the 1880s. Their scraps were marked with a 'W.H.' monogram. The firm had their own establishment in London between 1886 and 1916.

Heller, Emanuel – Vienna. Produced subjects such as Clowns, Boys and Girls in Fancy Dress, Prehistoric Animals, Koala Bear and Goats, Monkeys and Pets, Trees, Captors and Prey, Snakes, and Whale and Penguins.

Hildesheimer, Siegmund, & Co – London, 1877 to 1927. Published scraps, reliefs and chromos, including sheets of Bible history, Shakespearian characters and Queen Victoria's Jubilee.

Jerrard, John – London, *circa* 1862 to 1881. Seller of scraps and prints, scenes and views for cutting out. Sold scraps and prints of every description for albums, scrap books and screens. Published a catalogue. Some scraps are marked on the back.

Mamelok & Sohne – Originally in Breslau, Germany. Recorded from 1870 to the 1880s, but probably began production in the 1820s and thought to have been known as Mamelok & Adam. One of the largest producers of scraps, the firm is still in operation in Britain today. In the 19th century, they produced their own albums for scraps. Published sheets such as Wild and Farm Animals, Dogs and Cats, Little Girls with Presents and Toys, Gnomes and Oriental Youths, and children with boxes, baskets and dolls.

Myers, A. N. – London, 1800 to 1899. Sold sheets of lithographed scraps that were printed in Germany, with subjects such as Making a Snowman, Drawing a Caricature, The Clowns. Some of their scraps, including the 'Juvenile' series, were printed by K. Thienemann of Stuttgart.

Nathan, Michael Henry, & Co – London, 1878 to 1900. Published and imported scraps and other ephemera. Subjects included The Black Watch, King Harold and Robert the Bruce, Lord Berestord and HRH Albert Victor of Wales, Edward the Black Prince and Henry V, The Greeley Expedition to the South Pole, and The Greeley Expedition to the North Pole.

Below, left: **A pair of large relief scraps representing Edward the Black Prince and Henry V, printed by Michael Henry Nathan & Co. Late 19th century.** *Right:* **An effective relief entitled 'Woman Weighing Cherries'. This was one of the scraps published by A. N. Myers of London and reprinted by K. Thienemanns Verlag of Stuttgart. Late 19th century. Both Alistair Allen Collection.**

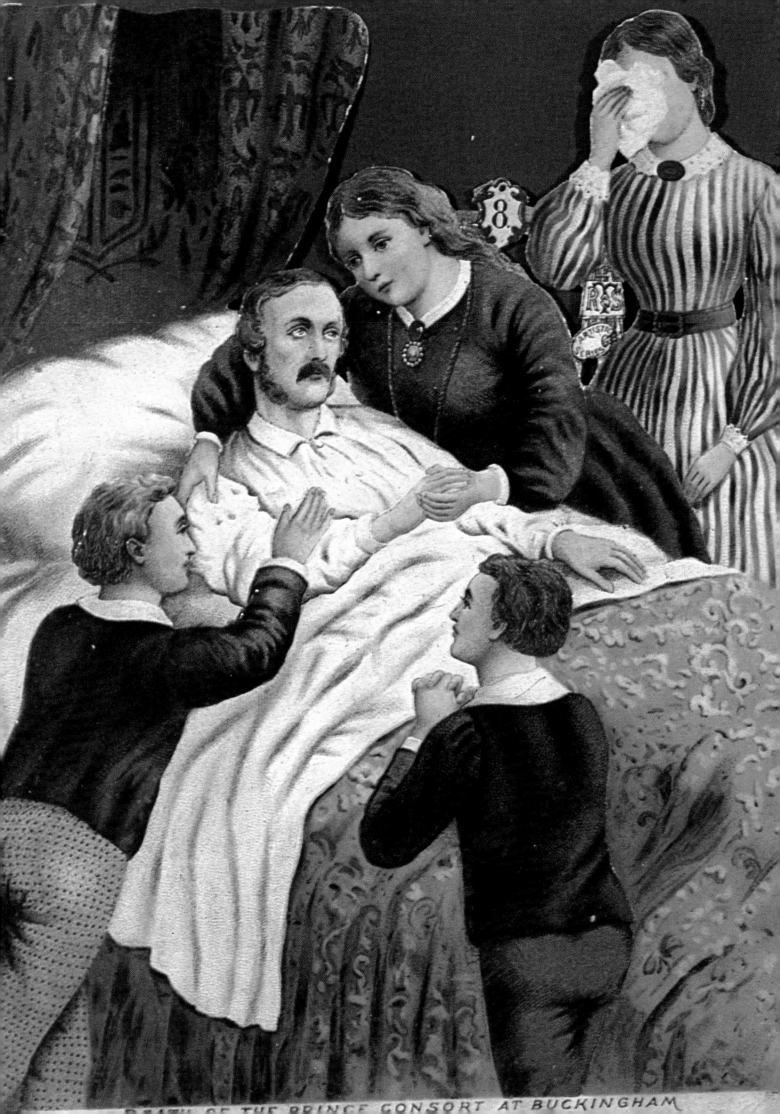

DEATH OF THE PRINCE CONSORT AT BUCKINGHAM

Priester, F., & Eyck – Berlin, 1870s to 1916. Printers of scraps, chromos and cards. This firm had a branch for distribution in London. Their trademark is 'MP' or an eye in a six-pointed star.

Tuck, Raphael – London, New York, Paris, Berlin and Montreal. Raphael Tuck left Breslau in Germany in 1865 and opened a shop in London to sell pictures and undertake picture framing. Three years later the company were publishing themselves and selling chromolithographs, black and white lithographs and oleographs. The familiar easel and palette trademark was used from 1880 and from 1881 the firm was known as Raphael Tuck & Sons. This was changed in 1895 to Raphael Tuck and Sons Ltd. The Royal Warrant of Appointment to Queen Victoria was granted in 1893 and used until her death in 1901. After this time, the names of succeeding monarchs appear. Books, wall charts, cards, paper novelties, marionettes and paper dolls were all produced as well as scraps. Their 'Jubilee' sets issued in 1887 were particularly fine, and sold in a wrapper inscribed, 'The Victoria Jubilee in twelve reliefs showing some of the principal events during the fifty years reign of Her Most Gracious Majesty Queen Victoria. Painted by Arthur and Harry Payne'. Their scraps were printed at their Fine Art Works in Bavaria or sometimes in Saxony. The colours are almost invariably good. Other subjects include sheets of the soldiers of England, France, Germany, Russia and Italy. Several impressive tableaux sheets such as the Fire Brigade, The Royal National Lifeboat Institution, Leading the Field and Britannia were issued. Also 'Construction' sheets such as a Negro and a Caucasian doll and dressing figures, and 'Panorama' sheets such as Robinson Crusoe, Snow White and Buttercup Farm. Of interest are the special editions such as Going to the Derby by George Cruikshank and the advertisement editions, which include one for Sunlight Soap. Scrap books and boxed sets of scraps were also sold. A large percentage of the firm's work was sold in America. The firm is still in operation today.

Vallet Minot & Cie – Paris. Published subjects such as A Dancer and a Lady of Fashion, Woman and Country Scene, Fruit Picking.

Zoecke & Mittmeyer – Berlin, 1896 to the present. Published good quality reliefs and many floral subjects, Raphael Angels, Flowers and Instruments, Insects and Leaves.

In 1887 Raphael Tuck & Sons published a set of twelve reliefs commemorating the Golden Jubilee of Queen Victoria. Here we see the cover of the set (*above*), and three of the reliefs, depicting 'Queen Victoria receiving General and Mrs Grant, 1887', 'Queen Victoria in the Highlands' and 'The Queen holding a drawing room at Buckingham Palace, 1886'. *Facing page*: Another relief from the Jubilee set, 'Death of the Prince Consort at Buckingham Palace, December 14th, 1867'. All Alistair Allen Collection.

Doll's dressmaking

Doll's dressmaking has formed one of the main occupations for girls since the beginning of civilisation, and whereas idle play with dolls was frowned upon in the 18th and 19th centuries by the more puritanical adults, the girl who made carefully stitched garments was much praised and assisted. Examples of 18th century children's work can be found on some doll's clothes, as well as in the often complex samplers that were made to illustrate their mastery of various stitches and techniques. Child-sized needlework boxes and needle cases are sometimes found decorated with motifs that are obviously intended for the young. However, there was little commercial interest in the subject until the early 19th century, when a book appeared written by Mme Malès de Beaulieu, which attempted to teach the child the correct dress for various social occasions by means of different doll's costumes. *La Poupée Bien Elevée* was first published around 1819 but subsequent editions can be as late as the 1850s and there were some English versions. The educational importance of making doll's clothes was also stressed in *The American Girl's Book or Occupations for Play Hours*, written by Mrs Leslie, which appeared in 1831. In this book, the descriptions of the actual construction of the clothes were not very clear and patterns were apparently not supplied, so that the child had to copy them from the illustrations.

The ladies' magazines which were being published in most European countries and America by the 1850s occasionally included special articles for children with instructions for knitting or sewing. In 1860 Frederick Lesser's *Dolly's Dressmaker* appeared both in Berlin and in London. This was a most definite advance on earlier publications, as it provided twelve sheets of patterns as well as instructions. The book's cover showed a child seated at a full sized three-legged sewing table and was obviously intended to show that she was learning an adult activity. Though the sewing machine was used in many homes in the mid 1860s, illustrations of the period invariably show the child industriously sewing by hand and we must assume that the toy sewing machine did not appear until very late in the century.

Several magazines appeared almost simultaneously in France in the 1860s, just at the time when French lady dolls, dressed in the height of fashion, were very popular. As several of these papers had links with the doll sellers, they probably assisted in advertising their products. *Gazette de la Poupée* and *La Poupée* were soon amalgamated but *La Poupée Modèle* was to continue until 1923. They were intended for girls between the ages of six and twelve and included patterns as well as encouragingly attractive pictures. *La Poupée Modèle* was produced by Mme Lavalée Péronne, whose shop, A La Poupée de Nuremberg, sold trimmings for small hats and mantles.

After 1865 there was a wealth of published designs. In 1870, *Demorest's Young America*, a magazine published by the American News Co of New York, advertised patterns that were obtainable by post and commented on those available at fairs and markets, so commercially producing patterns were evidently appearing in some numbers by this time. Designs intended for costuming dolls as babies also appear at this period and reflect the manufacturer's new found interest in the creation of dolls that resembled children rather than adults. One book published in Philadelphia in 1898 made the suggestion, rather startling for the period, that boys as well as girls should learn to sew dolls' clothes. Another much more commercial idea of the same year was to sell a doll and then supply patterns for its clothes. This idea also originated in America, where it was offered by Youth's Companion. A gift box that was sold in 1902 and entitled 'Die Puppen-Schneiderin' (the doll's dressmaker) contained a doll, patterns for clothes, fabrics, thread, scissors and needles, while another enterprising American

'Dolly's Dressmaker', a set of patterns printed on substantial paper, together with an instruction booklet 'translated from the German of Frederike Lesser by Madame de Chatelain'. Published in London by Joseph Myers & Co., and in Berlin by Winckelmann & Sons. *Circa* 1860. Betty Harvey-Jones Collection.

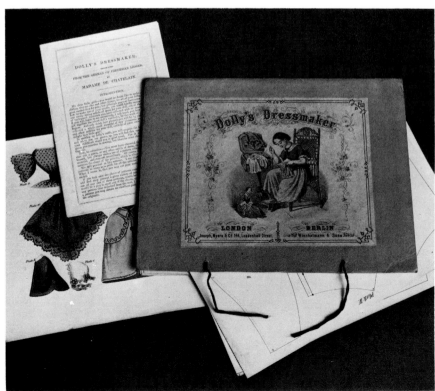

The extremely high standard of doll's dressmaking in the 18th century is illustrated by this fine embroidered silk coat and waistcoat, dating from 1725. Saffron Walden Museum, Essex. *Below:* This picture sums up the concept of doll's dressmaking in the 19th century. The toy sewing machine, usually made in Germany, was an essential part of nursery equipment. Patterns, instructions and advice were published in many magazines to help the young needlewoman. The doll is German. Author's Collection.

firm sold fabric printed with designs that could be cut out and assembled. Comparatively few of these instruction books are now available and even fewer dolls complete with their unsewn wardrobes. However, the sewing machines that were regularly illustrated in catalogues after 1900 have survived in some quantity and were evidently popular. It is sometimes difficult to estimate whether some of the small machines were actually toys or intended for specialised adult use. Both types are whimsically decorated and some of those shown in toy catalogues have surprisingly heavy wheels and bases intended for screwing to a tabletop. Very occasionally, treadle machines are found made by firms such as Singer, with details exactly mirroring those on adult machines of the time, including Art Nouveau ironwork supports. One of the main producers of toy machines was F. W. Müller of Berlin, who created some twenty different models, the cheapest sewing in chain stitch while the more expensive made two to four stitches at each turn of the wheel. Special boxes of cotton 'Dolly's Silkies' were sold in England by Ralph Dunn of the Barbican, London,

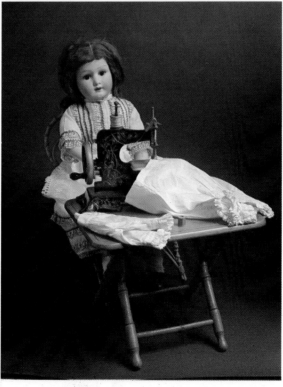

Mending Day

HOW quickly children's clothes
will rip and tear!

Each time I put off mending till
so late,

I re'lize that a family of eight

Can give a loving mother lots
of care.

If more get born I really do declare

I'll put 'em into bed and make
'em wait.

My brother hopes to learn to
operate,

But there is not a child that I
would spare.

HE'S borrowed three that he
pertends are dead.

But I won't even think of such
thin'!

And yet at mending time I've
often said

I almost wished—though p'raps
it is a sin—

That God has sent *some* paper
dolls instead

Whose clothes are only painted
on their skin.

—Burges Johnson.

Instructions for children's needlework often appeared in postcard form. *Above:* **An American postcard published by Reinthal & Newman of New York. It carries the notice 'Copyright 1908 Campbell Art Co.'. Author's Collection.** *Right:* **A business-like toy sewing machine with a chain drive, dating from the 1870s. Unmarked; height 4 inches. Luton Museum and Art Gallery, Bedfordshire.**

Facing page, left centre: **More obviously intended as a plaything is this heavy iron toy in the form of a clown, with a nodding head and a moving arm which functions as a sewing machine. Unmarked; *circa* 1885; height 8½ inches. Tolson Memorial Museum, Huddersfield.**

WATSON'S "HOW TO DO IT" SERIES (GIRLS'-4).

PATCHING

CALICO PATCH

RIGHT SIDE

1

WRONG SIDE

2

FLANNEL PATCH 3

while doll's patterns, packaged identically with those intended for adults, were sold by Blackmore of Camden Town, London, at a penny each and known as the 'Little Mother' series. They were all intended for a doll 10 to 16 inches long. Other firms, such as Gray & Nicholls of Liverpool, a games manufacturer, made millinery sets and even a 'Packet of Patchwork'. Ralph Dunn's Pets series of boxed crafts and games also included 'Pets Bonnet Box', which bears the wording 'Here is a nice box for all little girls: real dollies' hats with the material for trimming them. Pretty flowers, ribbon and even cotton are all provided in this box. Now buy this and give your dolly a treat.' The box lid shows the head and shoulders of a figure with long hair, on which an equally long haired child is fitting the hat. This set had come a long way from the original intention of child dressmaking, being intended to inculcate taste

into the child so that she could 'judge as to the desired combinations of colours which might be worn and thus avoid what often appears glaringly vulgar and common'.

Sewing machines in toy size continued to be produced for some years after the First World War. The designs were surprisingly old fashioned, with the exception of those made by Singer, which followed quite closely the advances made in full sized machines. After the 1940s, the child's sewing machine became more of a toy and less of a working model.

Very few surviving examples of child's sewing machines carry a maker's name, again with the exception of Singer, but the majority of the decorative examples are usually considered of German origin. They are collected mainly on the basis of their visual attractiveness rather than on their effectiveness as models.

Top left: **'Patterns for the Little Dressmaker', published by H. Schubert of Berlin. The set is contained in a red leather-cloth case and includes cartridge paper patterns for a 10-inch jointed doll.** *Circa* **1870. Betty Harvey-Jones Collection.** *Above:* **How to apply a calico and flannel patch, from one of a series of advertising post-cards distributed by Watson's Soap Works, Leeds.** *Circa* **1905. Author's Collection.**

Optical toys

A few optical toys are included in most general toy collections, but the true enthusiasts in this area are usually those interested in the development of photographic processes, as many items of this type in some way illustrate the theory of the persistence of vision, which is of course the basis of the cinema. Many toys of an optical nature, such as peep-shows and the magic lantern, began as adult amusements and only when their novelty value was expended did they become nursery equipment. In some instances it is difficult to ascertain the original intention of a piece, though usually if it is cheaply constructed the item is described as a toy.

Peep-shows were among the first toys of this type to achieve widespread popularity, and 15th century examples are recorded in which changes of lighting were used to create the effects of daylight, storm and moonlight. Travelling showmen set up their raree-shows until the mid 19th century and exhibited scenes such as 'The Tournament of the Field of the Cloth of Gold'. The peep-shows that the collector is likely to acquire are those often described as 'perspective toys'. These consist of a concertina-folded picture which can be opened at arm's length and when viewed through a peep-hole give an effective perspective view of such scenes as 'Westminster Abbey at the Coronation of Victoria' or 'The Thames Tunnel'. Some early 19th century examples are hand drawn and coloured, but there were many cheap printed versions on sale by the time of the Great Exhibition of 1851. Several interesting devices were manufactured in the USA by Milton Bradley of Springfield, Massachusetts, who in 1868 published a 'Historoscope. A Panorama and History of America from Columbus to the Civil War.' This was a box-like affair with an opening cut in the side in which appeared a series of panoramic pictures illustrating great incidents in American history. Another device, the 'Myriopticon', consisted of a panorama wound on rollers and illustrating incidents in the Civil War.

The magic lantern was invented by Athanasius Kircher around 1640 and its principles outlined in his book *Ars Magna Lucis et Umbrae*. Kircher was a particularly skilled showman who was able to alarm and terrify his simple audiences with the scenes he projected and was considered something of a sorcerer, despite the fact that he was a Jesuit priest. The magic lantern was still regarded with some suspicion in the early 18th century and mainly considered as an adult form of entertainment, though some educationalists advocated its use as a means of instructing the young. The finest lanterns were heavily ornamented in steel, copper and brass, which contrasted well with the gleaming polish of the woodwork. Expensive adult versions of this parlour type continued to be made into the 20th century, often by firms of instrument makers, though by this time the main producers were the great German toy-making companies. It is thought that the first true toy version was made by August Lapierre, a Parisian tinsmith, as a present for his children in 1843. His toy was basically a tin box fitted with a candle holder, a concave mirror and a lens, but this was gradually improved upon and he began to produce lanterns commercially from 1850. The firm was in operation until 1914 and eventually added a cinematograph to their range.

Early lanterns were lit by lamp or candle light and the flickering of the picture must have added greatly to the mysterious atmosphere they created. The cheaper children's lanterns were still lit by candles as late as 1910, though by this time there were several alternatives for the more expensive toys including petroleum lights, gas light, acetylene lamps, electricity and methylated spirit burners. The cheap lanterns were made of black-painted tin or polished Russian iron and fitted with three lenses, a paraffin lamp with a glass chimney and a

A panorama peepshow of a military scene decorated on the outside with scraps of the kings and queens of England by Raphael Tuck (*left*). The main picture shows the view through one of the peepholes. Unmarked; *circa* 1845. Bethnal Green Museum of Childhood, London.

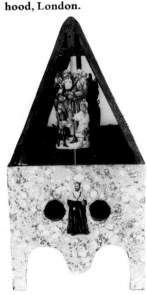

An ornate magic lantern contained in a leathercloth-covered box with slide compartments. The slides shown are of the long, narrow type first introduced in the early 19th century, which were drawn slowly across the lens of the lantern. Some show a continuous scene, others are split up into individual subjects. *Left:* The label from the same lantern, bearing the maker's trademark – the initials J.S. (for Jean Schoenner of Nuremberg, see page 173) and a star and a winged wheel. German, late 19th century; height of box $12\frac{1}{4}$ inches. Ipswich Museums.

245

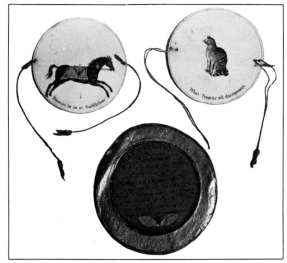

Above: **A group of five Phenakistoscope discs by Ackermann & Co. of London.** *Circa* **1835.** *Right:* **Two discs from an early optical toy known as the Thaumatrope, with their original box. When each disc is rotated by means of the threads, the two related images on either side appear to merge. The box bears the inscription 'Thaumatropical Amusement to illustrate the seeming Paradox of Seeing an Object which is out of sight, and to demonstrate the faculty of the Retina of the eye to retain the impression of an Object after its disappearance. Vide et Crede.' Both Science Museum, London.**

two separate removable cases for the slides. Included in the set were twelve coloured glass slides, one chromotrope (see below), a transformation scene and a moving landscape.

Slides illustrating a vast number of subjects of educational and religious interest as well as stories and children's rhymes were available, and while many collectors only wish to own a single lantern, the slides, which are often highly decorative objects, usually sell very quickly. In the early 19th century, long narrow slides with a scene painted over the whole surface were slowly drawn across the lens. They were painted in soft colours with some considerable skill. By the late 19th century, however, the majority of slides of this shape were separated into a series of single scenes and the remaining surface of the slip was painted black. Large square slides showing a single scene were also made, and these are the types most frequently found today, as they were produced for the more expensive lanterns and were carefully preserved by their owners. The range of subject matter was great and included 'Life and Work in America', 'A Tour through Switzerland and the Rhine' and innumerable religious and children's subjects. There were also mechanical slides, which enabled simple movements, such as a head nodding or a child on a swing, to be imitated. One of the commonest forms was the lever or slipping slide, which consisted of a frame with several movable pieces of glass that could be pulled to the side or pass across one another. Rackwork slides were more expensive but produced a smoother movement. Some of these were simply printed with brightly coloured patterns and known as chromotropes; they were particularly useful in between stories or to bring a show to an end and never fail to impress even modern audiences. After 1860, most slides were reproduced photographically and hand coloured. Some were sold with only the outlines printed and the purchaser then bought specially made paints for their decoration.

The high cost of many slides was commented upon in 1891 in *The Children's Friend*, and instructions were given for their construction, including some of the lever type which must have taxed even the cleverest child. Ordinary slides were painted by placing a slip of glass over a design drawn on a sheet of paper and tracing the outlines carefully in Indian ink. Any very fine detail could be scraped in with a needle-like tool. Colour was then added and again the highlights were picked out with a needle point, so that, for instance, the

few slides, while the better versions were packed in wooden boxes with a compartment for the slides. An example of the more expensive type is Georges Carette's 'Best Quality Magic Lantern', produced just before the First World War, and described in his catalogue as having 'excellent definition'. It was made with a body of 'polished blue steel plate, with an automatic slide holder to keep either thick or thin slides properly in focus. It also had 'a fine brass objective with rack and pinion movement' and was supplied with 'a superior new design two flame paraffin lamp' which was claimed to give a brilliant light without smoking. Carette's lanterns were sold in covered wooden cases with effect of sunlight on the edge of a cloud could be given. The slide was then varnished with a mixture of Canada balsam and turpentine and the plain sections of the slide were covered with lamp black mixed with gum water.

When cinematographs first appeared, the magic lantern makers quickly added them to their range, though they seemed unsure that they would remain popular. The noise that the film made when running was one of the main problems, though most of the firms claimed that their precision-made instruments were the quietest on the market. Some of the toy versions were lit by candles and with these it was extremely difficult to obtain any reasonable effect. High class projection instruments intended for adults were included in the toy catalogues of Bing and Carette, presumably so that fathers could entertain their children with subjects such as 'Tight Rope Walkers' or 'The Clumsy Servant'.

The cinematograph had developed from a variety of simple methods of simulating movement which had been experimented with from the beginning of the 19th century. The Thaumatrope, introduced in 1826, consisted of a circular disc, on either side of which were related images, such as a horse and a rider, When the disc was rotated rapidly, the eye united the two, so that a man appeared to be riding. The Phenakistoscope was invented in 1832 by Plateau, and simultaneously by Stampfer, who called his invention a Stroboscope. This was the first device to give the appearance of a moving picture, and consisted of a cardboard disc with a series of drawings in slightly different positions which was viewed through a mirror. Viewing was through slots that were cut around the sides of a disc, one slit to each drawing, so each movement was seen separately. The eye retained these impressions and the effect of continual movement was given. Ackermann & Co of the Strand, London, were among the leading producers of such toys, which they marketed under the title of the Fantascope. This design was somewhat modified in 1850 and the mirror was sometimes abandoned in favour of slots on a separate disc, this improved device being known as a Heliocinegraphe.

The Zoetrope or wheel of life was originally described in 1834, but the first model, produced by Desvignes, did not appear until 1860. It was eventually included in the catalogues of most leading tin toy makers and the first American version was patented and made by Milton Bradley. The Zoetrope was basically a modification of the

Above: **Among the forerunners of the cinematograph was the Praxinoscope, originally patented in 1877. This is a French example, complete with several bands of images and the original box and viewer. The succession of pictures seen in the mirrors of the viewer produces a moving picture.** *Left:* **The Zoetrope or wheel of life also used bands of images, which were viewed through the slots in a metal cylinder. Unmarked;** *circa* **1865. Both Science Museum, London.**

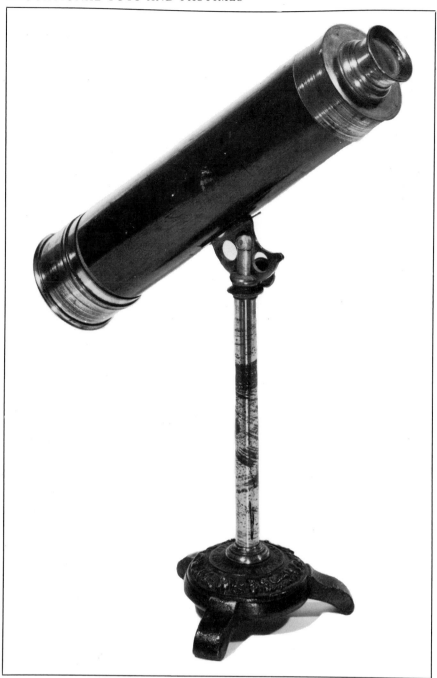

This handsome kaleido-scope is mounted on a cast iron stand which is marked 'Chadburn Brothers, Sheffield'. Late 19th century; height 14½ inches. Ipswich Museums.

slotted disc device, but here the diagrams were placed in a hollow cylinder which was rotated on a vertical axis so that they could be viewed through slits in the metal sides. The distortion that necessarily accompanied primitive simulated movement of this kind was limited to some extent by Reynaud, who in 1877 invented the Praxinoscope, with a band of pictures placed in a metal cylinder in the centre of which was a set of mirrors equal in number to the pictures. Images viewed in the mirror were much better lit and therefore appeared clearer. Such fairly basic devices could be developed further after the experiments of the American Eadweard J. Muybridge, who developed a moving picture from a series of photographs of horses in movement in 1879. Nevertheless it was some twenty years before cinematographs appeared in most of the toy merchants' lists.

Quite apart from the main-stream development of the moving picture, culminating in the cine-matograph, there were a number of novelty toys of an optical nature, such as the transparencies

that were available in the 18th century, repre-senting a simple scene which changed when held up to the light. Pictures with simple movements activated by the trickling of sand on a wheel were a popular form of nursery amusement, though there were also many versions made for adults by firms such as Brown Blondin & Co. Their dis-advantage was that in order to set the toy in motion the picture had to be taken from the wall and tilted so that the sand was returned to the top section. These devices seem to maintain their popularity, as they are often expressive primitive pictures as well as toys and have an appeal that is not limited to toy collectors.

The London Stereoscopic Company sold an interesting toy in the early 19th century which consisted of a length of wire bent into an outline and set in a metal spindle so that when revolved it appeared whole.

The invention of the kaleidoscope by Sir David Brewster in 1817 introduced one of the most popular nursery toys; it consisted of three mirrors set in a tube which contained sections of coloured glass or metal. When rotated, these formed colour-ful symmetrical patterns that still have the power to surprise modern children when they first en-counter them. The cheap later versions were simply shaken to rearrange the patterns, but the more expensive ones were provided with handles to turn them. Those made by Carette stood on polished wooden bases, rather like those on which telescopes are mounted, and were provided with a turning mechanism. A few contained 'child scenes', created by the use of photographs, but the majority obtained their effects by the usual glass pieces. The term 'Kaleidoscopic Colour Top' was used rather pretentiously by one firm in 1858, to describe a coloured spinning top which when set in motion showed how the visual mixing of the primary colours created the secondary colours such as green. This simple device was packed in a fine rosewood box and was probably intended for the amusement of adults almost as much as the young.

'Les Anamorphoses or polyoptic pictures' was another novelty visual toy, though the amuse-ment gained from it must have been limited. The device, sometimes also known as 'Les Méta-morphoses', consisted of a highly polished metal cylinder that was set in a circle drawn on a highly distorted picture. When viewed in the polished vertical cylinder the picture appeared completely normal. Ordinary distorting mirrors of the type now seen in fairgrounds were also sold in small

A device for viewing
anamorphic or distorted
pictures, made in Germany
in the 19th century.
Bethnal Green Museum of
Childhood, London.

sizes as children's toys in the early 20th century, but did not retain their popularity for long.

The stereoscope is another instance of an optical device that began its development as an adult amusement, embodying the phenomenon of binocular vision that had been known from the time of Leonardo da Vinci. In 1832, Sir Charles Wheatstone invented a means of simulating this sense of depth by the use of mirrors or prisms, and the optical instrument makers, Murrey & Heath, constructed a stereoscope to his specifications. Improvements in photography enabled the device to be developed. One scene or person was photographed from two slightly different angles and when the two photographs were viewed simultaneously the brain registered them as one, giving a three-dimensional effect. There were several improvements on the basic design, and it became widely popular after Queen Victoria showed great interest in the device at the Great Exhibition of 1851. A few years later the London Stereoscopic Company was founded. Using the slogan 'No

home without a stereoscope', this company became one of the main producers and as early as 1858 was claiming to have 100,000 photographs in stock. The prestige of the company was so great that the members of the royal family were happy to pose for them and these cards were sold all over the world. Children were usually given the cheaper versions of the toy, made of hardwood with folding handles and a sliding view-holder, or even the small pocket stereoscopes made of japanned tin. The adult pieces were much more sophisticated, made of brass and mahogany with velvet-lined viewers. Although the majority of stereoscopic cards were of the landscape type there were also a number of educational photographs such as 'Original views of interesting groups of animals in the Zoological Gardens', and 'Scenes of natural history'. When adults tired of this form of amusement, the stereoscope was often given to the children and some fine examples are often found among the nursery equipment when the contents of large houses are offered for sale.

Craft and constructional toys

With the exception of simple sets of building bricks, a few paper dolls for dressing and cut-out figures such as soldiers, there was little manufacture of craft and constructional toys before the 19th century. Children of the Georgian era were obviously encouraged to build, sew and engage themselves in the various crafts which the adults also enjoyed, but the supply of materials for these pursuits was left strictly to the child's family or their servants. Early 19th century prints, however, show children playing with bricks that are obviously commercially made and represent sections of castle walls, doors and windows. All these are made to a surprisingly large scale, so that a child may be seen standing alongside a wall which reaches to shoulder level. Wedge-shaped bricks were also available in the early 19th century and these could be put together to form small towers and cottages. Sheets of paper printed with baby house furniture were available from the 18th century, when they were produced in Strasbourg, while American settlers soon created constructional toys specifically for the needs of their children. An example of the latter is a log cabin construction set with some ninety-four separate pieces of wood now in the Museum of the City of New York, which dates from around 1850.

Educationalists such as Maria Edgworth and her father made some impression on the upbringing of children from educated families with their encouragement of rational toys, created from the natural materials that lay at hand, but of far greater influence was the work of Friedrich Froebel, whose first kindergarten was set up in 1837 near Rudolstadt in Germany. The children were here encouraged to experiment with cane, raffia and various puzzles, and commercial producers of toys with educational pretensions were to claim until well into the 20th century that their frequently mundane and unimaginative toys were made according to principles laid down by this famous educationalist.

During the 19th century, manufacturers concentrated upon the constructional type of toy, but from around 1900 there was a tremendous upsurge of interest in toys that helped the child to master simple skills and it was obviously considered almost improper to suggest that a toy was purely for amusement. One firm in 1910 was even producing a blue enamelled machine with brass cog-wheels, in which children could make their own ice cream, while flower making at home, weaving and paper plaiting, and a bead weaving loom to make such 'useful' items as book marks appeared in every toy seller's catalogue.

Boys seem to have been provided with much more interesting items than girls. In 1913 for example, they could buy sets for the construction of a whole range of aeroplanes including a Bleriot Monoplane and an Etrich-Rumpler, as well as

Doll construction sets are only very occasionally discovered uncut. This example, 'Construction Sheet Negro and Caucasian Doll. Sheet 667', was printed by Raphael Tuck. Alistair Allen Collection.

Facing page, bottom left: **A painted wooden constructional toy with glazed windows and furnishings. The painted decoration is typical of folk products of the Erzgebirge. Contained in the original box;** *circa* **1835–40. By courtesy of Christie's South Kensington, London.** *Bottom right:* **A constructional toy of a wooden church with the original box and toy catalogue issued by a Nuremberg toy merchant.** *Circa* **1836; height 20½ inches. Victoria and Albert Museum, London.**

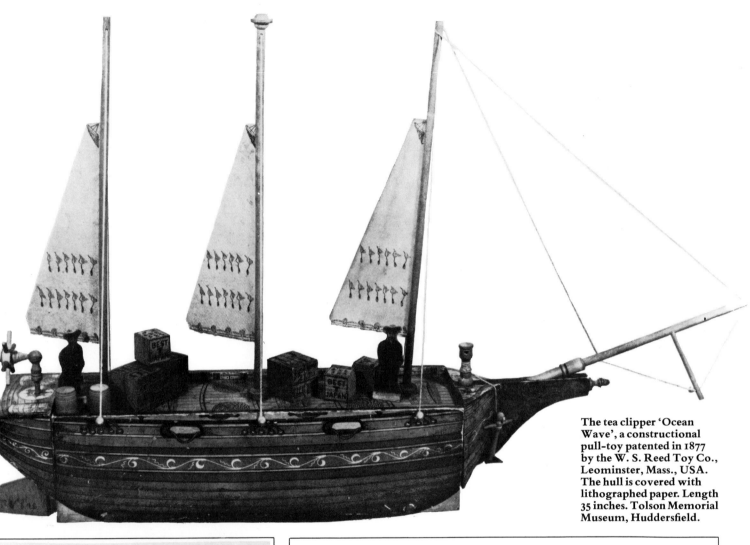

The tea clipper 'Ocean Wave', a constructional pull-toy patented in 1877 by the W. S. Reed Toy Co., Leominster, Mass., USA. The hull is covered with lithographed paper. Length 35 inches. Tolson Memorial Museum, Huddersfield.

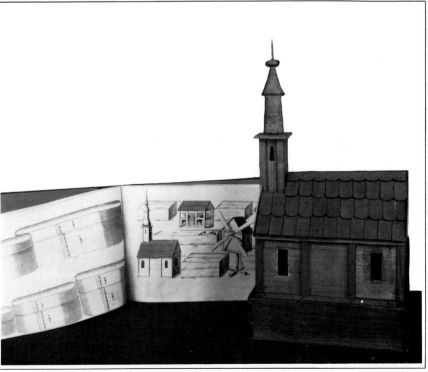

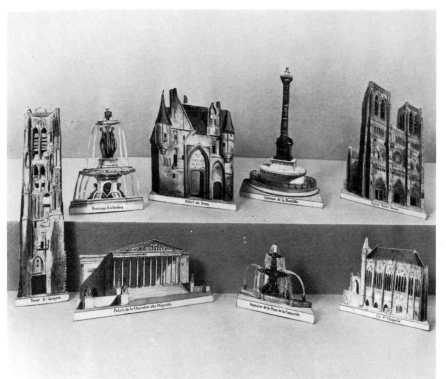

all sorts of accessories, including floats for 'Hydro Aeroplanes'. 'The Young Motor Maker', 'The Young Engine Builder', 'The Forge' and very complete carpentry sets provided the Edwardian boy with a host of interesting projects, while his sisters had to be content with their 'Bead Pleasures' or 'Art and Fancy Needlework'. Many of the box lids of these sets made claims that the contents proved impossible to support, though the toys probably helped in a small way to foster very basic but often completely useless skills.

Constructional toys, except those produced by the makers of tin toys, do not usually cost a great deal as they are often incomplete, but sets of Richter building blocks, attractive Epinal sheets and of course paper dolls can be reasonably expensive. The auction room price of quite complex constructions is often kept low, as few dealers and collectors have the time to check through the pieces to make sure the set is complete. Some of the German sets have the most attractively decorated boxes, but unfortunately very few are attributable and their value and interest to collectors depends purely on their visual appeal.

Above: **Models of buildings in Paris made around 1860 and including the Hôtel de Sens and Notre-Dame Cathedral. Printed paper on card; height of tallest building 5½ inches. Saffron Walden Museum, Essex.** *Right:* **Instructions and cut-out sections for making doll's house furniture, from** *La Poupée Modèle* **(see page 240), July 1868. Betty Harvey-Jones Collection.**

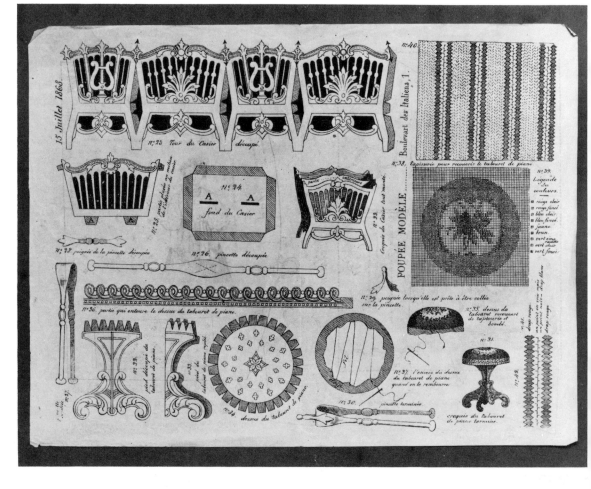

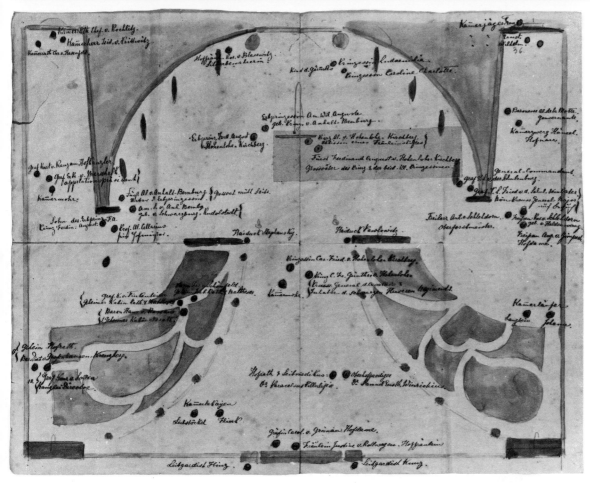

Above: **A princely construction made by Johann Jacob Uebelin, who was born in 1793 and was a private tutor to the Fischer von Reichenbach family. It was presented to Prince August von Hohenlohe-Kirchberg, who is represented with his family and retainers in the grounds of his palace. The tutor's gift was accompanied by a plan which showed how the 47 figures and 37 items of scenery should be arranged** (*left*). *Circa* **1820. Historisches Museum, Basel.**

The "CHAD VALLEY" GAMES.

MODEL CARD HOUSE AND FORT BUILDER
(Patent applied for)

A new and most ingenious invention. Each set comprises a large assortment of printed Card Sections of various sizes and shapes, with Clips for fixing them together. With these a number of charmingly designed Houses, Villas, Castles, Forts, Churches and Schools may be built. Numerous building plans are included which may be varied at will. The sets may be added to from time to time thereby enabling more complicated buildings to be made. A delight to every intelligent boy and girl.

No.			Trade Price.
6327	1/-	Set containing materials for building Houses, Villas, Cottages and Schools	12/- Doz.
6330	1/-	Set of materials for building Castles, Forts and Towers	12/- ,,

THE BRIDGE BUILDERS
(Patent applied for)

Sets of printed Card Sections of various sizes and shapes, with Clips for fastening them together with which most realistic model Bridges may be built, large and strong enough for model Carts and Trains to run over

No.			Trade Price.
6338	1/-	Girder and Suspension Bridge	12/- Doz.
6340	1/-	Pier and Draw-Bridge	12/- ,,

Manufactured at CHAD VALLEY WORKS, HARBORNE, ENGLAND.

A page from the Chad Valley catalogue of 1913–14, showing two of the constructional kits which they manufactured. By courtesy of Chad Valley Ltd.

CRAFT AND CONSTRUCTIONAL TOYS: BRANDS AND PRODUCERS

American Model Builder – Early 20th century. Almost an exact duplication of Meccano. A nine year legal battle over copyright was eventually won by the British firm and it was decided that American Model Builder was an improper copy. There were also several Continental imitators of the Meccano principle.

Augsburg – Sheets of printed furniture for baby houses, cut-out soldiers and dolls were produced in this area. Among the publishers at the end of the 17th century was J. Ph. Steudner. The main production of sheets came in the 18th century when animals, people and buildings were printed and usually sold uncoloured to be painted by the purchaser. Peep-show pictures and cribs were also printed for assembly at home.

Austin's Toy & Doll Counter – Pantheon Bazaar, London, circa 1830 to 1840. Sold building kits of plain wood which when assembled formed items such as a stable with a farmhouse and farmer. Other sets included a church and a bridge.

Bartlett, Alfred James – Gloucester, England. Working in the 1920s, Bartlett produced building and constructional sets under the trade name 'Bangaroo'.

Bassett-Lowke & Co – England, founded in 1899. Made a series of models of ships, aeroplanes, and locomotives just before the First World War. These were used for training purposes by the forces during the war but in the 1920s were on public sale.

Bing, Gebrüder – Nuremberg. Produced the 'Bing Structator, the up-to-date construction toy', which consisted of aluminium sections accompanied by drawing books full of designs. In the 1920s the firm produced their own range of stone building bricks.

Boussac, Kratz – Paris. In 1902 was producing construction games in great variety using the trade name 'Eureka'.

Burlington Building Blocks – England, late 19th century. Hardwood slats with small holes drilled through to be fastened together by pegs. The whole structure was held very firmly once constructed. Churches, houses, windmills, etc, could all be made.

Chad Valley – Birmingham, England. This firm was established before 1820 by Anthony Bunn Johnson. Early products were mainly printed material and stationery, but the company was certainly selling toys and issuing a catalogue by 1897. It was in this year that a new factory was opened by the Chad stream at Harborne outside Birmingham, by Joseph Johnson and his eldest son Alfred J. Johnson. The firm began using the Chad Valley trademark around this time, and traded as Johnson Brothers, Harborne Ltd. In 1913, they were offering among their construction sets 'The Card House and Fort Builder' composed of a large assortment of printed card sections of various shapes and sizes, with clips for fixing them together. Houses, villas and schools could all be added to supplementary packs at any time. In 1914, Chad Valley 'Bridge Builder' sets appeared; these again consisted of printed card sections with fixing clips but were much sturdier than previous models, and it was claimed that model carts could be run over the assembled structure. A suspension bridge, a pier and a drawbridge were included in this set. The firm became particularly interested in craft sets in the 1930s and sold them attractively

boxed and with titles such as 'Canvas Embroidery', 'Bead Ornaments' and 'Basket Making'. They also offered a construction toy which was a sectional model of the Queen Mary. It was designed by G. H. Davis, an artist who worked for the *Illustrated London News*. In 1947 the firm marketed the metal 'Ubilda Motor Car', which was ready for assembly by means of screws.

Crandall, Jesse A. & Charles M. – Brooklyn and New York, USA. Charles Crandall (1833 to 1905) designed a system of tongued and grooved building blocks that he patented in 1867. This idea was extended and a number of toys featuring interchangeable and interlocking parts were produced. In a later explanation, Crandall described how he had investigated ways of constructing croquet set boxes using tongued and grooved joints instead of nails. He took the unassembled sections home for the amusement of his son, who was recovering from an illness, and their visiting doctor saw and admired the 'blocks' and ordered the first set. Crandall followed the off-cut blocks with figures such as a school, a menagerie and 'Great Show Acrobats' in 1867, and the 'Hero or Veteran of '76' in 1876. All these figures were

packed into a box and consisted of flat printed wooden sections from which it was claimed thousands of figures could be assembled by slotting together the interchangeable arms, legs and torsoes. The box lids claimed the sets to be 'Full of Fun and Frolic and Most Brilliant in Costume', adding 'Will Exhibit at the House of the Purchaser Afternoon and Evening, no postponement on account of the weather'. These sets were exported in some number and can be found in Europe as well as the USA.

Charles Crandall's Great Show Acrobats', patented in 1867, each consisted of six parts which fitted together to form a figure, with colourful lithographed paper designs on the front and back. Margaret Woodbury Strong Museum, Rochester, New York. *Below:* Another Crandall constructional toy, 'John Gilpin'. Painted wood with original box and instruction leaflet. Late 19th century; height 14 inches. Victoria and Albert Museum, London.

Deezy, Bill, & Company – Boston, Mass., USA. This firm was making constructional toys at the beginning of the First World War.

Dover Toys – England. Manufactured by A. G. Owen of Sheffield in the early 20th century. These were craft sets, mainly for boys, including a blacksmith's shop – basically a hammer, anvil, wheels and nails packed in a box – and a small potter's wheel and accessories.

Epinal – The collector's term for sheets produced from the early 19th century by the firm of Pellerin, which was based at Epinal in eastern France. The range was very wide and consisted of often extremely complex printed constructional models such as villages, stations, aeroplanes, submarines, picture galleries and shops. Instructions for assembly were printed on the sheets which could be pasted to cardboard for strength.

Erector, 'The Master Builder Set' – USA. A constructional toy which was invented and manufactured by A. C. Gilbert in 1913. Gilbert was a doctor, amateur magician and sportsman and his intention in creating the toy was to 'Teach boys the principles of Construction and Engineering'. He claimed that 'It is the only construction toy with girders like real structural steel'. In direct contrast to the early Meccano sets, Gilbert included pinions and gears and electric motors for his first models. In 1913 he bought the American interest of Richter Building Bricks (see below) and in 1920 bought the American branch of Meccano. He later made children's telephone and telegraphic sets.

Possibly the most famous of all the constructional toys is Meccano, patented by Frank Hornby in 1901 and manufactured in Liverpool, England. These pages are from *The Book of Hornby Trains & Meccano Products,* **dating from 1935. Reproduced by courtesy of New Cavendish Books.**

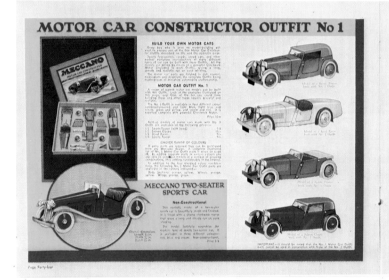

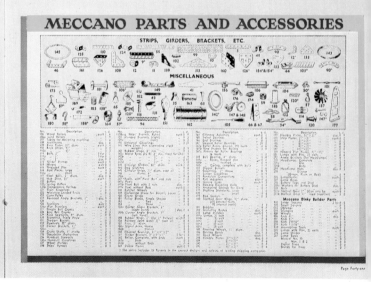

Firma Falk – Nuremberg. Made construction sets packed in boxes labelled 'Industrie'. Another similar set was produced by Märklin. Both early 20th century.

Groovette – Trade name for a system sold by Ralph Dunn of the Barbican, London, around 1908. Grooved unpainted lengths of wood that locked together and could be used to build structures as diverse as doll's furniture and bridges.

Harbutt, William – Britain. In 1897, Harbutt invented Plasticine, a cheap and clean modelling substance that has remained highly popular to the present time and is one of the best toys of this type. The early substance was attractively boxed and carried slogans such as 'Plasticine is something new, and hopes to make a friend of you'. Later the firm found it necessary to make far greater claims and it was stated to be of use in 'Nature Study and Object Lessons, Geometric modelling and maps'.

Jean-Jean – England, *circa* 1910. Trade name for constructional houses made from cardboard sections such as walls, outer and inner doors, staircases etc. These pieces were formed into a solid structure by metal clasps fixed on the inside.

Joiboy – Trade name of Wallis Brothers and Wicksteed, Stamford Rd, Kettering, England. They made a variety of building sets which used printed interlocking cards.

Journet, R. – Harrow Road, London *circa* 1905. Maker of kindergarten occupations and puzzles and a 'How to Build' range. Made the 'Bead Basket Maker' set and an interesting 'Little Clockmaker' which included all the pieces needed to make a working wall clock. It was advertised as 'Clockmaking Made Easy. Complete parts to make a 30 hour clock with wood case, brass wheels, escapement and metal back'. Journet also sold gilt doll's house furniture which could be slotted together by the child.

Kliptiko – England. Trade name used in early 20th century for a system that was 'Simple enough to interest a young child with possibilities expansive enough to prevent that interest from flagging as the child grows up'. Cranes, towers and bridges could all be made with 'No irritating parts to get into the wrong place. Standard units the same in each set so that all pieces are interchangeable'.

Lott's – Watford, England. Makers of 'Stone Bricks' and 'Tudor Blocks'. Their thin rectangular blocks are believed to have been at first made from ground-down Italian marble. The firm's founder E. A. Lott later bought up the Richter plant and was advised by the architect Arnold Mitchell to cut the bricks into shapes that were suitable for constructions such as cathedrals. Later, smaller sets for cottages were also made. These cottage sets were originally sold only in black and white but they were not over popular and so red bricks and later other shapes and colours were added. At the British Industries Fair in 1918, Queen Mary purchased the first box of Lott's Bricks. Various arches and buildings could be made and the later boxes included embossed bricks, mullioned windows, and a Tudor style set.

Märklin – Germany, founded in 1859. Märklin produced constructor set aeroplanes in the 1930s with clockwork motors. They had diecast ailerons and rudder, and composition figures. In the 1934 to 1935 catalogue Märklin Constructor car sets are shown. The chassis was sold separately and different bodies were then bought and assembled. A few were issued after the Second World War.

Marples, William & Sons – Hibernia Works, Sheffield, and Ivy Lane, London. Produced a very wide and good quality range of boy's carpentry tools before the First World War.

Meccano – Trade name for metal construction sets produced mainly at Binns Road, Liverpool, England. This is by far the best known of all construction sets and is still in production today. It was patented in 1901 by Frank Hornby, who had been fascinated by the lives of inventors as a child and had continued to build models himself well into adult life. The system as he originally conceived it consisted of metal strips half an inch wide with equal holes at half-inch intervals. These sizes were never changed, which meant that a father could amalgamate his own set with that of his sons. The use of wheels and metal rods enabled working models to be produced. The wheels in early sets were fitted with a 'key' which clipped on the rod and held the wheel in position, though this was soon replaced by a specially made set screw. Hornby called his invention 'Mechanics made easy'. At first he had the parts made by other firms, but soon set up a factory to produce them. The name 'Meccano' was registered in England in 1907 and Germany in 1912. Manuals of instruction were

supplied with every outfit from the beginning, and every effort was made to ensure that these were written in correct technical language. The early strips were made of tin with turned-over edges, and were finished by being dipped in acid and then varnished. Soon, however, the material was changed to rolled steel, which was heavily nickel plated. In 1926, Meccano in colour was introduced, with the plates and pulley wheels enamelled in red, and strips, girders and brackets in green. The Meccano Guild was set up in 1919 for boys of all ages. Prestige working models were specially supplied for use in shop window displays. The *Meccano Magazine* was first issued in 1916, appearing every two months until 1922 and then monthly. The Meccano 'Constructor Plane' sets introduced in the 1930s were a departure from the established system, and when made up looked like ordinary toys. A variety of planes were made and in 1940 and 1941 camouflage models and others in service grey were introduced. 'Motor Car Constructor' outfits were also made in a range of bright colours. The manufacturer's description claimed that they were 'perfect miniature reproductions' of sports cars, four-seaters, sports coupés and others, and added: 'A powerful electric motor that gives the models a long run on each winding is enclosed in each outfit. The parts are painted in rich enamel and nickel plated'.

Metalcraft – St Louis, USA. This firm marketed a constructor plane, 'The Spirit of St Louis after Lindberg's Ryan Monoplane in which he made his first flight in 1927'. The box contained materials to construct twenty-five planes and the cover was attractively decorated with a picture of the Statue of Liberty.

Pajeau, Charles H. – Chicago. Was working in 1914. Made toys, games and building blocks and a particularly effective wooden construction toy with interlocking spools and rods that could be assembled into either animal or abstract shapes.

Peacock, A. – Clerkenwell, London, Established 1853. Made a series of construction sets and marketed Skaymo bricks.

Peugeot – France. In 1928 Peugeot sold automobile constructor sets in metal which could be used to make up three chassis and a cabriolet vehicle. All the mechanical parts worked and optional equipment included a spare wheel, bumpers and other items of a similar nature.

Pin-Tung or Model Making Made Easy – England, early 20th century. This system consisted of metal sections drilled at regular intervals.

Richter Building Bricks – Rudolfstadt, Germany. Marketed by F. D. Richter & Co in London and New York. The firm is thought to have been founded in the Middle Ages, but their first registered sign was in 1879. Their building bricks were patented in 1880, though they were on sale before this time. An advertisement in the *Illustrated Sporting and Dramatic News* in 1887 read: 'Royal Playthings. Toy Makers to their Majesties the Emperor of Austria and the Kings of Italy, Portugal, Bavaria etc. Anchor Stone Building Boxes. As supplied to the little princes and princesses of the Royal and Imperial Nurseries of Europe. Building bricks in real stone. Blocks in stone colour, red, brick and slate. A clever toy for every child. A never ending source of enjoyment for young and old. The large box weighs over half a hundredweight. There are 328 different shapes and sizes of stones. An interesting book entitled "The Toy the Child Likes Best" containing a catalogue of sizes and prices. . . . The Public are warned against common and dangerous imitations of the Anchor blocks made with QUICK-LIME. Will make castles, towers, bridges, streets and villages. 1/3 to 64/- a box.' These bricks

Sets of Richter Building Bricks were a part of almost every European child's play between 1880 and the 1920s. The set shown here dates from around 1905. Bedford Museum.

Facing page: The toys produced by Citroën Cars in the 1920s and 1930s were part of a publicity programme for the full-sized machines. Here we see a constructional toy in the form of a 1929 Citroën C6 chassis, still in its original box. Eric Morgan Collection. Reproduced by courtesy of New Cavendish Books.

A set of Skaymo bricks with their original box and a booklet of plans for making 'real scale models'. All the sections were multiples of one unit, so that the components in the different sets produced were compatible. *Circa* **1920. Author's Collection.** *Top right:* **A constructional toy produced by J. W. Spear of London, 'The "Spero" Troupe of Table Acrobats', advertised in** *The Toy and Fancy Goods Trader* **of October 1909.**

were to become almost an essential feature of Edwardian nurseries and they are so attractive that most toy collectors like to own at least one set. The 'Anker-Steinbaukasten' won medals at Paris in 1900 and St Louis in 1904.

Schuhmann, Adolph – Nuremberg, early 20th century. Produced metal building bricks, constructional toys and others and used the trademark 'Combinator'.

Skaymo Rgd – Altrincham, Cheshire, England. Trade name for wooden bricks that were used for the construction of realistic models in the 1920s and 1930s. The bricks were hardwood, mainly with a polished natural finish, but some pieces were painted black or red and important sections such as a cupola might be silvered. 'Recognisable architectural scale models' could be made and the system of interchangeable and related parts enabled large and small boxes to be combined. The boxes all measured $12 \times 10\frac{1}{2}$ inches but varied in depth. A book of plans was supplied with each and extra books could be purchased separately. Real glass windows in wooden frames were supplied and the models attempted to be completely modern in style.

Smith, Bailey & Co – Birmingham. Supplied loose parts for building model locomotives and horizontal, beam and marine engines.

Spear, J. W. – Germany and London, founded in 1878. Made a wide variety of constructional toys mainly of printed paper or card that were designed for the British market but printed in Germany. Paper dressing dolls were also sold in great numbers. In 1913, 'Paper Cutting and Pasting' was advertised as well as basket work and stick building sets. The firm is still in production.

Strasbourg – Alsace. Traditional centre of the printing industry. In the mid 18th century the main production was of cut-out soldiers with a few dolls printed by firms such as Seyfried and Jean Frederic Striedbeck, whose factory was established in 1786. Later, sheets were sold either plain or coloured and printed with subjects such as farms and animals, houses and all sorts of figures.

Tuck, Raphael – Bavaria, London, Sydney and New York. Established by Raphael Tuck, who came from East Prussia in 1866. Many of their toys state that they were printed at the 'Fine Art works in Saxony' and the standard is usually good. A large number of dressing dolls were made and also constructional toys such as boats, aeroplanes and ambulances. Some were printed on paper but others were on richly coloured and embossed card with the pieces joined by tabs. Uncut sheets are of course preferred by collectors as the assembled models were fragile and soon became damaged when they were played with.

Money boxes

Simple earthenware money boxes are found in the remains of early civilization and there was often little change in the basic wheel-turned shape until the 18th century. Many of the slip-decorated examples made in country districts even in the early 19th century are so archaic in appearance that their date is easily mistaken. There were also a number of potters associated with the Arts and Crafts movement of the late 19th century, such as Edward Bingham at Castle Hedingham in Essex, who produced pieces in a deliberately ancient style and even used the early dates as the main form of decoration.

That the seasonal trade in money boxes was well established in the 16th century is indicated by a reference in 1585 to a box of 'Potters clay wherein boyes put their money to keepe, such as they have in the shops towards Christmas'. The development of more colourful containers began with the production of Delft ware, such as that made at Lambeth from the 1670s, but the Staffordshire potteries in the early 19th century were to manufacture the most brilliantly coloured versions in the form of flower bedecked cottages and castles. These were mainly chimney ornaments for adults, but they also exist in very small sizes, surely intended for children as they hold so very little. As there was no easy means of retrieving money from such items, if the usual expedient of a flat-bladed knife failed, they were frequently smashed, and as

a result examples in good condition are considered to be very desirable.

Wooden money boxes, or banks as they are termed in America, have a history that is probably as long as those made of earthenware, but as they are obviously more subject to decay they have rarely survived. Both Georgian and Victorian examples can however be discovered, though they rely for their interest on their degree of ornamentation. The child's name and date of birth was sometimes engraved on a brass plaque but at other times this information was carved on the box itself. These sturdy containers were often provided with a leather guard inside the slot to prevent the removal of money by the knife method. Many of the boxes that were made to appeal to adults are extremely effective and decorated with marquetry, mother of pearl, straw-work and shells or inlaid with brass, silver, ivory or bone. The German wood turners sold a range of sturdy, gaily painted figures with slits cut in the tops of their heads, which resemble Russian nesting dolls in construction.

The toy collector's main interest in money boxes dates from the introduction of metal models and it is the trick and novelty boxes of this substance that command really high prices, despite the fact that they were mass produced. The American manufacturers tended to favour cast-iron boxes, and good examples can be found much more

Two examples of the simplest form of money box. *Far left:* A salt glazed earthenware money box made in Derbyshire in the early 19th century. Height 4 inches. Victoria and Albert Museum, London. *Left:* A child's Staffordshire money box brightly decorated in orange and red. Height 3½ inches. Author's Collection.

easily in the United States than they can in Europe.

In 1816 the first Chartered Savings Banks were opened in the US and these almost immediately caused the manufacturers to create banks shaped like small buildings, so the child could pretend that he too was visiting the savings bank. The English Penny Bank was not introduced until 1850, and this may also probably account to some extent for the American supremacy. The banks were cast by hand and made by pouring molten metal into a sand mould, producing the characteristic slightly rough texture of cast iron. One of the most famous firms associated with the manufacture of this toy was J. & A. Stevens of Cromwell, Connecticut, established in 1843. This company's initial production was of boxes in the form of bank buildings and one of their most popular models showed a figure that appeared at the top of the bank every time a deposit was made. Another of Stevens' best-sellers was the 'Bread-winner's Bank', showing a labourer striking an anvil which bore the legend 'Monopoly'. This money box had an obvious adult appeal and was doubtless purchased by many thrifty and hard-working artisans to encourage their children to follow their ideals. The same company issued a box in 1873 which parodied the Tammany Hall swindle that had shocked many Americans. The box showed a plump, well-dressed gentleman, representing William Marcy Tweed, sitting in an armchair and nodding his thanks when any deposit was made. Tammany Hall was the headquarters of the controlling organisation of the Democratic

American cast iron money boxes are highly prized by collectors. *Above right:* **An 'Uncle Sam' mechanical money box in cold painted cast iron. The figure drops coins into the portmanteau. Height 11 inches. By courtesy of Sotheby's Belgravia, London.** *Bottom and facing page:* **Two American mechanical boxes, one, very rare, representing an opium smoker, and the other a dentist with his patient. Pollock's Toy Museum, London.**

Party of New York City and State, and Tweed, with his party of politicians, had succeeded in swindling the city of millions of dollars. The Tammany Bank was still produced some forty-five years later and long after its significance had any real impact. In the later period it was often referred to as the 'Fat Man's Bank'.

The greatest number of novelty banks were produced between 1880 and 1910, and American toy catalogues of the period give some idea of their variety and ingenuity. The 'Minstrel Bank' contained dancing figures that were set in motion by the dropping of a coin. Another type had a monkey in whose hand the coin was placed; a handle was turned and a chime of bells rang as the monkey revolved and placed the coin in the bank. This bank was the work of G. W. White of Philadelphia, a company that also produced a 'Dime Register', a combination of a mechanical and a registering money box in the form of a pump and water bucket. The pump handle was moved up and down and the amount deposited was registered on the top of the bucket, which could be removed when $5 had been deposited. Another popular cast iron box represented an eagle feeding her

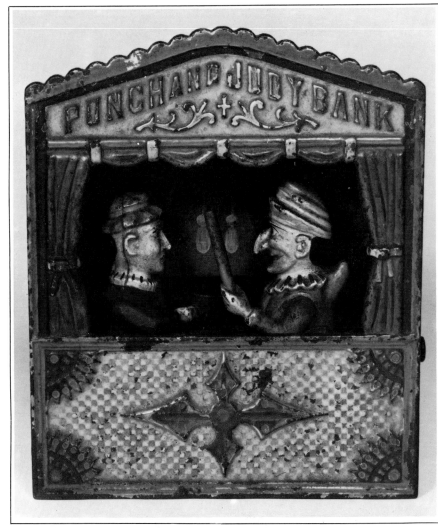

The 'Punch and Judy Bank', made in America around 1900. By courtesy of Phillips, New Bond Street, London. Many of the American cast iron banks are now reproduced, so care must be taken in purchasing.

Near right: **A coloured tinplate money box in the form of a sweet shop which advertises 'Noblett's Everton Toffee'.** *Circa* **1910; height 4½ inches. By courtesy of Christie's South Kensington, London.** *Centre picture:* **Two pages from the 1892 catalogue of the American mail order firm of Marshal Field, advertising a series of mechanical banks with musical movements. Also included is the 'Evening News Baby Quieter' mentioned on page 90.** *Bottom left:* **An American mechanical bank in cast iron, painted brown. Height 10 inches. Pollock's Toy Museum, London.**

young, the figure bending forward with the coin in its mouth. One of the most dramatic represented a dentist with a black patient. When a button on the patient's footstool was pressed the dentist lunged forward and rammed a coin down the patient's throat.

Money boxes based on black themes were common and among these the most frequently found are those entitled 'The Jolly Nigger'. The figure holds out his hand for a coin and after swallowing it rolls his eyes either with relish or horror. A companion model to this represented a much more realistic woman known as 'Dinah'. Simple tableaux representing black minstrels and other figures were also popular, including one in which a brightly dressed man dances at the door of a hut. It appears that Irish jokes had some appeal even in the 19th century and one box introduced in 1882 represents 'Paddy and his Pig'. A coin is placed on the pig's nose and this is then tossed in the air, whereupon Paddy thrusts out his conveniently long tongue to catch it and swallows it while his eyes roll in delight. Such amusing mechanical boxes are understandably expensive, though some made in aluminium and cast in the 1930s are much cheaper. Many of the figures, including some once considered extremely rare, are now reproduced in large numbers, so great care has to be exercised when buying.

The collecting of money boxes has been popular in the United States since the 1920s and the enthusiasts have coined specific terms to identify the various forms of the toy. A 'still bank' is a box of the simplest traditional type in which the coin is merely dropped through a slot, in contrast to the 'mechanical' versions in which figures perform simple movements. In a 'registering bank' a mechanism records the total amount of

TOY BANKS AND WHEELTOY.

money deposited, and though in general these are less decorative as objects there are still many enthusiastic collectors.

Some of the most effective of the mechanical banks were made by the firm of Shepherd; one of them consists of a figure of Uncle Sam standing by a briefcase into which he drops a coin. Stevens used a similar mechanism for their monkey bank, in which a coin was dropped from the animal's hand into a nut. Most famous of the banks made by this firm is the 'Greenbacked Frog'. This was produced around 1880 as a satire on General Butler's advocacy of the issue of very large amounts of paper money to counteract the after-effects of the Panic of 1873. The green frog represents his association with the Greenback party for whom he ran as a presidential candidate in 1884.

The more realistic banks, often representing safes, are much less attractive than those with amusing figures and are consequently less lucrative propositions to the manufacturers of reproductions. In 1895 the American mail order firm of Marshall Field showed readers of its catalogue some eminently practical models, such as a milk churn entitled 'The Dairy' which was nickel finished with brass bands and a 'puzzle padlock'. The 'Presto Trick Bank' represented the building of a very substantial town bank and contained a trick drawer. A coin was placed in this drawer which was then closed; a button was pressed and the drawer flew open to show that the coin had disappeared. Others were completely correct miniatures of actual safes such as the 'Security', which was provided with a money guard 'to make the abstraction of money an impossibility'. Touches of humour sometimes appeared, as in 'The Watch Dog Safe', where a dog sitting on a ledge at the front barked when a deposit was made.

Banks are now so popular that almost every design of interest is reproduced. Some of the makers mark their work so that the casual buyer cannot be deceived by an unscrupulous dealer. But the majority, especially those encountered in Europe, are completely without identification and the buyer has to be very wary. Some forgers will add several coats of paint to a bank so that the upper layers can be convincingly chipped away, while others resort to forms of distressing with acids and abrasives. The very large number of fakes has caused something of a depression in the value of the less unusual banks, a similar effect having been seen when Staffordshire figures began to be remade in quantity.

Vending banks are another popular field for today's collectors; in these, foil-wrapped sweets or chocolates were displayed behind a glass panel and could be obtained by putting a coin in the money box. The greatest number of these toys were made somewhere between 1910 and 1930, usually of lithographed tinplate, so that they are attractive items. The majority appear to have been produced in Germany, though they were lettered and decorated to the specifications of the various countries. A box made by the Stollerwerk Brothers, for example, is found in English, German and French versions. Individual companies also ordered banks to contain their own goods; one example carries the slogan 'The Glory of Devon in a packet', advertising Pascall's sweets. The banks all worked on a similar principle, whereby a coin was dropped into a slot, engaging a release mechanism, and the drawer containing the treat then opened. One machine which was obviously intended for children because of the nature of its decoration even vended cigarettes in the less health-conscious period of the late 1920s.

Improvements in the processes by which tin plate was lithographed meant that very simple containers could be realistically decorated to represent houses, banks, treasure chests and wheeled vehicles, all of which could be provided with a slot and sold as money boxes. The suppliers of tea, biscuits and chocolates often packaged their wares in this way and the lettering of the company's name often formed an effective part of the design. The small, bright red pillar boxes bearing the monarch's initials which remain so popular with British children sometimes bear a manufacturer's slogan which may help in more accurate dating. These tinplate boxes are difficult to restore if badly scratched, so only examples in good condition should be purchased.

BIBLIOGRAPHY

Allen, Alistair: *Scraps*, exhibition catalogue, Bethnal Green Museum, London, 1977.

Altes Spielzeughaus Basel, Historisches Museum, Basle, 1973.

Ariès, Philippe: *Centuries of Childhood*, Jonathan Cape, London, 1962.

Athletics, Sports, Games and Toys, London, October 1895.

Bachmann, Fritzsch: *An Illustrated History of Toys*, Abbey Library, London, 1966.

Bossi, Marco: *Autohobby*, Priuli & Verlacco, Ivrea, *circa* 1976.

Bing, Gebrüder: German catalogues, 1906 and 1909; English, 1912.

Boehn, Max von: *Puppets and Automata*, Dover Reprints, New York, 1972.

Britains, William, Ltd.: 1905 catalogue reprinted by Britains Ltd., 1972.

Britains Toy and Model Catalogue, 1940, reprint, Almark Publications, London, 1972.

Burkij-Bartelink, A.: *Antiek Speelgoed*, Van Dishoeck, Bussum, 1973.

Carette, Georges, The Great Toys of, reprint of 1911 trade catalogue, New Cavendish Books, London, 1976.

Chad Valley Ltd.: catalogues from 1897 to 1954.

Chapuis, A., and Droz, E.: *Les Automates*, Neuchâtel, 1949.

Coleman, D., E. & E.: *The Collector's Encyclopedia of Dolls*, Robert Hale, London, 1970.
The Collector's Book of Doll's Clothes, Robert Hale, London, 1976.

Cook, Olive: *Movement in Two Dimensions*, Hutchinson, London, 1963.

Culff, Robert: *The World of Toys*, Hamlyn, London, 1969.

Daiken, Leslie: *Children's Toys Throughout the Ages*, Spring Books, London, 1963.

Dean's Rag Book Company: catalogues from 1911 to 1938.

Ellis, Hamilton: *Model Railways, 1838–1939*, Allen & Unwin, London, 1962.

Everybodies Book of the Queen's Doll's House, published by *The Daily Telegraph*, London, 1924.

Fraser, Antonia: *A History of Toys*, Weidenfeld & Nicholson, London, 1966.

Freeman, Ruth: *American Dolls*, Century House, New York, 1952.

Gamage's Christmas Bazaar, 1913, reprint, David & Charles, Newton Abbot, 1974.

Garratt, John G.: *Model Soldiers, a Collector's Guide*, Seeley Service Co. Ltd., London, 1965.

Greene, Vivien: *English Doll's Houses*, Batsford, London, 1955.
Family Doll's Houses, G. Bell, London, 1973.

Greilsamer, Jacques and Azema, Bertrand: *Catalogue of Model Cars of the World*, Edita, Lausanne, and Patrick Stephens, London, 1967.

Grober, Karl: *Children's Toys of Bygone Days*, Batsford, London, 1928.

Hannas, Linda: *The English Jig Saw Puzzle*, Wayland Publishers, London, 1962.
Two Hundred Years of Jig Saw Puzzles, London Museum catalogue, 1968.

Hart, Louella: *Directory of British Dolls*, privately printed, USA, 1964.

Haskell, A., and Lewis, M.: *Infantillia. The Archeology of the Nursery*, Dobson, London, 1971.

Herz, Louis H.: *Messrs Ives of Bridgeport*, Mark Heber Co., USA, 1950.

Hillier, Mary: *Automata and Mechanical Toys*, Jupiter, London, 1976.

Hobbies Handbooks, Hobbies, Ltd., Norfolk, 1934–1940.

Hornby, Frank: *The Life Story of Meccano*, facsimile reprint of *Meccano Magazine*, 1932–1953, New Cavendish Books, London, 1976.

Howarth-Loomes, Bernard: *Victorian Photography*, Ward Lock, London, 1974.

Hughes, Bernard and Therle: *Collecting Miniature Antiques*, Heinemann, London, 1973.

Illustrated Sporting and Dramatic News, selected issues, London, 1887.

Jackson, Mrs F. Nevil: *Toys of Other Days*, White Lion Reprint, London, 1976.

Jacobs, Flora Gill: *History of Doll's Houses*, Scribners, New York, 1965.
Doll's Houses in America, Scribners, New York, 1974.

Jacobs, Flora Gill and Faurholt, Estrid: *Dolls and Doll Houses*, Charles E. Tuttle, Rutland, USA, 1967.

King, Constance E.: *A Collector's History of Dolls*, Robert Hale, London, 1977.
Price Guide to Antique Dolls, Antique Collectors Club, Woodbridge, Suffolk, 1977.
Toys and Dolls for Collectors, Hamlyn, London, 1973.
Dolls and Doll's Houses, Hamlyn, London, 1977.

Ladies Home Journal, New York, selected editions 1924 to 1926.

Latham, Jean: *Doll's Houses. A Personal Choice*, A. & C. Black, London, 1969.

Levy, Allen: *A Century of Model Trains*, New Cavendish Books, London, 1974.

Mackay, James: *Nursery Antiques*, Ward Lock Ltd., London, 1976.

MacClintock, Marshall and Innez: *Toys in America*, Public Affairs Press, Washington, 1961.

McClinton, Katherine Morrison: *Antiques in Miniature*, Scribners, New York, 1970.

Märklin: *Technical Toys in the Course of Time*, reprinted catalogues, Hobby Haas, Frankfurt a. M., 1975.

Marshall Field Toy Catalogue, 1892–1893, edited by Dale Kelley, Wallace Homestead Book Company, Iowa, 1967.

Mateaux, C. L.: *Wonderland of Work*, Cassell, Petter, Galpin & Co., London, 1883.

Mechanisches Spiel und Theater, catalogue, Stadtmuseum, Munich, 1972.

Maingot, Eliane: *Les Automates*, Hachette, Paris, 1959.

Moderne Kunst in Meister Holzschnitten, Richard Bong, Munich, *circa* 1910.

Mogridge, G. S.: *Sergeant Bell and his Raree Show*, Thomas Tegg, *circa* 1845.

Naegelsbach, Barbara Emde: *Antiquitäten-Spielzeug*, Heyne, Munich, 1974.

Oberammergau Folk Museum Guide, published by the Community of Oberammergau, 1963.

Ortman, Erwin: *The Collector's Guide to Model Tin Figures*, Studio Vista, 1974.

Pearsall, Ronald: *Collecting Mechanical Antiques*, David & Charles, Newton Abbot, 1973.

Powell, Rosamond Bayne: *The English Child in the 18th century*, John Murray, London, 1939.

Prasteau, Jean: *Les Automates*, Grund, Paris, 1968.

Pressland, David: *The Art of the Tin Toy*, New Cavendish Books, London, 1976.

Puppen & Spielzeug, No. 3, Stuttgart, 1977.

Quayle, Eric: *The Collector's Book of Children's Books,* Studio Vista, London, 1971.

Reder, Gustav: *Clockwork, Steam and Electric. A History of Model Railways,* Ian Allan, London, 1972.

Remise, Jacques & Jean Fondin: *The Golden Age of Toys,* Edita, Lausanne, 1967.

Roe, F. Gordon: *The Georgian Child,* Phoenix, London, 1961.

Roh, Juliane, and Hansmann, Claus: *Altes Spielzeug,* Bruckmann, Munich, 1958.

Schiffer, Herbert F. and Peter B.: *Miniature Antique Furniture,* Livingston, USA, 1972.

Strong Museum, Margaret Woodbury, leaflet produced by Lincoln First Bank of Rochester, New York.

Speaight, George: *The History of the English Toy Theatre,* Studio Vista, London, 1967.

Tallis, David: *Musical Boxes,* Frederick Muller, London, 1971.

Taranovskoi, N.V.: *Folk Toys of Russia,* 1968.

Teaching Toys, Norfolk Museum Service Booklet, 1975.

Thomas, D. B.: *The Origins of the Motion Picture,* Science Museum, HMSO, London, 1964.

Tilley, Roger: *A History of Playing Cards,* Studio Vista, London, 1973.

Playing Cards, Octopus, London, 1973.

Toller, Jane: *Antique Miniature Furniture,* Bell, London, 1966.

Toy Trader and Fancy Goods Review, London, 1906 to 1930.

White, Gwen: *Dolls, Automata, Marks and Labels,* Batsford, London, 1975.

Antique Toys and Their Background, Batsford, London, 1971.

Whitehouse, F. R. B.: *Table Games of Victorian and Georgian Days,* Priory Press, Royston, and Chad Valley, Birmingham, 1971.

ACKNOWLEDGEMENTS

Many museums, firms, libraries and auction houses have assisted in supplying photographs for this book, and their assistance is credited in the picture captions, but the author and publishers would particularly like to thank the staff of the Margaret Woodbury Strong Museum in Rochester, New York, who themselves suggested unusual and relevant items for the American sections, and provided very adequate caption material. In Britain, they would especially like to thank Betty Harvey-Jones and David Pressland, who kindly allowed objects from their private collections to be photographed.

Picture credits
t = top; c = centre; b = bottom; l = left; r = right.

Copyright the American Museum in Britain, photo Derek Balmer, 59t; Atwater Kent Museum, Philadelphia, 71t; Author's Collection, photos Simon de Courcy-Wheeler, 11, 20, 28b, 29b, 38, 43t, 45, 47, 48, 49, 50, 51, 53, 55b, 74, 80b, 82tr, 88b, 89, 108b, 109b, 111t, 116, 117t, 122b, 153b, 154–5, 158b, 173t, 193bl, 212t, 218lc, 230b, 231c, 232cr, 233c, 241b, 242t, 243r, 260r, 264–5t; Bedford Museum, photos Simon de Courcy-Wheeler, 42, 60, 205tl, 213, 216b, 259; Blenheim Palace, 143; Bowes Museum, Barnard Castle, 96; British Museum, Dept of Prints and Drawings, 214, 215b, 217t, 228; William Bulwer Long, photos Trevor Wood, 24, 25b; Copyright Centraal Museum, Utrecht, 22t; Chad Valley Ltd., 73, 254; Christie's South Kensington, photos Mike Fear, 77, 90, 92, 93, 97, 100, 102, 123b, 138t, 168t, 178b, 184t, 190c, 192–3t, 193br, 205tr, 251bl, 264tl; Colchester and Essex Museum, 111b; Mrs M. Eccles-Holmes, photos Simon de Courcy-Wheeler, 83; H.M. Queen Elizabeth II, 31; Escher Foundation, Haags Gemeentemuseum, The Hague, 22b; Michael Ellis, photos Simon de Courcy-Wheeler, 177t; Germanisches Nationalmuseum, Nuremberg, 17, 18, 39, 41t, 44, 66, 67, 137b, 139, 143t, 146c, 163t; Betty Harvey-Jones Collection, photos Trevor Wood, 2, 21, 32, 46b, 58, 61, 62, 65b, 109t, 112, 175t, 201b, 240, 243tl, 252b; Historisches Museum, Basle, photo M. Babey, 253; Historisches Museum, Frankfurt am Main, 16; Reproduced with the permission of the Controller of Her Britannic Majesty's Stationery Office, 70l;

Bill Holland, 95bl, 182, 185, 186; Ipswich Museum Committee, photos N. J. & L. Cotterell, 9b, 10t, 28t, 29t, 30, 40, 41b, 52, 95t, 107, 113, 117b, 119, 120, 157tr, 167t, 203, 205b, 206c, l & r, 210, 212b, 217t, 218–9, 226–7, 228–9t, 230t, 232t, 245, 248; Kirklees Libraries & Museums Service, 129t, 162b, 172b, 175b, 190b, 191c, 243lc, 251t; Kunsthistorisches Museum, Vienna, 103; Leeds City Art Gallery, 86; Luton Museum, photos Simon de Courcy-Wheeler, 27, 65t, 82br, 136, 147t, 162c, 174, 192b, 242b; Milwaukee Public Museum, 36; Musée d'Art et d'Histoire, Neuchâtel, 94, 98, 99; Museum of Childhood, Rottingdean, 127; Museum of the City of New York, photo Helga Photo Studio Inc., 37b; Copyright reserved, Museum of London, 121, 145, 207, 216b; National Motor Museum, Beaulieu, 129br, 130, 131c; National Museum of Wales, Welsh Folk Museum, 9tl, r, 13, 64, 88t, 106, 108t, 126b, 138c, 162t, 198, 200, 202, 208t, 209, 211b, 215t, 219bl, r, 228–9b; Copyright National Trust, 25t, (photo Jeremy Whitaker) 26; New Cavendish Books, photos Rob Inglis, 147c, 149t, 156, 158t, 165, 170t, 173b, 180t, 181, 191b, 195t, 256, 258; Phillips, New Bond Street, London, 87, 135, 140, 141, 144, 178t, 179, 263t; Pollock's Toy Museum, photos Simon de Courcy-Wheeler, 71b, 222, 223, 224, 225b, 226l, 227, 262–3b, 264b; David Pressland Collection, photos Simon de Courcy-Wheeler, 6, 147b, 151, 164, 165t, b, 166t, 169, 170, 171, 172t, c, 177b; Copyright Foto-Commissie, Rijksmuseum, Amsterdam, 19, 23; Saffron Walden Museum, Essex, 55tr, 59b, 122c, 201t, 211t, 229br, 241t, 252t; Crown Copyright reserved, Science Museum, London, 146b, 246, 247; Miss N. Smith, photo Simon de Courcy-Wheeler, 82tl; Sotheby's Belgravia, London, 75, 78, 80b, 91, 128, 148, 149b, 150, 152b, 152–3t, 183b, 188, 189, 262t; Courtesy of the Margaret Woodbury Strong Museum, 10b, 12, 34, 35, 37t, 70r, 72, 76, 101, 138b, 142, 183t, 184b, 187t, c, 199, 204, 208b, 233t, 255t; Society of Colonial Dames, New York, 33; The Toy Trader, 79, 110, 126t, 131tr, 157tl, 166b, 260tr; Victoria and Albert Museum, Crown Copyright reserved, 8, 43b, 54, 56, 95br, 218tl, 251br, 255b, 261l, (Bethnal Green Museum of Childhood) 7, 46t, 55tl, 57tl, b, 63, 81, 84, 85, 115, 118, 122t, 123t, 125t, 134, 137t, 160, 161, 163b, 167c & b, 206t, 225t, 231t, 244, 249, endpapers, (Alistair Allen Collection) 234, 235, 236, 237, 238, 239, 250; Courtesy, The Henry Francis Dupont Winterthur Museum, 57b.

POL...

NEW AN...

STAGE...

To be

THESE PIECES TO BE PLAC...

TO MAKE IT HIGHER.